PN 1992·8·D48
ALV

...ing of a TV series

the making of a TV series

Manuel Alvarado
Edward Buscombe

British Film Institute
in association with

First published in 1978
by The British Film Institute
127 Charing Cross Road, London WC2H 0EA
in association with
Latimer New Dimensions Ltd
14 West Central Street, London WC1A 1JH

Copyright © British Film Institute 1978

ISBN (hardback) 0 85170 075 6
ISBN (paperback) 0 85170 076 4

The opinions expressed in this book are those of the authors
and are not necessarily those of the British Film Institute,
nor do they represent official BFI policy.

Designer: Paul Bowden
Hazell logo: Bernard Allum
Cover photo: Pat Dyos
Typeset by TNR Productions 11, Greek St, London W1
Printed by Brown, Knight & Truscott, Tonbridge, England

Contents

Acknowledgements

Above all we have to thank June Roberts, who had to put up with us for longer than anyone, who had little to gain from our presence and most to lose. We are also very grateful to Jeremy Isaacs for allowing us inside Thames in the first place, and to Verity Lambert for having us in her department. We owe a special debt to Nicholas Ball, Richard Harris, Frank Van Raay, Terry Venables and Gordon Williams not only for formal interviews but for many conversations and much assistance during the production. We are also grateful to the following for many kinds of help: Bernard Allum, Moira Armstrong, John Bedells, Jack Breckon, Colin Bucksey, Liz Cadley, Sue Cassell, Irene Cullen, Donald Cullimore, Arthur Duff, Peter Duguid, Brian Farnham, James Faulkner, Dave Ferris, Jim Goddard, Felicity Grant, Janice Guild, Celia Gregory, Willis Hall, Mandy Harper, Stan Hay, Bill Henderson, Tony Hoare, R. I. Hughes, Oscar James, Don Leaver, Bill Lee, Mary Lewis, John Lopes, Sue Mahoney, Ian Martin, Roddy McMillan, Desmond McNamara, Andrew Nickolds, Derek O'Connor, John O'Keefe, Bill Palmer, Mike Phillips, Peter Piddick, Trevor Preston, Del Randall, Peter Ransley, Alistair Reid, Maggie Riley, Joan Rodker, Liz Sadler, Adrian Sumption, Ken Tester-Brown, Sally Thorpe, Denver Thornton, Sheila Trezise, Brian Walcroft, Jo Ward, Kenneth Ware, Barbara Young.

Thanks also to Judy Houldey for transcribing the taped interviews and to Erich Sargeant for help with the illustrations.

We should also like to record the assistance we received in the production of this book from the British Film Institute and the Society for Education in Film and Television, and in particular from Angela Martin and Susan Honeyford.

Last and by no means least, this book would never have appeared without the help of Sarah Boston and Scilla Alvarado.

Illustrations by kind permission of Thames Television.

1 Introduction

This book was written to fill a gap. So far as we know there has been no full-length study written by independent observers of the making of a British television drama series. This may seem surprising in view of the part that television now plays in our daily life, and the centrality of drama within the spectrum of television output. One reason for this lack must undoubtedly be the fact that although it is over forty years since regular television transmissions began in this country, television has yet to acquire the status of earlier forms of communications such as the press, theatre and cinema. Thus its study still lags way behind what would be justified by its cultural, social and political importance.

It is true that books about television are now starting to appear in increasing numbers. But most of them are concerned with the most obviously 'important' forms of programming such as news and current affairs. This is despite the fact that well over half of the top twenty most popular programmes each week are drama productions (the rest being mostly light entertainment shows), and that in one average week we counted over 80 separate drama productions on television, including in that figure programmes such as situation comedies (which may originate in Light Entertainment Departments) but excluding schools broadcasts. Any one of these shows would have drawn an audience several times greater than the total number of people who went to the theatre that week.

Neither the sheer amount of television drama nor its popularity are reflected in the critical attention paid to it. Very few of those 80 productions would have received any kind of notice at all in the press, and virtually none outside it. In the tabloid press there is no television criticism as such, only brief descriptive phrases of forthcoming programmes and regurgitated publicity hand-outs. In the so-called quality press coverage of drama concentrates heavily on the single play and prestige productions such as the BBC2 classic serial.

It's easy enough to argue that the greater part of this output is not worthy of recognition; yet the West End stage receives as much attention in the press as the entire output of television. Is the average quality of its productions so high?

But to us arguments about artistic quality seem beside the point. Surely the forms, the styles, the dominant concerns of the mass of television drama deserve some attention if so many people spend so much time watching it and so many resources in terms of time and money are expended on its production.

The reasons why such cultural prejudices persist would make an interesting study in themselves. More directly relevant to the concerns of this book are the reasons why there have been so few studies of the production process in television. In part this must be because dominant critical theories have not traditionally ascribed much importance to the knowledge that such study would produce. The critic's job as it has usually been conceived has been to examine what is there on the printed page, the screen or the stage. What does it matter how it got there? People want to see a show; they don't want to know about all the problems there were behind the scenes.

In fact a lot of evidence is against such a view; witness the recent spate of books about the making of *Jaws* or *King Kong*, the weekly articles in *Radio Times* about how a football match is covered for television or on the wonders of the Make-Up Department, and the long tradition in the theatre and cinema of back-stage musicals. But, it will be argued, satisfying people's curiosity has nothing to do with critical judgement. The job of the critic is to offer his or her perceptions, values and taste to the public in the hope that the public, and perhaps the artists, may profit by comparing the critic's views with their own. Knowledge about how the work came to its present form could only prejudice a judgement on its artistic qualities. The critic's function is to deliver a verdict; extenuating circumstances are not admissable as evidence.

If one accepts that the role of the critic is primarily to judge then there may be something in this argument as applied to particular cases. This is one reason why we offer no critical judgements on *Hazell*. Because we know so much about how the programme was made, we would perhaps be too indulgent of its faults (knowing possibly the unavoidable circumstances in which some of them came about) or too critical of its virtues (knowing maybe in what ways it could have been even better). And our personal contacts over a period of many months with the people who made it would make an objective assessment very difficult, whether we wanted to praise or criticise. But it does not follow from this that knowledge of the production *process,* as opposed to particular instances, inhibits critical perception. And in any case we would argue that the kind of criticism which television most needs is not one which is primarily concerned with handing out prizes or brickbats to individuals. It seems to us that what television most requires is a kind of criticism which is concerned above all with understanding, with trying to find out how television works, what it means and why it is what it is. We don't advocate such a criticism in the spirit of *tout comprendre, c'est tout pardonner,* since the ultimate objective of such criticism would be to make television better than it is. But judgements based, as most criticism currently is, on taste or moral values, or more frequently on purely personal likes and dislikes, without any consideration of how those tastes and values are formed and how they are perpetuated or subverted by television as a system, must in the end tell us more about the judges than about what is judged.

This book, then, is intended not as an aid towards more informed critical judgements about *Hazell,* but as a contribution to a better understanding of television as a whole. We hope that the kind of information we have been able to provide will, firstly, help people to see that television programmes are *made*; that they do not simply emerge, fully formed, out of the ether. This may seem like an obvious point, and we don't seriously suppose anyone believes that the actors make it up as they go along. All the same, we ourselves find even now after having made this study that it is all too easy as the flow of television programmes slides past the eye to remain comparatively oblivious to the extent to which is on the screen has been put there for a reason by people who have designs upon us, benignly or not, consciously or not.

Secondly, we have tried to identify some of the forces at work within the system which make television programmes what they are. In part these forces are the result of people working towards deliberate ends; in part any television programme is determined by structures beyond the control of the individuals who produce it. But the fundamental assumption we have made, and which we hope this book goes a little way towards demonstrating, is that television programmes are produced not within a vacuum but within a highly organised system. At what one might call the macro-level, this system is a tissue of political and governmental controls, legal obligations, commercial imperatives, institutional structures. At a micro-level there is an interlocking network of everyday working practices, artistic and other cultural demands, the beliefs and actions of individuals and social groups. Television can be spoken of as a system in the sense that programmes do not take the form they do by chance (and to those who would insist on the role of chance we would say that this is only a name for what is not yet understood). It's also a system in the sense that each part of the whole both affects, and is affected by, the other parts. This does not mean that we, or indeed others, understand how the complete system fits together; or even that it *does* fit together like a well-oiled machine. The stresses and strains, the disfunctions, are obvious enough — not least to those who work in television. But the tendency of the system is to try and make everything fit, since the survival of the system itself, and those who benefit from it, depends on it.

Of course we're well aware, after talking to many of them over a long period of time, that television programmes are made by people. But the focus of this book is not on personalities as such, but on the way that these personalities operate within the institutionalized structure of the production process. *Hazell* would have been a different programme if it had been made by different people. But our interest in writing the book has been in what is typical about *Hazell,* what it reveals about the way in which television works, rather than in what the individuals who produced it are 'really like'. We may therefore disappoint those readers who are looking for a 'good story', with heroes and villains, amusing anecdotes and melodramatic set pieces. Personality plays its part; it might even be said that in certain areas such as writing or acting it is individuality which creates the value of the product. But our emphasis in looking at the production process has been on the constants rather than the variables — always bearing in mind that variables are constantly present.

This raises the question of how far *Hazell* is typical. What, in fact, can be learnt about television as a whole through the study of one programme? Where possible we have tried to contextualise our observations. But inevitably our opportunity for generalisation has been limited. This book not only can't tell you everything you need to know about television. It can't tell everything about television drama, or even about *Hazell* itself. Nevertheless we think that the kind of detail which a particular case study makes possible has its own value, and could not be arrived at by any other means. The solution to the problem of the limited and partial view obtained through this method surely lies in the production of many more case studies, not only of individual programmes but possibly of the entire output of a department over a period of time, and indeed of a company.

Whether such studies will appear is hard to say. One reason why

4

there have been so few in the past is the sheer difficulty of this kind of work. And there are several aspects to this. One has been the undoubted problem of gaining access. Relations between television companies and researchers have frequently been marked by a degree of mutual hostility, with the companies often behaving as though revelations of the 'secrets' of production must at all costs be prevented for fear of some dreadful but unspecified consequences. At this point we should say that we have had the fullest possible co-operation from Thames at all points and any faults of omission which the book contains are our responsibility, not theirs.

Getting inside, however, is only the first problem the researcher encounters. There is also the sheer scale of the operation. *Hazell* employed some 74 different actors and actresses, 7 directors, 9 writers and 3 designers, not to mention the scores of people involved in camera crews, sound crews, lighting, make up, wardrobe and so on. To talk to all of them in detail about their work is a near-impossible task, though we have tried to say something about every field of activity. And the work goes on for a long time. The production cycle of *Hazell* began in the spring of 1976 and at the time of writing (November 1977) is still not complete, with dubbing still continuing and work on publicity hardly begun. Even for researchers who are able to work on their project full-time, which we have not been able to do, this represents a very large investment of time — and, on the part of those who are paying them, of money. A further difficulty caused by the scale of production is that with so many people involved much of the work is going on simultaneously, and even though there were two of us we couldn't be everywhere at once. Thus we undoubtedly missed some of the things we should have liked to observe.

A problem of a rather different kind was raised by our own status. Both of us have a long-standing interest in television. We have written about it and taught classes in television studies. We have made programmes on ½" video equipment. But we would be the first to recognise that at least before we began our research we knew very little about professional television production. It is true that there was some advantage in our ignorance. We intended writing a book for readers who, like ourselves, knew next to nothing and so at least we were in no danger of assuming our readers would understand what had not been explained. But we were frequently aware that if we had known more we would have understood more. This was particularly true in the case of the electronic technology employed in the studio.

Another aspect of our status needs to be posed here. Not only were we amateurs in a world of professionals; we were also non-participants. Non-combatants, one is almost tempted to say; certainly there were times when we felt a little in the position of United Nations observers in the middle of a battle anxiously watching the shells whizzing overhead. The neutral observer's role is a familiar problem in social science. Does the presence of an observer change the nature of the situation which is being observed? Do people in fact behave differently when they know they are being watched? Does the request to explain to someone what you are doing and why affect your thinking about your work and the way you do it? When people know they are being watched are they inhibited from doing or saying things they might have otherwise? When people are asked to describe their areas of responsiblity are they inclined to paint a favourable picture of what they have achieved? In other words, does the 'objective observer' get an objective view?

The answer of course must be no. Much of what takes place the observer can see directly (though seeing, especially when one has limited prior knowledge is clearly not the same as understanding). But for much of our information we were dependent on what people told us, and they, inevitably, were not objective. This would be true in any situation, but it is exacerbated in television by the high degree of job insecurity. People won't readily admit anything that might be damaging to them if it is going to affect their future chances of employment, and who can blame them? Besides this, much of the work that people are doing involves a heavy investment of their personalities. Self-criticism does not come easy in such a situation and criticism of others' work can appear to be a personal attack. So understandably enough people have not always told us exactly what they thought. And sometimes where they have we have not, in part because of the laws of libel, been able fully to report it.

It seems important to raise such questions not only to indicate some of the necessary limitations of this kind of work, but also because having investigated how other people do their work it seems only fair to expose our own 'process of production'. The information in this book was gathered both by watching people at work and by questioning them about what they do, in formal taped interviews and in countless casual conversations in studios, offices, rehearsal rooms, homes and bars. Some kinds of work are more observable than others. Thus we have watched directors directing and actors acting, but we have not watched writers writing. Similarly some people find it easier to talk about their work than others. A set designer can explain why his set has to be a certain size (to fit into the studio, to accommodate a fixed number of actors). But if one asks a writer why he wrote a certain line or a director why she cut together a scene in a particular way, one may merely get the answer 'it felt right'. When faced with such replies we usually tried to go further, to find out why it felt right, and on occasion we have speculated on why, in our opinion, it should feel right. But to go very far in this direction would have taken us into an analysis of the programmes themselves. For reasons already outlined we have chosen not to include such an analysis; such work would be best left to a separate study.

In writing the book we have selected from a large amount of material: notes taken by ourselves, transcriptions of interviews, scripts, memoranda, letters and other written documents, together with visual material. The selection and arrangement of all this in itself constitutes a 'view' of what happened and much of it, we believe, speaks for itself to the intelligent reader; but we have also not hesitated to comment where it seemed appropriate. On the other hand we do not offer many very general conclusions because we believe that such generalisations can only be shakily based on a single case.

Thus it seemed to us, for example, that the production process was of such complexity and involved so many people carrying out specialised functions that it often eluded the control of those working in it. *Hazell* turned out to be something a little different from what was originally intended. But it is very difficult for us to say that this is generally true, and to what extent special factors produced such a situation. To be specific, because of changes in schedules and other difficulties more directors and writers were used than the producer thought desirable. So *Hazell* might not be a typical example of the problems of control. Only further studies of this kind could make meaningful comparison possible.

Various other general observations about the nature of the production process presented themselves; for example, that it is very hierarchical (despite the efforts of the producer in this case to involve more people than would usually be consulted about production decisions); that people's functions are highly specialised, leading to a kind of fragmentation (several people complained to us that they didn't feel involved or that they didn't get much feedback on their work); and that television is a very enclosed world (thus the publicity people and the programme liaison officer claimed to us that they were closer to the

7

audience than the people who made the programmes). Again there is the problem of generalisation. Made at a very abstract level these observations are in danger of being no more than cliches. But we would be loathe to say to what extent the actual manifestations of such characteristics on *Hazell* were typical.

Two further points in relation to our work may be made, one in relation to the gathering of material, one in relation to its presentation. We have already indicated some of the difficulties of being an observer. But a further kind of problem results from not being a part of the production team. While collecting information we tried very hard not to get involved in the work by offering comments or suggestions on what was going on, despite on occasion being invited to do so. Thus while the producer was trying to make a decision on the casting of the central part she showed us some studio tests and asked what we thought. We don't flatter ourselves that our comments on that occasion were of much value (and in any case we gave contradictory opinions).

But it's worth recording one instance where our determination to remain outside the production became an issue, because it illustrates a point we would wish to make: that non-involvement is in itself a kind of involvement and that to assume that an observer can simply be a fly on the wall is seriously to misunderstand the realities of the situation. Non-involvement, and hence the 'truth' of our account, can only be relative.

A situation arose on the production where certain personality differences threatened to disrupt the work. Several of the individuals concerned had been interviewed by us and expressed their views. The producer was worried by what was happening and put it to us that her understanding of the situation would be improved if she could read the transcripts of our interviews. This placed us in a dilemma. If we showed her what had been said this might compromise our position of neutrality and make it harder in future for us to gain the confidence of those we wanted to talk to. They might not tell us things if they thought they would go straight back to the producer. On the other hand not to let the producer see our material might damage our relations with the person on whom we most depended for continued access to the production. And there was also the possibility that the success of the series might be impaired if the producer, through lack of information on what was happening, was impeded in her efforts to resolve the situation. Was our book more important than the series?

In the end we decided the only think to do was to explain to the producer the nature of the problem caused by her request and to say if she insisted we would let her see what we had but would prefer not to. Eventually she decided that she would do better to talk directly to the people involved and thus our problem, if not hers, went away. The point seems to us to be that the position of a neutral observer can come into conflict with other considerations. Adopting such a role seems the only way to get a clear overall view of a production, but one has to recognise the possibility that one might become involved and be prepared, in certain circumstances, to compromise.

In relation to our presentation of the material, we have chosen to make frequent use of transcribed interviews. This is partly because people sometimes explain things better in their own words than we could. Reproducing verbatim what they said also indicates, as an interpretation or summary might not, that this is *their* view of things and the reader can therefore make allowances, if he or she thinks fit, for the position of the speaker.

The book is intended for all with an intelligent interest in television, though within that audience we have particularly addressed ourselves to teachers at secondary and further education level who may be teaching television, possibly in the context of a media studies course. We hope that for them this book will provide some basic material on the television production system, material which is difficult for them to obtain by themselves.

One last point; why *Hazell?* The answer is simple enough. We wanted to write about a popular series; at the time Thames were prepared to let us in *Hazell* was just about to get under way. It seemed a good choice (not that we were in a position to demand a choice). It still does.

2 Institutional Structures

A comprehensive account of the workings of British broadcasting would be out of place here; the reader seeking more information on the structure of the industry is referred to the bibliography. What this chapter offers is a sketch of some of the institutional factors which can be seen to have influenced decisions on the making of *Hazell*.

The ITV network

The fact that Britain has two separate television networks, the British Broadcasting Corporation and Independent Television, means inevitably that there is competition for audiences. This would be so even if one of them, ITV, were not a commercial system. The need for ITV to maximise its audiences is clearly a major factor in any decision about which programme to make, and as we shall see *Hazell* was no exception to this. To what extent the people who actually make the programmes see themselves as competing with the other channel is more difficult to judge. For one thing, while a programme is being made, over a period of months or even years, they cannot know which particular programmes on the rival network will be scheduled against their own, and so competitiveness can only take the form of a general desire to make their programme as good as they possibly can. And 'good' may not mean quite the same as 'popular' (though no-one sets out to make unpopular programmes). On the other hand there was undoubtedly on the part of some of those involved a desire to outdo past and future programmes of a similar type (thus while *Hazell* was in production there were occasional references to crime series which the BBC and other ITV companies were known to be planning).

It's also true that people working in ITV know perfectly well that their prospects of future employment depend on the continuing financial success of the company they work for, which depends in turn on how many viewers, and hence advertisers, ITV can attract. It's also worth mentioning that directors and actors are paid 'residuals', i.e., repeat fees, and the more popular their programme the more repeats it will get. The production team, therefore, cannot afford to ignore the ratings, which may be said to operate as a fact of existence for all those working in television. For most people, even in ITV, it's not necessarily the first or the only thing they think of. But it's always there in the background. The high priests of the company, the executives, think of it rather a lot and often feel the need to remind those lower down the scale, whose minds are dwelling on other things, of its importance.

ITV is a regional system, with each of the 15 companies having a monopoly of the ITV channel in its own area, though filling its air time with programmes from other companies in the network and outside it. Companies therefore do not compete with each other for audiences (although Thames and LWT, uniquely in ITV, do compete in the same advertising market since they are the only companies broadcasting in the same area); indeed, each stands to benefit from a successful programme produced by another company if it is networked, as almost all major programmes are.

Doubtless for this reason there is close co-operation between companies in the organisation of production, through the working of the Programme Controllers Group. This consists of the programme controllers of the 5 largest ITV companies (Thames, London Weekend Granada, ATV, Yorkshire, who between them produce the bulk of ITV's most popular and expensive programmes) together with an official of the Independent Broadcasting Authority and the head of the network programmes secretariat, representing regional companies. It is this group which constructs the schedules. Companies announce their production plans to the group, but do not agree specific programmes with it since it is assumed that all major productions will be networked, even if a company may occasionally be less than enthusiastic about the ratings potential of another company's production.

The pressures on the decision makers in each company are not wholly economic. ITV schedules have to gain the approval of the IBA (hence the IBA representation on the Programme Controllers Group), which is responsible for seeing that companies fulfil their obligations to provide what it calls 'a balanced variety of programmes', these obligations being placed on the companies by Parliament through the IBA Act. The IBA also, as we shall see, exercises some control over the actual content of the programmes (see chapter 5). But perhaps more crucial than this in terms of deciding what actually gets made is the question of the company's status both within the ITV system and outside. Prestige can be important not only for the psychological satisfactions it may give to the company's employees and shareholders but also for other reasons. Producing programmes which are acknowledged to be good as well as popular helps a company attract talented people. Recognition of that talent may come from critics (though many in television affect to despise them, they are cultivated none the less); or it may come from fellow professionals at such events as the annual BAFTA (British Academy of Film and Television Arts) awards. Either way such feed-back is valued as an endorsement of both the individual's and the company's purposes and performance.

But prestige can also impress the IBA when the next allocation of contracts comes round. And it can also impress advertisers. Not all of them are concerned with reaching the largest number of viewers; some may have products which they wish to sell to a smaller but more up-market public. So Thames produces glossy promotional material emphasising not only the company's large audiences but also its cultural achievements, and the foyer of their Teddington Studios has a display of awards won by Thames programmes at international festivals.

The ITV system, then, both in its competition for ratings with the BBC and its status rivalry among the commercial companies, influences the decisions that are made about what to produce. But there are of course differences between the individual companies, and some of these can also be seen to have their effects on decisions about programmes. A comparison between the different companies is outside the scope of this book, but some characteristics of Thames seem relevant to this enquiry.

Thames Television

Thames is the biggest of all the ITV companies. It employs 1800 people, produces some 1200 programmes a year and in 1976/7 had a turn-over of nearly £50 million (see diagram for a breakdown of how the money was spent). Its sheer size perhaps enables it to make programmes which are not only outside the capabilities of smaller companies but which carry an element of risk. Somewhat like the old Hollywood film studios, it can afford to make some programmes which might not make the top of the ratings because it is also making lots of programmes which *will* be popular. As we shall see *Hazell* was to be one of the more popular shows providing the necessary breathing space for others of more specialised appeal. Size, of course, does not necessarily make for adventurousness, but it does offer the *opportunity* to

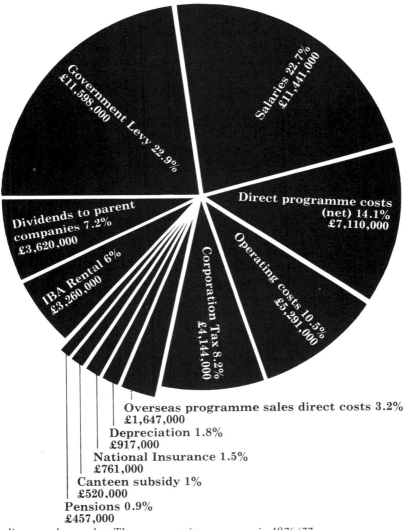

Salaries 22.7%
£11,441,000

Government Levy 22.9%
£11,598,000

Direct programme costs (net) 14.1%
£7,110,000

Dividends to parent companies 7.2%
£3,620,000

Operating costs 10.5%
£5,291,000

IBA Rental 6%
£3,260,000

Corporation Tax 8.2%
£4,144,000

Overseas programme sales direct costs 3.2%
£1,647,000
Depreciation 1.8%
£917,000
National Insurance 1.5%
£761,000
Canteen subsidy 1%
£520,000
Pensions 0.9%
£457,000

diagram shows what Thames spent its money on in 1976/77

experiment, and with shows such as *Rock Follies* and *Bill Brand* in the last couple of years Thames would certainly claim to have taken that opportunity.

Another factor in determining production policies, though of limited relevance to any particular programme, is the company's declared

13

intent of not diversifying out of television into other kinds of business, as some ITV companies have done. Granada, for example, have invested some of their profits from television in publishing and restaurant chains. The Directors in a promotional brochure, take pride in a single-minded concentration on programme-making: 'We have set our face against diversification out of film and television production and broadcasting. That is our professional business and that is where our aspirations lie.' Such declarations may have the effect of focussing the company's energies squarely on programme production. But they are also making a virtue out of necessity. Thames is jointly owned by two of the giants of British industry. EMI (Electrical and Musical Industries) own 50.01% of the voting shares and BET (British Electric Traction), through its subsidiary Rediffusion Television Ltd., holds 49.99%. EMI has extensive interests in hotels and catering, film production, distribution and exhibition, electronics, records and other musical businesses. BET is involved in printing and publishing, transport, building and construction, mining and electronics, including the manufacture of television sets. The company also owns Wembley Stadium. Other television companies have diversified because of the claimed uncertainty of the television business — there is no guarantee that their contracts will be renewed by the IBA. But EMI and BET are already secure enough. And there would be little point in Thames forming subsidiaries in the industries favoured by other television companies, such as the electronics and leisure fields, since this would be to compete with the existing activities of the parent companies.

Thames does in fact have 3 subsidiaries, though all are concerned with television or film production. Thames Television International markets its television programmes overseas. Cosgrove Hall Productions makes children's cartoon films for an international market. And Euston Films, named after Thames' main offices in Euston Road, makes film series for television, such as the highly successful *The Sweeney*. Euston Films have also recently branched out into feature film production with *Sweeney!* (distributed by EMI) and have other features planned. If there were ever to be a feature film of *Hazell* it would probably be produced by Euston Films, and distributed by EMI.

Another aspect of production policy, explicitly promoted by the Thames board, is its concentration, in television production, primarily on the domestic market. Thames say that they have no intention of making programmes designed to appeal to overseas buyers (as other ITV companies such as ATV have done). This policy is confirmed both by Jeremy Isaacs, Controller of Programmes, and Verity Lambert, Head of Drama.

VL: '... We are here to make the best possible television for the people of this country. If it's good my feeling is that it will sell abroad, though that doesn't mean everything will. But I think it's very dangerous for programme-makers to sit down and say we'll do this programme because maybe it will sell abroad. Because then you start making compromises in order to make it more acceptable. And you end up with something which is perhaps not even acceptable to your home audiences.'

To date, however, Thames Television International has sold the company's products in 95 different countries and last year did £2 million worth of business; and a company brochure takes pride in having it both ways:

'We are gratified that our policy of making quality productions uncompromisingly for British audiences has nevertheless brought us huge export successes.'

It wouldn't be true to say that no thought at all was given to a possible foreign audience for *Hazell*. In 1976 Thames took the novel step of hiring the air-time of a New York station for a whole week to show its programmes, and we were told that after this (highly successful) experiment word did come through to the people working on *Hazell* to go just a bit easy on the cockney rhyming slang. But the effect appears to have been marginal; some of the dialogue in *Hazell* is sufficiently cockney to cause problems to British audiences north of Watford.

This brings us to another aspect of Thames which has some bearing on decisions about what programmes to make. Thames is London based; producing programmes which are shown throughout the network, its immediate target audience is the 14 million people who live in London and the surrounding area. This audience is shared with London Weekend Television, Thames being responsible during the week from Monday till 7 p.m. on Friday, after which LWT takes over. 43% of programmes shown in the London area originate with Thames. Verity Lambert believes it important to create a regional identity:

'Somehow or other we try to do drama that comes from our region, to get a kind of feeling about our drama that couldn't have come from any other company, that had to come from London.'

Certainly *Hazell* fits into this pattern.

The Drama Department

Thames has 6 programme-making departments: Drama, Light Entertainment, Current Affairs and Documentaries, Children's Programmes, Education and Religion, and Outside Broadcasts. Drama is
one of the most important. Its budget for direct costs in 1976 was
£1,928,000, only very slightly less than that of Light Entertainment and
two-thirds as big as all the other departments combined (see diagram).

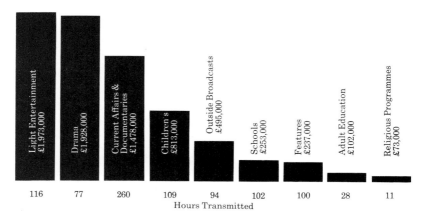

Hours Transmitted

diagram shows proportion of production budget allocated to each department

The department employs about 20 people on its permanent staff at
Teddington. At any one time there will be about half a dozen producers
employed in the department, one responsible for single plays, one for
day-time drama and the others working on series. All are employed on
a free-lance basis. Verity Lambert's argument is that the freelance
system best allows her to fit producers to projects. Producers tend to
be better suited to certain kinds of drama than others, she feels. If the
producers were on the staff permanently she might find herself having
to give them productions which someone outside the company might be
better suited to. Some ITV companies, however, such as Granada, do
have staff producers in the Drama Department.

Thames contributes about 50 hours of drama a year to the network.
This is the amount which the company can reasonably cope with in the
three studios at Teddington, bearing in mind that these studios have to
be shared with Light Entertainment and Children's Programmes. (The
other departments operate out of the Euston Road studios.) The

16

normal pattern is for two shows to be in production at any one time, with others in preparation. An hour-long show will usually 'turn round' in 2 weeks; that is, from the start of rehearsals to the final recording day in the studio is 2 weeks. A 13-episode series will thus take about 6 months to record, four such series thus making up the 50 hours or so achieved during the year. *Hazell* was worked on for something like 20 months, including preparation and post-production, and so during this period a considerable number of other productions were going on at the same time in the Drama Department. These included, for example, *Rock Follies* (second series), *Romance, Rooms, The Crezz,* some single plays, *Rumpole, Armchair Thriller, London Belongs To Me, Born and Bred* and *Edward VIII*: a mixture of costume drama, thrillers, period and contemporary drama and comedy.

We have already referred to Thames' policy of producing drama with a London flavour. We asked Verity Lambert if there were any other policy guidelines:

VL: 'When I took over in 1974 I decided not only that we would try to do drama drawn from our region but that I didn't want to do any costume drama. I felt it was very important to do contemporary drama; there wasn't enough of it about. What those decisions brought forward in the first year was the first series of *Rock Follies, Bill Brand* and *Plays for Britain,* which were attempting to tackle in one way or another modern problems and life. That took care of the first 2 years in fact, because it takes a year from when you take over before anything of yours filters through. At the end of that 2 years I re-examined things with Jeremy Isaacs and we decided that we'd done rather well in a certain way but that we hadn't got the mix quite right in terms of providing entertainment. We were always lucky in that Thames had *The Sweeney* coming from Euston Films, which in a sense catered for that area. But within the things I had chosen to do there were difficulties. *Rock Follies* was difficult because people reacted very strongly for or against it, *Bill Brand* was difficult because it was a very serious programme. I think it was extremely good, but for some people who had been working in a factory all day it was perhaps a bit much to come home to. And so that's why we decided to do *Romance* and *Hazell.* We wanted something that was entertaining, a little less heavy. So the policy does change. You have to keep looking at it and saying, have we missed out some area? That doesn't mean you have to do crap, you can do very good entertaining programmes, but you do have to think of your audience as a whole.'

The fact that Thames is a commercial company, then, doesn't necessarily mean that every drama production has to achieve the greatest possible audience. Some margin for experiment is possible. On the other hand this margin must be limited in a way that it need not be in a public service broadcasting company. It is unlikely, for example, that Thames Drama Department would ever do a production of Samuel Beckett one-act plays, as the BBC did in its *Lively Arts* series, since the audience would be below what any ITV company would consider acceptable.

The unions

Few areas of televison raise such contentious issues as those which are involved in the organisation of labour within the industry and its relations with management. There is certainly room for a thorough study of the subject, which can hardly be given adequate coverage in the few pages we are able to devote to it. Later in the book we describe an industrial dispute which arose in the course of the production of *Hazell* and which had certain consequences for the programme. What this section aims to do is to give a general outline of the relations between Thames and the various unions with which it deals.

It should be realised at the outset that industrial relations in television are characterised not only by the factors which govern such relations in any industry in Britain at the present time, but by certain special factors (though these are not necessarily only to be found in the television industry). In particular, there is the problem of the introduction of new technology; new kinds of electronic editing facilities, light-weight portable equipment, new sound systems and so on. Even where the main purpose of new technology is not to increase productivity by cutting down the number of workers required (and some of the new equipment is precisely designed to do just that) it may still have that effect. The companies need to introduce such equipment in order both to cut their wage costs and to keep abreast of their competitors technically. The unions on the other hand must protect the jobs of their members as well as ensuring that where changes are justified there is adequate retraining or, if necessary, compensation. Whether one regards the interests of management and unions as essentially incompatible or whether one takes the view that there is a long term identity of interest, it must be clear that from time to time conflict will break out.

The ITV companies' policy is to attempt to manage potential conflict by operating a series of agreements with the unions. Though they do not refer to it as a closed shop, this is essentially the system in operation within ITV. Thames has agreements with 4 major unions representing its staff employees; these are the Association of Cinematograph, Television and Allied Technicians (ACTT), the National Association of Theatrical, Television and Kine Employees (NATTKE), the National Union of Journalists (NUJ) and the Electrical, Electronic and Telecommunication-Plumbing Trades Union (EETU-PTU). It has further agreements with the various performers' unions: Equity, for actors; the Musicians' Union; and the Writers' Guild.

ACTT organises what are known as production staff: casting directors, floor managers, directors, production assistants, lighting directors, designers, etc., and also technicians such as camera and sound crews, engineers and so on. NATTKE members are make-up and wardrobe, props, scene shifters, certain secretarial posts and others. The NUJ involves reporters on current affairs programmes. Studio electricians and plumbers are in the EETU-PTU. With these unions, and with the performers' associations, there is an understanding that the company will not employ workers who are not members (though in the case of the Writers' Guild the agreement takes the form of an undertaking by the company that though they will accept one piece of writing by a non-member they will not accept a second without requiring that the writer join the Guild).

The agreements cover a number of areas, such as the procedure to be followed in the case of disputes, working hours (where appropirate), general conditions of employment and, of course, pay. However, the agreements over pay usually concern minimum rates and therefore do not necessarily reflect actual wages and salaries. Thus in the ACTT agreement the minimum rate for a director after the first year of employment is £7135 plus £6 p.w. but one can assume that the experienced directors employed on *Hazell* got more than this. The agreement with the Writers' Guild provides for a minimum fee of £1100 for a 51 minute episode of a series for an experienced writer, though it can be seen from the budget detailed later in the book, writers on *Hazell* were usually paid more than this. There is also a minimum rate for actors of £15 a day during performance, but only extras are likely to be on a rate as low as this.

The Equity agreement also provides definition of the different types of role artists may be required to perform, and these again are related to minimum rates. Thus an extra is defined as 'a performer who is not required to give individual characterisation nor to speak any word or line of dialogue except that crowd noises shall not be deemed to be dialogue in this context.' Crowd noises 'can include singing of well-known songs where the words do not have to be learned and also congregational hymn-singing of well-known hymns from hymn books.' Walk-on parts, on the other hand, involve performing 'individually in medium shot, or more closely, a special function peculiar only to the trade or calling that his character is supposed to represent, e.g., a bus conductor collecting fares on a bus, a policeman on point duty, a bartender serving drinks . . .' Such a part is known generally as a 'walk-on one'. A 'walk-on two', in addition to performing such functions, 'is also required to speak a very few unimportant words.' Walk-on ones are paid more than extras, walk-on twos more again.

With the performers the companies negotiate a fee for two screenings of a programme within 2 years. There are appropriate payments for overseas sales, depending on the size of the market. (A sale to one of the American networks would require a payment to the artist of 150% of the original fee.) Any further showings after this have to be renegotiated with each and every artist in the programme; i.e., actors, musicians, writers. Directors also are entitled to extra fees for a repeat of their shows. (It should be said that these agreements apply to ITV only; the BBC makes its own arrangements.) These agreements relate only to television showings. If Thames wanted to release one of their programmes in the cinema they would be obliged to secure a separate agreement with everyone involved.

The ITV companies also have an agreement with the ACTT covering the minimal crew that shall be used during filming (there must be 2 on camera, 2 on sound, plus 2 production staff and floor or unit manager). There is no formal agreement, however, covering crewing levels in the studio. Such matters are dealt with by what is known as 'custom and practice', which means that there are generally recognised levels of crewing in the studios and any changes to these would involve consultation between unions and management. So, for example, *Hazell* used 4 cameras, with 6 people to operate them. Had the company suddenly decided the show could be done with only 2 cameras, this would have broken with custom and practice.

Although the agreements with the unions are made with each company separately, in a formal sense (since it is the individual companies which are the employers, not the ITCA — Independent

Television Companies Assn.), negotiations on terms and conditions of employment are carried out at a national level where appropriate. In some instances, however, this does not apply. Thus Thames became the first ITV company to install fully electronic editing and this, as we shall see later, involved the company in separate negotiations with some of its employees to cover new working conditions. Such negotiations are likely, though, to have a 'knock-on' effect if and when such equipment is installed by other companies.

In conclusion, one point about the unions seems relevant to a case study of one programme. The unions are one aspect of the way in which television production can be said to be institutionalised. Many of the decisions which were taken during the production of *Hazell* were made with a fair degree of freedom, though always within a range of options. But the agreements between the employers and the unions meant that certain things were fixed and could not be changed. Thus the budget was to an extent dictated by the agreed rates of pay for the various jobs involved. The number of cameras was fixed, and so on. If you choose to make a programme within the ITV system, certain things are decided for you in advance. This is intended simply as an observation, and in no sense a criticism, since in our view the benefits to their members of strong unions and firm agreements are obvious.

3 Preliminaries

How It All Began

In 1974 Macmillan published a novel, *Hazell Plays Solomon,* written under the pseudonym of P. B. Yuill. The novel was a thriller dealing with the adventures of a cockney private eye called James Hazell. The book was well received and successful enough for Macmillan to commission another based on the same character. It was called *Hazell And The Three-Card Trick* and appeared in 1975. The following year a third Hazell book, *Hazell And The Menacing Jester,* was published.

The dust jacket of the second book revealed the authors to be Gordon Williams and Terry Venables. Gordon Williams, a Scot, was originally a journalist and is now a full-time writer with a dozen or so novels to his name, among them *The Siege Of Trencher's Farm,* subsequently made into the film *Straw Dogs.* Terry Venables, after playing football for Chelsea, Spurs, Queen's Park Rangers and England, is now the manager of Crystal Palace F.C. They first met while Terry was playing for Chelsea and Gordon was doing some ghost-writing for footballers. Some years later they collaborated on a novel about football, *They Used To Play On Grass.* Their decision to use a pseudonym for their crime fiction was the result of the reception of that book. Terry Venables explains:

TV: 'We wrote the football novel under our own names and everyone thought it was just cheap publicity, that I was sitting there saying this and that happens and Gordon was writing it all down. In fact I suppose I actually wrote forty per cent of the book. But they thought it was a gimmick, no-one would believe I was really involved, a sweaty moronic footballer who couldn't put two words together. So we thought we'd take a pen name, actually the name of an uncle of Gordon's, so that the next book could be judged on its merits.'

We asked Terry to say how the Hazell books came about and how the collaboration works.

TV: 'Gordon was going to ghost a story for me, something about playing for England and what did I think about it. And he said to me, why don't you write it yourself; you get a hundred per cent of the money instead of only fifty. So there was a motivation for a start. Then I wrote a short football story about a London boy called Sammy Small who gets sent to the North-East, and that's how we got together on the football novel. I was training in the morning out at Ruislip with Rangers, who I'd moved to by then, and without having a bite or anything driving straight into town where Gordon's office is and leaving there about 7 at night. I started off saying, I can only do 2 days a week, because I was trying to resist it. I thought I'd be far too lazy to get involved with writing books. But once I'd started I couldn't stop until we'd done it. Then we did the next one and I was in every day in the end.

Hazell started out as a bit of a fluke. I had the idea for *Hazell Plays Solomon* as just an out and out tear-jerker, just at the time *Love Story* was earning fortunes. I had an idea about two children and what would happen if one mother found out years later that she'd got the wrong baby — a kind of "not a dry eye in the house" sort of thing. We got about three-quarters of it straight down, but it was useless, we were far too cynical. We laughed most of the day. Then up came the idea of weaving a cynical young chap into the plot, a private eye. So up came Hazell, a bit like us. But he was there just for the plot; the book wasn't a vehicle for him. Then when the publishers saw the book they thought he came through stronger than the plot, so they wanted another one about him.

The idea for the second one, *The Three-Card Trick,* was mine and Gordon's; the third one, *The Menacing Jester,* was mainly Gordon's. But it's one of those things where you can't split it in the end. We used to make jokes about it; that's your bit and that's mine, but in the end you can't remember who's done what. We enjoyed doing it; Gordon found himself making all sorts of Hazell remarks in the pub, it took him over completely.

The way we work is, we think up a plot, talk it over, get it strong all the way through in our minds. Then we work out a lengthy synopsis, in detail. Then we knock it into sections, chapters near enough, and decide who will do each bit. So I will do a section, say where Hazell pulls up outside the high-rise flats in Bethnal Green, and I take it until he comes out and gets back in his car again. Then Gordon will write him getting in his car and going back to the office and seeing Gregory (the solicitor for whom Hazell works). If one of us gets caught we ask, what would Hazell say here? Or, this is a great chance for Hazell to say one of his remarks. So we'll put things down until we think of one, then go at it again until it's finished. Then we'll go through the two pieces to make it nice and sweet, and then go on to the next piece until the whole thing's finished. Then we'll rewrite it. With the jokes in it and his sense of humour we felt we'd got away from James Bond, Supercock or whatever you want to call him, and from people like Marker of *Public Eye*, who was real but quite depressing. We wanted someone who was as real as Marker with the problems he had and we all have, but at the same time had a sense of humour.'

What happened next was that *Hazell Plays Solomon* was sent by a literary agent to the television companies. The book arrived on the desk of Joan Rodker, who is the Script Executive in Thames' Drama Department. Her job is to sift incoming ideas and scripts for programmes. Much of the unsolicited material, of which there is a great deal, is farmed out to readers who then send back a report. If this is favourable Joan will read the material herself. If not, Joan explains:

JR: 'If it's a dud, and we get a high percentage, I just put a little R on it, and we have a very sweet letter, which is not really a brush-off; we give some reason. There are a couple of formulas: this is well-written, but unfortunately we have no openings . . . which is true most of the time. But if there is any promise I actually go into why it works or doesn't. I'll give you an example; there's a bloke here, this is about the seventh script he's sent me. I'm not going to say anything rude, but I am getting a little bored with his name. He's a smallish talent and I doubt now that on this showing he'll get any bigger. But I will see him because he's so persistent and desperate to write. He keeps asking, where do I go wrong. And I tell him. But he hasn't got enough what I call real talent to make it. He has a little gift, but it's too competitive a field, too many people chasing too few slots. I fear he's going to have to learn the hard way; it's like with a child, you have to let them do it, if you tell them they won't believe you. It's tough.

I pass on a lot to other people I think could use it. Very often I write to a person and say, this is strictly a radio play, why don't you try the B B C. I've even got an old man who wrote, a pensioner, who did some rather pleasant little anecdotes, reminiscences. Nothing we could use, but they were well-written and unpretentious. I said why don't you try your local paper. I mean, I'm an advisory bureau — I call myself a social service because a lot of people that write are only getting rid of their troubles. Well, this old man wrote back and said he's doing a nice little side-line in anecdotes for the local paper now. I get rude letters too sometimes, saying I haven't understood someone. Often when I'm dictating a letter I say, we're going to get a come-back on this one, this is a nutter. We might get a whole page of someone saying he's a genius, and I've got to write to him saying the play doesn't work. And I know he's going to come back, just from the way he writes.'

Joan Rodker reads a lot of books, to keep up with what's being published. But a great deal of what eventually gets produced comes from writers already known to her, or from agents who know the kind of thing she is looking for. And this is what happened with *Hazell*.

JR: 'It came to me through an agent with whom I've had quite a bit to do. We have a certain affinity, shall we say, because she knows what I'm interested in. She just sent it along with a batch of other things. One of the first things I did when I came here was to say, we really ought to be looking for a totally new detective character. She knew I was looking, all the agents knew. I liked *Hazell Plays Solomon*, to be honest not so much for the story, which I don't think is the best, but because he had something. He had the kind of quirkiness that Colombo has done so well, but an English kind. He was a nice human character and you could identify with him. One of the things that was attractive was the dialogue, not only the voice-over but this kind of quirky humour which you could see would work. The quality of speech which would translate into television. So then I wrote to Verity a page or two of how I liked it and said at the bottom, let's talk about it, and we did. I usually more or less leave it there unless she wants to talk later. But presumably, it lodged in the back of her mind because in due course I heard we were doing *Hazell*.'

The actual decision on whether to buy a property is Verity Lambert's. As she remembers, the agent originally sent it to Thames as a suggestion for a one-off ninety minute play or film, and it was read by Barry Hanson, then producer of single plays within the Drama Department. He, like Joan Rodker, thought it would make a good series and also passed it on to Verity. She recalls:

VL: 'I found it very difficult to read, for some reason. I just wasn't in the mood. So I left it and came back to it eight or nine months later. I liked the character, I thought it was original. It was different from most TV detectives. It had a kind of freshness, I found it amusing and ingenious. I think *Hazell and The Three-Card Trick* is a very well-written and ingenious book, where he comes across a situation you think is one thing and it turns out to be something quite different.

That's interesting writing. The best thing is something incredibly funny that turns into something that's not. And I rather like things with humour in them. I think too much of what's on TV is not funny but rather heavy and unappealing. This was fresh; you're always looking for something that's not quite like everything else. I would like to think *Hazell* had a kind of reality, where you believed in the story as well as following the character. The story should be real; it should show something of the underbelly of London. If you go up to Soho at night and you see the sort of people who hang about, they may be 'characters' but underneath it's all rather unpleasant. I hope we'll manage to get both elements in; though Hazell has the cockney sense of humour he's actually quite a hard man and is dealing with situations that are unpleasant.'

This, then, was what Verity Lambert first saw in the book. Later, other people were to put forward slightly differing conceptions. But though the decision to buy was Verity's, she normally consults with Jeremy Isaacs, who explains the nature of the consultation:

JI: 'Verity is expected to put to me the proposals she intends to make into programmes. It's so important what she does that I would have to approve the deal; not because the money might be all that crucial, because by now she will have what she probably didn't have when she started in the job, an idea of the range of expenditures within which I'm not going to quibble. She makes two kinds of proposals to me: one is, I'm thinking of buying this and it will cost us roughly so much. Is that OK? And I say yes. The other is, I'm thinking of buying this but I have to warn you now that it might cost us a great deal. What do you think? That obviously is a much more difficult decision. But on the whole I accept her view of what a thing is worth. I have to because she knows a damn sight more about it than I do. So I do have to approve how much we spend to purchase the rights to a property, but the sums of money we're talking about are comparatively small as a proportion of the total budget of the Drama Department. There's ample money in the drama budget for the development of ideas; we spend a great deal more on scripts than we ever transmit. One of the things I said to Verity at the beginning was, we've got to get into a situation where half the scripts you commission you are able to reject if you want to.'

So what attracted Jeremy Isaacs to *Hazell* and made him approve the purchase of the property?

JI: 'In my view there is a rough cheerful bloody-mindedness about London crime and some London people that wasn't contained in the very starched crime series that commercial TV used to do, like *No Hiding Place*. It's touched on in *The Sweeney*, which is about how some very strong people do live. It seems an almost limitless area of subject matter. And it seemed that the man Hazell might take us into this world. You see, you have to realise that I come from Glasgow and Gordon Williams is from Paisley. I admire him; I think he writes about people in a tone of voice that I respond to. So when this particular proposal came up I read the books and liked them and I said, right, let's do it.'

Thus the decision to go ahead with *Hazell* was based on the enthusiasm of three people: Joan Rodker, Verity Lambert and Jeremy Isaacs. But such a decision has to be seen in a context, the context of Thames' drama requirements. The company was at the time already on the look-out for something of this sort. We have seen that Joan Rodker was keen on a new detective series and that Verity Lambert's department had certain production policies. But, as Verity has already suggested, there were certain schedule requirements. This is one of the primary areas of Jeremy Isaacs' responsiblities.

JI: 'I hired Verity Lambert as Head of Drama. She and I began by saying let us do drama in the next couple of years that will make everybody sit up and take notice. As soon as we'd commissioned the material and it had begun to happen I started to say to Verity it might be a good idea if we did some drama for 2 years beyond that, which spoke to an audience of the same sort of size as this company used to attract with series like *Callan, Public Eye* and so on. I said to Verity, you can do what you like with *Plays For Britain*, I don't mind if they don't get an audience. But please give me some more drama series that will appeal to a very big audience, and which if they work will have enough life in them, enough guts about them, to suggest to us that we should do more than one series of them. We need something of which viewers will want to see at least, 39 (i.e., at least 3 series), and of which we'll want to do at least 39. Which means it can't be just cardboard cut-out formulas, it's got to have growth areas in it: growth in character, growth in the use of locale. Even if there's an element of repetition there's got to be some sense of deepening of the story. So I said please find something that will help me do my job, which is to pull in an audience that will keep people advertising on Thames and which will therefore fund the programme-making. And this will enable us to do some things we want to do even if we don't think we're going to get an audience for them. So, knowing it's impossible to guarantee success or popularity, please make me some suggestions which are in the area of what might be popular as opposed to areas which, however interesting, stimulating or provocative, breaking new ground or whatever, don't seem likely to dominate the ratings.'

It's perhaps only fair to say that at the time we spoke to Jeremy Isaacs in the autumn of 1976, ITV was under severe competition from the BBC and was in fact losing audiences. The question of ratings was therefore even more on his mind than it otherwise might have been. But whatever the particular situation may have been, *Hazell* was always designed to be a series which would come near the top of the charts. With the agreement of the Programme Controllers Group, who were informed of Thames' plans for the series some months before it went into production in the studio, *Hazell* was to be assigned one of the prime viewing slots of the week.

JI: '*Hazell* is designed to go out at 9 p.m. That's where most of Thames' drama goes. It will be outside what is called family viewing time (up to 9 p.m.) so it will have whatever licence it needs in terms of bawdiness or violence. We want it to command a very large audience. At the moment we make a habit of playing a strong series, often a crime series, at 9 p.m. on Mondays when the BBC is playing a feature film. Things may change between now and when *Hazell* appears, but the likelihood is that we will still need a strong series at that time, and that is what *Hazell* is intended for, to be placed at 9 p.m. in the Thames schedule on Monday nights and to get a rating of 40 if it can every night it appears.' (i.e. 40% of the total potential audience for an ITV programme). This slot in the schedules would not necessarily always be filled by a Thames programme, but 'we have been able to fill it with *The Sweeney* and before that we had *Special Branch,* and *Van Der Valk,* and the feeling is that we *can* fill it. If other people came along and helped fill it that would be very acceptable to me, and I think very welcome to others. But I do know there will be a need for something like *Hazell* at 9 p.m. on Mondays.'

Verity Lambert, though well aware of the requirements of the schedules, finds that she cannot necessarily decide in advance on the precise kind of programme she wants:

VL: 'I find it's very difficult to say things like, I need a private eye series, because then you never find it. It's like going out to buy a dress saying I want a dress exactly like that. You can never actually find it. Maybe it's a catch-as-catch-can way of doing things, but I'm much more inclined to say that's a good idea. I'd like to do it. And then find some way of fitting it into the mix. Although of course in the back of my mind I must have an idea of what I'm looking for, otherwise I might end up with all the programmes exactly the same.'

Thames, then, were looking for something popular to fit into a slot, and to an extent for something that would fit into a formula of known popularity, the crime series. And at the same time they wanted something that would also provide a variation on that formula. *Hazell* fitted in very well. London Weekend were also at one time strongly interested in the books, but Thames were first with a definite offer. Thames therefore bought the rights. This consisted of the right to use the first novel, *Solomon,* as the basis of one or more episodes, and to use the character of Hazell himself in 26 scripts. Thames were not committed to using Gordon and Terry as script writers and could in fact do anything they liked with the character once they had bought him. But Gordon and Terry were subsequently commissioned to write one script with the possibility of more, and were to advise on the series generally. There was also talk of buying the second novel, *Hazell and The Three-Card Trick,* to use as the basis of a later *Hazell* 'special' (a longer show or possibly a feature film), but nothing has so far come of this.

A few tentative conclusions suggest themselves at this point. The fact that the book came to Thames through an agent indicates the existence of well-worn channels through which new material for television flows. Obviously if the books had been no good an agent wouldn't have been much help. But in television one suspects it's not enough to be good. You also have to be in the right place at the right time, and the agent knew what Thames were looking for at that particular moment. (Though it should be said that even so Thames took several months to make up their minds.)

A further point is that work has not only to be good but of the right kind. The available models are comparatively few and television, particularly popular television, works to formulas. This is an observation, not a criticism. Popular formulas or *genres* aren't necessarily bad — or good. *Hazell* fitted in because it looked like the basis of a private eye series though in several respects it goes against the usual formula.

There is also within television as it exists at the moment, as will be clear from this chapter, an inbuilt tendency towards the series, towards an idea that is capable of reproduction. If Hazell had been shot dead at the end of *Hazell Plays Solomon* the novel would not have been bought for a series. The threatened demise of the one-off play has not yet taken place here (as it has in America — though in a sense it has been born again in the made-for-T V film). But series and serials do dominate the ratings, and undoubtedly part of Hazell's attraction was that the nature of a private eye's work allows for an almost infinite number of adventures. Whereas even a novel as long as *War and Peace* can't be extended beyond a limited number of episodes.

Starting work: the producer

Once a definite decision has been made to go ahead, the first step is the appointment of a producer. The producer is responsible, in the last analysis, for everything except in so far as certain crucial decisions may have to be referred upwards. In particular the producer will, together with the script editor if there is to be one, develop and set the concept of the series. What will it be about, what kind of a show? What kind of style will it have? Vital here is the choice of writers, actors and directors, and these choices are ultimately the producer's. But s/he will also attempt to get the most suitable designers, lighting directors and others for the job. This may not always be possible since apart from writers and directors most of the people working on the production will be on the permanent staff of the company, and their availability will be subject to the requirements of other productions.

The choice of producer is Verity Lambert's. How does she make the decision?

VL: 'The first thing is if *I* think they're right for it. It will vary from series to series. Sometimes producers bring me ideas they want to do, but that doesn't happen as often as I'd like. Very often they don't have a lot of time; they're working so hard that their actual thinking time is very limited. The reason I chose June Roberts was that she'd just had her first job as producer, doing *Couples* (a day-time series based on the work of marriage counsellors). She'd done that quite well, I was pleased with it. But the tone of *Couples* was quite downbeat and heavy, dictated by the subject matter. I thought it would be a good time for her to do something different. Also I knew that she was very conscientious and works very hard, and that she would really try and make it very successful and commercial, which is what I want it to be. I felt she was at the moment when she would bring a lot to it. She hadn't done that sort of thing before and because she was a new producer she wouldn't come to it thinking it's got to be like this or like that.

Then after I've decided I've got to see if the producer feels that they're right for it. If you have someone who doesn't feel for what they're doing you end up with something not very good. June was very ambivalent until she read the books and then she decided she could do it, wanted to do it. This doesn't mean we don't have differences about how it should be done. But basically I think she will try and get it right and she's tough enough to argue if she feels strongly enough about something. She's not someone I can actually push around, which is good. She is her own person, she will fight for something she believes in.'

We asked if there was any particular reason for picking a woman*

VL: 'No, I didn't go into that. I didn't think about it. It's quite possible that Gordon and Terry would have preferred it not to be a woman when they were originally presented with the idea, since Hazell's basically a male chauvinist pig. But it just didn't enter my head.'

Taking our cue, we asked Terry for his reaction:

TV: 'It surprised me, but then anything could have surprised me because I don't know anything about television. I met Verity first and I saw that Verity had done *Budgie* and I think you've got to have respect for track records. I thought that was excellent. And when she spoke it made a lot of sense. So having the programme produced by women didn't really bother me one way or another once I'd got over the initial shock.'

As with the decision to buy the property, Jeremy Isaacs is consulted on the choice of producer. He had this to say, before *Hazell* went into the studio:

JI: 'I think one of the absolutely critical decisions about *Hazell* is the appointment of June Roberts as producer. I have a funny kind of

---

* The sexual division of labour within television is still acute, most jobs being confined to one sex only. For a full analysis of the situation see the report *Patterns of Discrimination*, written by Sarah Benton for the ACTT. In this book we have tried where possible to indicate which sexes do which jobs. Where the reader finds a specific sexual pronoun used, this can be taken as indicating either that a certain function on *Hazell* was in fact performed by a member of that sex, or that in ITV it invariably would be. This is not to be taken as implying that we think it *should* be.

relationship with June. She's not quite sure that I'm a fan of hers. I remember her as a marvellous editor of the house magazine, the best we've ever had. She chucked that and became a story editor in the Drama Department. Then she did *Couples,* which was very brave but didn't really work. I mean, it worked in the sense that it was enormously valuable to me because it managed to get by with the utter minimum of resources and facilities because it was virtually one, or very few, sets. And a lot of dialogue that could be done on very long takes. So it was inexpensive. And it was well worth doing; it was abrasive and altered the possibilities of day-time drama. But what it didn't succeed in doing was what one hoped it would do, which was to tell running stories so that the same marriage problems would keep coming back and you would have ongoing relationships between the counsellors and their clients. And it wasn't very popular.

That was the first thing June had produced. Then Verity said she thought June should produce *Hazell.* I accepted and am backing Verity's judgement, but it's a very bold decision because *Hazell* is such an important series to us. The safest thing might have been to appoint a senior producer with an experienced track record in that field. But I believe in giving people a chance and I believe in Verity's judgement. All the same, there's so much riding on it; and there's also the male chauvinism thing about it. I've never met Gordon Williams or Terry Venables, thought I look forward to doing so. But I'm hoping June's tough enough to see them off, because she's going to need to be.'

Budgets

Before the producer can actually start work on the series, however, some key decisions have to be made which will materially affect its future course. To begin with, June had to know what kind of budget she was expected to work to. One might suppose that because *Hazell* was to be a very important show in terms of the ratings battle it would have an extra large budget. But it doesn't work like that, Verity Lambert claims:

VL: 'It will have an adequate budget to do what is required. You can't say that because something is major that it will get extra. Money isn't the thing that will make *Hazell* work. *Enough* money will make it work, but an enormous amount poured into it won't necessarily make it good. It won't have, for example, the kind of budget *Rock Follies* has, not because *Rock Follies* is more important than *Hazell,* because as far as

I'm concerned everything we do is important. There isn't one series I could point to and say we're doing that because it's cheap. But something like *Rock Follies* has an enormous amount of music and a lot of costume design, both of which are very expensive. *Hazell* is fairly standard in those area; it doesn't have music and the clothes have got to look real rather than amazing. So I've put a price on *Hazell* which I think is adequate. [The producer is given an approximate figure to work to by the Head of Department, then goes away and consults with the relevant sections on what each area will cost.] But later on June will come to me when she's worked out what she thinks things are going to cost. If it's more than I've given her I will ask her how she arrived at the figures. If she needs more for a valid reason I will try and find it for her. But some departments often come back with figures which cover them for every eventuality, and you have to examine whether in fact they really do need all the money they're asking for. Quite often they don't but they add an extra thousand because they think, well if something goes wrong I'm not going to be the one who comes in over budget.'

Hazell of course had to fit into a total Drama Department budget for the year. This budget had been set some time in advance.

VL: 'This is actually quite difficult because I have to do the budget for the department nearly a year before the shows that I'm budgeting for come up. I know from experience not totally accurately but roughly how much a particular kind of series will cost. Something like *Romance,* which is all costume drama except for one episode and has extremely lush set designs, is going to cost a lot of money. In actual fact with *Romance* I made a guess and it was way under what we needed, so I had to make an extra allocation. With something like *Hazell* it's not too difficult, because it is to be scripted to fit into certain studio recording times. This is another thing you have to do: the writers are briefed that they can have so much location film in it and that it must be capable of being done in 2 days in the studio. Also when I budget I build in a rise of costs and materials and work (the average is about 20%), which you add on to last year's costs. I know that I have to do about 50 hours of drama a year. But I might put in things for a year ahead which are still only TBA (to be announced), because I may not have a series idea that I want to do at this point. But this makes it very difficult because you budget for something at a certain cost saying it will be this kind of thing and then you change your mind and do something else, which might be more expensive.'

The actual budget for each episode of *Hazell* worked out at between £28,000 and £29,000 for above the line (direct) costs. ITV, unlike the BBC, works on an accounting system which charges only direct costs to a production budget. Studio overheads, the salaries of permanent staff and so on do not appear on the budget sheets. In fact those amount to approximately £1.70 for every £1 of direct costs. Thus *Hazell* can be reckoned to have cost Thames something like £80,000 an episode, or £800,000 in all for the 10 episodes that were eventually recorded. The cost of one particular episode breaks down like this:

	£
Script	1,450
Cast	8,586
Music	80
Film (3 days)	1,200
Design and Sets	14,000
Titles and Stills	100
Wardrobe, Hairdressing, Make-Up	660
Additional Facilities	900
Production Staff Expenses	1,200
Insurances	15
Hospitality	150
Camera Tubes	300
Total	28,641

Note: Most of these headings are self-explanatory. A proportion of the budget for the music and graphics of the opening titles is charged to each episode. Production staff expenses will be things like fares. Film includes only stock and equipment; salaries will be below the line (indirect). For design the costs will be of materials and the labour involved in making them up. Additional facilities will be such things as a wardrobe van for actors on location, or security services, or whatever. A set figure for camera tubes appears to be charged against all programmes. We never discovered why.

Though it is the job of the producer to ensure that the show is brought in within this allocation, there is a system of financial control to assist in this. Tony Rowlands is what is called the programme cost assistant in the Drama Department. He first heard of *Hazell* in the spring of 1976, when nothing much had happened beyond the appointment of a producer. At that time he was helping Verity Lambert draw up the departmental budget for the next financial year (Thames' financial year starts on 1 July). A sum had to be set aside for *Hazell*. based on the kind of programme it was going to be. His next involvement came once June Roberts was in a position to draw up details of the budget she was intending to ask for; together with June and the heads of the relevant sections, such as design, he produced figures for the various headings of the budget, and was then involved in the discussions between June and Verity which resulted in the budget allocation being finally fixed. Then once production starts his job is to collect information on what is being spent and, ten days or so after the completion of the recording of each episode he will send the producer a cost sheet giving details of what has actually been spent. If during the course of the production anything starts to go over budget it is his duty to warn the producer. Once money has been spent it can't be taken back, but savings will have to be made on other items of the budget to compensate, if at all possible.

Also involved with the budget is Brian Walcroft, the manager of the Drama Department. Every year he goes with the head of his department, Verity Lambert, to meet Jeremy Isaacs, the Director of Programmes, in order to present the Drama Department's budget request for the year. This figure is then submitted, together with the figures for the other departments, to the Thames Board of Directors, and the allocation for each department then comes back down from the Board. If subsequently any of the Drama Department's budgets for individual productions start to go over budget by more than five per cent Brian Walcroft has to send a report to the Managing Director, the Director of Programmes and the Director of Finance. Obviously over-spending is sometimes unavoidable because of equipment failure, rain on location or whatever. But only if savings cannot be made on other items will more money be provided.

Because of this strict control on overspending the planners have to get the budget as nearly right as possible in advance. This is not always easy, not necessarily because one is dealing with unpredictable artists, but because in design, for instance, much of the cost is labour and this can't always be predicted exactly, as Brian Walcroft says:

BW: 'With design you can get an estimate, but when you get the cost in it's almost invariably over. You can have a set built in the construction shop one week and it will cost, say, £1000. You can have a similar set built there in three week's time and it will cost £2000 and you say, why did it take longer and they don't know why. Maybe they went to a party the night before and they had a hang-over. But when you are dealing with people who are working with tools you can't always tell how long they are going to take, and if they take twice as long there's very little you can do about it. I can't go back to the construction people and say, you took twice as long, you can pay for half of our set. It doesn't work like that.' (Thames have a contract with a company in Manchester who build their sets. The contract specifies the number of hours of labour that will be bought, not the number of sets that will be built.)

The budget for *Hazell*, as far as we know, is about average for this kind of production. £800,000 may seem like a lot of money for one programme, but one has to consider, first, that such a sum would be cheap for one feature-length cinema film and second, that the cost is recouped not only by income from commercials but by payments for the programme from other companies in the network and sales overseas. Obviously at these figures Thames' programmes are profitable (remember that in 1976/7 the company made a profit of £7,764,000 before tax), otherwise they wouldn't stay in business.

The question arises of why the average figure for costs should be of this order. To answer this in detail would take us well beyond the scope of this book into general questions about the economics of television. But the answer lies in a relationship between a number of factors. The company will try to keep the costs down to a minimum, but its efforts are constrained in the first place by certain costs such as those of labour and materials which it can only marginally affect. The figure for the script fee is only a little above the minimum the ITV companies have agreed with the Writers' Guild, and that figure is the result of market forces, based quite simply on supply and demand, as modified by the fact that writers are in a trade union. Similarly the cost of labour and materials for the sets represents what it costs in the market to build sets of this kind. Against the desire of the company to keep down costs is the need to assure a certain 'quality' of production. *Hazell* could have been made with cheaper actors or skimpier sets, but then it would not have reached a standard high enough to ensure its artistic and commercial success. Producers can haggle with departmental heads and account-ants, but only within a very limited field of manoeuvre. *Hazell*, to use Verity Lambert's words, has 'what it needs', no more and no less, to reach the required standard, and the practice of television production is so established that these needs will be universally recognised as, roughly, the right ones. The cost of all the labour, materials and fixed capital (i.e., investment in studio facilities, etc.) needed to achieve the required standard has been established by long precedent.

The result of this standardisation of costs is, of course, that however 'different' *Hazell* was to be in its conception and execution, its economics would have to be the same as any other similar type of production. It wouldn't have expensive international stars or weeks on location in foreign parts because it was conceived from the start as conforming to the norm for a British TV crime series. Its 'differences' would therefore have to be managed within this similarity. It's also worth mentioning that the budgeting system also ensures another kind of homogeneity. Each episode of the series would cost approximately the same. The occasional episode did in fact go over the budget, but by a fairly small percentage. So that in terms of, say, sets or wardrobe each episode would conform to the pattern. Sets will change, but insofar as their look is dictated by their cost they will look the same. Thus the consistency which the producer, writers and script editor would try to achieve at the level of characterisation, plot and mood would be reflected and in a sense dictated by the budget.

Scheduling

Brian Walcroft's job also involves booking studio space for each of the Drama Department's productions. This is done at a meeting of all the departments at Teddington together with the various production services such as wardrobe and make-up, at which productions for the next 6 months will be slotted in to the available studio time. Jeremy Isaacs will also attend the meeting so that in the event of there being a clash on dates (and there is great pressure on studio space) he can decide which programme he has most urgent need of for the schedules and so which should have priority in the studios. Brian Walcroft will also need to book the services that will be required during the location filming; this again is booked up to 6 months in advance.

Studio 3 at Teddington is too small for drama. Of the other two, Studio 1 is considerably larger than Studio 2, and Light Entertainment tends to favour it because they can get a larger studio audience in. This means that the Drama Department will be obliged to use Studio 2 for quite a few of its studio dates, and this restricts the number of different sets that any episode recorded there can have, and the size of those sets. A series such as *Romance,* which had large sets, had to go into Studio 1 and was therefore scheduled there when it was available. *Hazell,* on the other hand, presented no particular problems in this respect, and was mostly made in Studio 2. What this means, of course, is that decisions about studios and decisions about scripts are mutually reinforcing. If the series is conceived of as demanding only modest set requirements then it will be earmarked for Studio 2. This in turn means that if someone then wanted to write an episode with several large sets it would not be possible. (It also wouldn't be possible in terms of the budget allocation.)

We can also mention here that Brian Walcroft is responsible for booking directors for each episode. It's up to June Roberts to decide which directors she would like, based on her feeling about which are suited to this kind of material and also, given that not every episode is the same in mood or style, which scripts to assign to which directors. It's then up to Brian Walcroft to see if they are available, and to agree a fee. (There's not much negotiation about a fee, it seems. Thames decide what they will pay and it's more or less take it or leave it after that.) He also fulfils the same function for script editors and production assistants, and for producers themselves.

Before each programme goes into production he will agree with the various heads of technical departments at Teddington what is called a 'norm' for the show. This consists of a break-down of the requirements of the programme for each day in the studio (see page 214).

Film versus video

One feature of *Hazell* right from the start was intended to be its use of authentic-looking London locations. This has always been a strong suit of its predecessor in the 9 p.m. Monday slot, *The Sweeney*. But *The Sweeney* is made entirely on film, with no studio work on tape at all. Why, then, was it decided to make *Hazell* largely in the studio on tape, with only 10 or 15 minutes of film in each episode?

This question of whether to make programmes on tape or on film or on a combination of both is a sensitive one both for Thames and for the industry generally. For Thames it involves not only aesthetic considerations, plus the fact that they have large amounts of capital tied up in studio equipment, but also the views of their employees, particularly the permanent staff at the Teddington studios, about future employment prospects. Our study of *Hazell* raised many interesting and important topics in relation to television generally which we would have liked to pursue in greater detail and the issue of film or video is one of them. There is much debate within television now as to their relative advantages. Many directors, for example, prefer to work on film because it allows them to set up each shot separately and in particular to arrange the lights in the best way for each single shot. Working on tape in the studio they are in general obliged to light a scene in a way that will suit 4 cameras, shooting from different angles simultaneously. The length of time available in the studio simply doesn't permit individual set-ups as a rule. Another advantage of film to directors is that during shooting they can be on the floor, close to the actors. In the studio, working on tape, though the director will normally be on the floor for the camera rehearsals, his or her presence is necessary in the gallery during the actual take because that is the only place the director can see how the shots are actually being mixed together. And a further advantage of film is that it has until very recently been much more flexible to edit. Not only has it been capable of more precise cuts but the fact that tape editing involves extremely expensive equipment has meant that the time available to each director for editing has been limited, in contrast to the situation with film, where the director and editor can spend hours arguing over a single cut if needs be.

The whole issue is complex: we can do no more here than report on how the situation affected *Hazell*. This is what Jeremy Isaacs had to say before any episodes had been recorded:

JI: 'If we had our present studio facilities and there was no continuing series being done by Euston Films and they needed one then we would pretty certainly have said that *Hazell* should be done on film. I think it will be more difficult to do in the studio and we'll have to see whether they can succeed or not. But we needed something strong from the studios. [The unions at Teddington had made forceful representations to the management that too many of the most interesting and prestigious programmes, such as *The Sweeney* and *Van Der Valk,* were being done on film, on location away from the studios, and that consequently there might not be sufficient work for the permanent staff at Teddington.]

Although we may gradually increase the output of Euston Films over the years without diminishing the output that comes from Teddington, it was just more convenient, because there was the need for it, to do it from Teddington. The facilities are there, we don't like to keep the studios empty. Equally we can't keep people idle and people don't want to be kept idle. Indeed, as you perceive, they are very alarmed at the thought that we should do work on film that they feel they could do, and that is a very proper concern on their part. They are extremely talented people and they are not to be deprived of work, or of interesting work, just because it is possible to do things on film. One of the trickiest things I have to do over the next few years is to make sure that however much we do on film there is still plenty of interesting work to be done at Teddington. I don't think *Hazell* will suffer all that much. There's so much of a kind of salty strength in the characterisation and the humour and I think a lot of that can be captured by casting and acting and dialogue in the studio. I would hate to see *Hazell* turned into something that was all action, in which you never get out of a motor car or never stopped hitting people hard below the belt.

The situation with the unions now is that it's pretty well impossible if we start at Teddington on tape for us ever to move it onto film. We have an obligation to consult, one which we're very willing to honour. I take the view that it might be more interesting to say, look, you've done that long enough in the studio, we're taking it out because we can give it more life on film, and we're going to give you something else marvellous instead. Some people will accept that; others won't see it that way. Some people enormously enjoyed doing *Shades of Greene* because technically it was rather different; enjoyed doing *Rock Follies* because it was stylistically different. They enjoyed doing *Bill Brand* because the subject matter was interesting; and they will enjoy doing *Hazell*. I myself think they won't particularly enjoy doing *Hazell* if it gets to a fourth, fifth or sixth series. But that is something I will be talking over with them as we go along.

Things like *Callan* and *Public Eye* were done in the studio and were highly successful, though they were done at a time when ITV was not doing chase series or investigative series on film. As soon as you do it on film you provide a whole new pace and zip. It makes it that much more difficult to do anything similar in the studio.'

Clearly on balance Thames would have preferred to do *Hazell* on film, simply because film is felt by most people in television to be a 'faster' medium than tape i.e., you can get more pace into a show on film. But if people didn't think it could be done on tape at all then it wouldn't have been; this was certainly Verity Lambert's view:

VL: 'If I'd felt really strongly that *Hazell* could only have been done on film then I would have put it off until *The Sweeney* ended and put it in that gap. But I didn't. I know it can be done in the studio because I've done series like it in other companies. It's a hassle, it seems like a nightmare to begin with, but it can be made to work and work well.'

Two more points are worth making. Firstly, technical developments in videotape have increasingly closed the gap between the two media, to the extent where tape now has much of the flexibility that people value in film. Lighter weight equipment, including hand-held video cameras for use in the studio and outside, and new editing technology have made it possible both to shoot with the precision and fluidity traditionally felt to belong to film and to piece the separate takes together with something approaching the pace and subtlety formerly achieved only in the cinema. As we shall see, both these new kinds of technology were to be employed on *Hazell*.

Secondly, *Hazell* was never intended by any of the people involved in its conception to be an 'action' series. ('Action' in television parlance is normally a euphemism for violence and car chases.) The intention was always to do something quite different, within the genre of the crime series, from *The Sweeney* and the American series such as *Kojak* which were its inspiration. There's very little violence in *Hazell* (he does kill one man, but this is seen as very much an exception to his normal behaviour) and though Hazell has a car he doesn't do much chasing in it. This may turn out to the programme's advantage. Certainly there is irony in the fact that while *Hazell* was in production there was talk of a new BBC series coming up, *Target*, which some felt would have an advantage, being entirely on film. As it turned out *Target* is merely a retread of *The Sweeney*, without any of the latter's saving sense of humour.

Two of the directors we talked to had contrasting views on the question of film v. tape. Alistair Reid shot more film for his episode than any other director and in the studio tended to use the television cameras like film cameras, setting up each shot separately. His preference for film seemed almost mystical:

AR: 'It's a philosophical question really of being actually able to hold the stuff and touch it, which I like, and of being able to chop and change it *ad infinitum*. Whereas up in the editing suite you're dealing with space-age technology, vastly expensive equipment, and the actual programme sitting on the machine is itself worth in the region of £50,000 and you can't touch it or smoke or anything. So there's a feeling of caution about videotape.

The other thing I have against tape is that it's really too good. It's too clear, it shows up all the faults. You can't get the light effects you can on film and the sound is too clear, you can hear you are in a studio. I'd like to go for rather rotten pictures and messy degraded images and all that. But it doesn't please the technicians.'

Alistair Reid also thought that it was easier to improve acting performances by judicious editing on film, and that in his episode he could have saved the cost of the sets (around £15,000) by going out on location. (Though as far as we can tell there is no particular cost advantage in film because while it may require less sets and technicians it also takes longer — perhaps 9 days shooting for a 50 minute episode compared to 2 days in the studio.)

Brian Farnham also took the view that if *Hazell* had been made on film it would have been more like *The Sweeney,* a point which Alistair Reid made, if only implicitly. But this for him would have been a positive disadvantage:

BF: 'I think the script would have been very different done on film, and I think not as good. I think there would have been a terrible tendency for it to have become a bit 'Sweeneyesque', it would have become all car chases and rushing around, that sort of stuff. And that was one of the things we were trying to get away from. What fascinates me is what you can do with television as an electronic medium . . .'

Brian Farnham was one of the two directors of the last series of *Rock Follies,* generally reckoned to be one of the most inventive taped television shows of the last few years.

But this was a minority view. June Roberts also would have preferred film, since, she argued, a production wholly on film would have used a smaller unit, which would in turn have made consistency from episode to episode easier to achieve.

4 The Scripts

Before work on the scripts began, then, certain parameters had been set within which they would be written. There were financial limitations: *Hazell* would have the budget deemed necessary for this kind of show, but no more. This precluded, for example, scenes involving large numbers of extras. In terms of how *Hazell* had been fitted into studio schedules, there were further dictates. Each episode had to be capable of being recorded in 2 days in the studio, and must have no more sets than could be erected within the studio space available in the case of Studio 2, up to about 5 sets of average size. Location work was restricted to what could be filmed in 3 days (10 to 15 minutes of screen time). Lastly, the decision to make the show largely on tape ensured that certain choices about the style and content of the series became virtually inevitable. It would be a mistake, however, to look upon these sets of contraints as simply negative in their effects. Although some people did at times wish for more money, more time in the studio or hanker after more film and less tape, to many the constraints were a challenge to ingenuity and inventiveness, even a positive advantage. Thus, though a mere 2 days in the studio seemed a very short time (albeit standard throughout television for a show of this length) there was a feeling by some of those involved, especially directors, that the very lack of time served to raise the adrenalin level of the actors and so improve performances.

Work on some scripts had begun while discussions on the matters referred to above were still proceeding, and continued right up to the time when the production entered the studio — indeed, in some cases beyond it. Most of this work was directed towards two objectives. Firstly, the concept of the show had to be defined in detail. What was *Hazell* all about, what was it trying to do? What made it different from other TV crime series? Secondly, once such a definition had been arrived at, scripts had to be made as good as they could possibly be. If these two objectives could not be achieved, prospects for the show would be slim; everybody agreed that good scripts were an essential foundation for success. For one thing, the better the script the better the artists you can get to realise it.

The question of what made for a 'good' *Hazell* script is discussed below. The immediate problem was to decide on a series format, to define a concept that would be original and entertaining, and which would come as close as possible to what those already engaged in the production wanted it to be.

Who Is Hazell?

It might be thought that the problem of deciding exactly what Hazell himself was like would be a relatively simple one, since there were already in existence three novels describing him in detail. All that had to be done was to transfer the character from the printed page to the screen. But as Gordon Williams himself pointed out, this isn't simple at all. In a novel the reader will accept a certain amount of imprecisions and inconsistency, fusing them in his/her imagination into a coherent whole. But what can be left vague in a novel has to be precise and consistent on screen. In print a character can have a long nose and it's left to the reader to decide how long. But once a particular actor is chosen for the role the length of nose is fixed precisely to a millimetre. This already makes for difficulties in casting, since no actor will ever correspond exactly to what is in the novel. But there is also the problem that the screen image has to embody a number of different people's conceptions: the producer, director, writer, script editor, actor, costume designer and so on. No two people's conception will be exactly the same; but for the sake of internal consistency throughout the series there must be as much agreement as can be managed.

Not only is Hazell a single character, but the world he inhabits must have its own unity. This doesn't mean, of course, that different facets of Hazell cannot be revealed or that his world cannot contain widely contrasting elements; indeed, the demands of dramatic variation require it. But virtually all television drama works within the dictates of narrative realism, in which both characters and the world they inhabit have an inner consistency and unity. In a series running for several episodes to be written by different writers it is important this this consistency and unity be hammered out at the start, so that everyone is working towards the same ends.

This problem is of course common to any television drama series, and one of the producer's most important functions is to solve it to the satisfaction of all concerned. The producer doesn't (generally) write or act or direct or design; the job is to a large extent to see that all these various functions are working in harmony. The concept of the show may not, in fact probably won't, be theirs exclusively; but theirs is the responsibility for seeing, first, that there *is* a viable concept, and second, that everyone is working to realise it. That responsibility can be exercised by virtue of the fact that the producer has the ultimate power of decision, except in so far as decisions may have to be referred upwards, and is the only person to be involved at every stage of the production.

All this is by way of saying that it was ultimately up to June Roberts what *Hazell* was to be like within the limits already described. With the three novels she had quite a lot to go on already. But the novels were only a starting point, there was considerable scope for altering what was in them.

Preserving intact a unified concept is clearly easier the fewer people you have involved. Thus at an early stage June attempted to keep down the numbers. Ideally there would be two or three writers, perhaps only two directors, and a single designer and lighting director responsible for the whole series. This ideal proved impossible to achieve; partly because other demands on the Design and Lighting Departments meant that the work had to be divided up, partly because unavoidable changes in production dates meant that other directors had to be brought in, and partly because of various problems with writers, which will emerge below. Ideally, too, a series would have the same technicians all the way through: the same camera crews, sound crews, film crews and so on. But this in fact is never possible, due simply to the number of productions carried out by the company. Camera crews can find themselves working on children's programmes, drama and light entertainment in a single week.*

Originally it was intended that Gordon Williams and Terry Venables would contribute the first script to the series. Neither had worked in television before but they were keen to make *Hazell* a success, and there was an obvious advantage in having the formulative scripts written by the two people who knew Hazell best. But then Terry was appointed manager at Crystal Palace, and pressure of work there made any further writing after the first script impossible. More writers had to be engaged. At this point Gordon was asked to produce a character sketch of Hazell which would assist new writers with their scripts. It's worth quoting this in full, partly as an indication of the kind of briefing

* Of course it's a question of priorities; if the company felt such continuity was vitally important ways would be found of ensuring it.

writers are likely to get on a series of this kind, and partly because it gives, as well as something of the flavour of the books, a good idea of the original concept of the character that everyone started out from:

Hazell is in early or mid-thirties, divorced, ex-police, big, good-looking, slightly battered, and has an intermittently painful ankle, heterosexual. He is heavy physically, deliberate, not exactly ponderous but solid to slow.

He has mass tastes — *Daily Mirror,* slightly old-fashioned pop music, films, paperbacks — yet he is aware of being conned by mass media and makes critical remarks of a commonsense, perhaps simplistic kind. Now and again he goes to football matches, having always supported West Ham.

His accent is variable, basically cockney but capable of social 'elevation' if necessary. In fact, this is a key point — he has left his Dagenham/East End origins both geographically and emotionally, yet they have not left him. Faced with snobs he drops his aitches and uses 'f' for 'th'. Faced with gorblimeys he goes the other way — using a sophisticated vocabulary in a self-conscious, self-parodying way.

He has certain set expressions, both verbal and facial. One of his expletives is 'Kinnell!' which is never elucidated on. Another is 'I'm more yer fish and chips.' ('Shall we lunch at Claridges?' 'If you don't mind I'm more yer wodge of stodge in corner caffs and that.') 'I'm more yer . . . ' Another is 'Call me a naive sentimental fool . . . ' e.g., 'Call me a naive sentimental fool but I don't actually like mass murderers . . . '

Facially he is typically East End — pleasant, open, smiling — in a droll, hypocritical way. He would go on listening to you with that frank, open smile right up to the moment he belted you. Artful Dodger, tell you the most awful lies with that straight open face, the eyes defying you to call his bluff.

Under all this is a tiredness and a disappointment brought about by the failures of his police career, his marriage, his lack of a home life. He is not cynical — given any chance he displays the usual incongruous East End humour — but he is by no means the jolly cockney. Isolation is his predicament, and a somewhat naive optimism about people who tend to let him down or try to cheat him.

London is his only possible environment. Birmingham he would think of as Siberia, Scotland as Zululand. Yet he is painfully conscious of the size and anonymity and unfathomable diversity of the vast sprawl. Caught in a traffic jam he'll describe modern

London as hell, a place to get out of if only he had the fare and if only there was anywhere else in the world to go to.

He is continually looking for Miss Right, for kids of his own, for a chance to push a pram down High Street on Saturday morning. Naturally he's not going to get these things.

He is well capable of extreme violence but whenever it occurs he feels degraded, particularly by his guilt at enjoying it.

The one certainty in his life is that he is not a bum and is determined to make his way in the world as honestly as possible. In some ways, generally to do with money and business, he is quite slow but he would not make the same mistake twice.

In general he reacts or counterpunches. If he hears a hard-luck story or meets a sad case he is genuinely moved and will help (e.g., he would dive straight in if he saw ten youths beating up an old man); if, however, he saw a pickpocket gang jostling a tourist on the tube he would put it down to 'one of those things' and not intervene on the basis that playing Sir Galahad would be a full-time unpaid occupation. In many ways he is Mr Average, keen on his car, keen but not too clever about buying clothes; he is reluctant to be so flash as to call himself a private detective, generally preferring to say he's 'going a bit of your enquiries and that' if forced to be specific. Indeed, he is never too sure how he drifted into private detective work and has a sensitivity about what he calls snooping and prying. He would like to be rich, with handsome shoes, cigars, a smart flat — but knows in all probability he'll never achieve it — and not like it if he got it. Given any encouragement he is *nice*.

This is a fairly accurate summary of Hazell as he appears in the novels, except that it tends to play up the darker side of the character: the sense of failure, the problems of his injury, his marriage, his drinking. June Roberts believes that there was always a split in the concept, which she interprets with some plausibility as relating to the personalities of his two creators. To Terry she attributes the concept of Hazell as a bit of a lad, an extrovert ladykiller, a winner. Gordon she sees as responsible for the darker side of Hazell. In his concept Hazell is a bit of a loner, for whom life has turned, if not bitter, then a little sour. It would be much too simple to suppose that there was any direct correspondence between the characters of Hazell and his creators; Hazell isn't the sum of the characters of Gordon and Terry. But June may have been right in supposing there was some connection. Gordon Williams, however, thinks this is entirely wrong and that it's Terry Venables who is the 'serious' one of the partnership.

June Roberts told us that she thought Verity Lambert inclined more towards the extrovert side of Hazell, though in fact the description of the character which Verity herself gave was of someone 'who was vaguely dissatisfied, quite disillusioned, and quite interested in money, a hustler in a way. Somebody who is on the whole unable to have good relationships with people, who's a loner, but also someone who has a terrific surface, of dealing with life through jokes, but quite hard'. Verity also told us she has met people like that, that Hazell was a life-like character. What is clear is that June herself, while not necessarily disagreeing with these views of the character, had very definite ideas about what the *style* of the show should be:

JR: 'I wanted to do a contemporary but very 40s-50s looking, extremely romantic private eye thriller. I wanted it to have a language of its own, be extremely witty, and I wanted people to recognise the conventions that we were putting on the screen. The reason I went that way in the beginning was, first, because of the Chandler influences that were there in the books anyway — not that strongly but they were there. And secondly because we were on tape. I knew therefore it would be a much slower show. You can't compete with action series, it couldn't be another *Target* or another *Sweeney*. And we'd already done *Public Eye*. If we hadn't done anything different it would have been another, younger, *Public Eye*.'

This argues a concept which is highly stylised, very much referring back to a certain *genre* of movies and crime fiction, and which would entertain by wit and elegance. It's a concept which deliberately owes more to a remembered fictional world than to any real world, and the kind of thing which is hardly ever seen on television, reduced as the medium is to more or less naturalistic*representations of what the world is supposed to be like. To an extent it overlapped with Gordon Williams' own feelings about what the series ought to do. The novels had in fact been written with half an eye on Chandler, with the hero transposed from Los Angeles to London. But Gordon also wanted to give a realistic picture of London life. He remarked at one point that the series should have two heroes, Hazell and London. He wanted to get a kind of authentic feel of London into the series in the way that Marlowe inhabits an identifiable Southern California.

* By naturalism here we mean an attempt to reproduce the surface appearance of everyday life.

The series 'Notes', prepared for new writers coming on to the show, indicated that it would explore 'areas unfamiliar but intrinsically London'.

Gordon Williams: 'I was anxious to get away from the old *No Hiding Place* style, where you turn a corner and there's Buckingham Palace and you look over your shoulder and there's St Paul's and Big Ben is chiming the time and there's two pearly queens on the pavement — this is really made for an American audience. And I think of things like *The Sweeney*, where the two Flying Squad detectives, working from Scotland Yard, are rarely, if ever, seen in Central London, W1. They are always in suburbia, Acacia Avenue, simply because it's very difficult to film in central London.'

Hazell certainly made attempts to find locations which were away from the tourist sights and which offered a genuine flavour of London: locations such as Acton, parts of the East End, Piccadilly underpass, Clapton dog stadium, Battersea heliport, Shepherd Market.

on location in Shepherd Market: l. to r. Vinnie Rae (Celia Gregory) Hazell (Nicholas Ball) Dot Wilmington (Barbara Young)

Stan Hey (one of the writers who worked on *Hazell*): 'You get the impression from television that 90% of the crime of this country is committed on British Rail wasteland. We're trying to use locations that mean something, which people can identify with. If Hazell's got to go up to Chigwell, then he's got to get a bus out from Finsbury Park and if necessary people can get out a bus map and follow him.'

Yet as it turned out a lot of the location filming was done in Soho, which is hardly unfamiliar to begin with and looks increasingly less so as one runs out of new shooting angles in what is after all a fairly small area of London. A problem about the use of London that was never perhaps quite resolved is that in Chandler's books Southern California is more a state of mind than a real place. There is actually relatively little description of location in the books, and the best known films of the period to be drawn from his books, such as *The Big Sleep* and *Farewell, My Lovely,* scarcely ever venture out of the studio. June Roberts' idea of a very stylised series ran counter to the impulse to show the 'real' London; and one reason possibly why the series keeps coming back from Acton and Chigwell to what is a slightly romantic view of Soho is that people who wanted realism and people who wanted style were both talking about Chandler and therefore thinking they were talking about the same thing, when in fact they weren't. For some Chandler meant realism, for others a certain stylisation.

This tension between differing concepts, both drawing on Chandler and the so-called 'hard-boiled' school of writers, and on the Hollywood *film noir* of the 1940s, but emphasising different aspects of it, was to surface later in discussions both about Hazell's character and about the kinds of situation he should find himself in. But in the early stages of talking about what kind of show it would be June Roberts was concerned to focus attention on the question of how far *Hazell* could be made to reflect on the conventions of the 40s crime film.

Hazell and the movies

One day in June the first 3 writers to be involved in *Hazell,* Gordon Williams, Terry Venables and Peter Ransley, were assembled at Teddington by June Roberts to watch a couple of movies: *The Big Sleep* and *Double Indemnity.* Two acknowledged classics of the *film noir genre*, they were intended to act as reference points for a discussion of style. If *Hazell* was to have some relation to Raymond Chandler, what

strong women and dark shadows (Jane Greer and Robert Mitchum in Out Of The Past, RKO, 1947)

could be learnt from watching these two films, one drawn from a novel of his, the other from a script on which he collaborated?

Film noir as a *genre* has a number of characteristics, beyond the fact that the films are almost invariably about crime. Visually the films are highly stylised, using low-key lighting, with its attendant strong shadows, and bizarre camera angles. The narrative structures are often convoluted, employing devices such as flash-backs and voice-over narration. The plots often feature strong women characters, frequently morally corrupt. Much of the action takes place at night; sometimes it's foggy too. Invariably the pictures are shot in black and white.

In the discussion which followed the viewings, which was also attended by Verity Lambert, one thing that fascinated the writers was the use of voice-over narration in *Double Indemnity*. Much of the distinctive feel of the film comes from the cynical, hard-bitten style of Fred MacMurray's voice as it recounts the story. The Hazell novels like Chandler's Marlowe series are also written in the first-person and there was a general feeling that the device could be used to advantage in the series. But no-one was precisely sure what its function was. Who is the narrator actually talking to? In this particular film this is not a problem, since MacMurray's narration is motivated by having him speak into a tape-recorder for the benefit of Edward G. Robinson, who will thus understand after MacMurray's death what has happened. But would Hazell be talking to himself in a kind of interior monologue, or speaking to the audience in the manner of an Elizabethan dramatic hero? Would he be commenting on the action as it happened or would he be recollecting events at a later date? Eventually it was decided that voice-over would be used as a convention of the series and would be an address to the audience, and that it would refer to events in the past; in other words, as though Hazell were telling the audience the story.

It's interesting to note, in passing, that though Hazell speaks to the audience he never looks at it. The convention of virtually all television drama, that the audience is looking in on events rather than having them directly presented to it, is preserved. Brian Farnham, who directed the last episode to be recorded, did include a shot in which, at the end of the episode, Hazell turns to the camera and winks. But the shot was never used*.

A note was composed for writers on the series indicating what functions the voice-over would fulfil: 'The function of this device is to set atmosphere; convey information quickly that could not be done more effectively in the context of a scene; provide opportunities for humorous or philosophical asides; comment on character; increase suspense by giving or witholding information.'

Further discussions between the writers and the producer brought agreement that the series would not only be built round Hazell's character but that each episode would be seen, as it were, through his eyes. Hazell himself would virtually never be off the screen and the audience would have no privileged information, only knowing what he knew. It seems there were two reasons for this. Firstly, though this was a private eye series, no-one was very interested in the paraphernalia of detection as such, in Agatha Christie-style clues and suspects. Interest was firmly centred on Hazell and the people he became involved with. Though there would be suspense, character was to be the focus of interest. Secondly, given that the books were told through Hazell and voice-over was to be used in the television version, it seemed a logical extension that events would be presented as Hazell's experience. In fact it seems for a time that June Roberts flirted with the idea of using subjective camera at certain points, showing things literally from Hazell's point of view. This was soon rejected and though in general one might be in favour of more experiments with technique, anyone who has seen the disastrous experiment of *Lady In The Lake,* a film from the Chandler novel which uses this device throughout, can only rejoice.

A footnote to this is provided by Verity Lambert. We asked her to

---

* The reason, we assume, was that it didn't fit in with the conventions that had been established whereby Hazell speaks to the audience but never shows visually that he is aware of them.

52

what extent she, as Head of the Drama Department, involved herself in decisions. Her reply was that she tried to preserve a balance between interfering on the one hand and letting producers fall flat on their faces on the other. As we shall see, she was involved in some crucial decisions, such as casting.

VL: 'I did put my foot down about subjective camera because I knew that it wouldn't work over a long period of time, it would have become very pretentious and boring and I just wasn't prepared even to allow that mistake to be made.'

One example, then, of a decision not left entirely to the producer.*

There's only one, rather odd instance of what might be called subjective camera in the series. In the first episode, *Hazell Plays Solomon*, Hazell goes to call on the Abrey family. The door of their flat has a peep-hole and we get a view through it, shown with a fish-eye lens, of Hazell as seen by Clifford Abrey. But there's also a view from Hazell's side of Abrey, giving a similarly distorted view. Of course you can't actually see through a peep-hole backwards. As far as we know this is the only time in the series there is a departure from 'realistic' visual conventions.

The problem of how to render the visual effects achieved in *film noir* in a television series made in colour was one on which a lot of thought was expended. Later we shall see what the outcome was, but at this stage the problem was left unresolved and the script writers were not explicitly instructed to write to any particular visual conventions, though they were briefed to write visually interesting locations. This possibly made it more difficult later to experiment visually.

Another Hazell

The fact that Terry had had to pull out of writing and that time had been spent in wrestling with the problems of first-person narratives, flashbacks and so on led Verity Lambert to suggest that June Roberts appoint a script editor. At first she had fulfilled this function herself, but increasing demands on her time meant that she was unable to

---

* June Roberts later remarked to us that she never intended to use the device throughout, only in the opening shots of the first episode, up to the moment Clifford Abrey opens the door of his flat. She says that after discussion with Jim Goddard, the director, she herself abandoned the idea, feeling that as it was the start of a new series introducing Nick Ball to the viewers, the whole sequence should be shot tightly on his face.

devote her full attention to the new writers who were being brought in. The job of the script editor will be discussed later. At this point we are concerned with the effect of this appointment on the concept of the series. Kenneth Ware, who took the job, describes his own view of Hazell and how in his opinion the character changed during the time he was in the job:

KW: 'I got a phone call saying was I interested? Since at that time they were talking about quasi-Chandler I was very interested. But the concept of what the series is about has gone through so many changes, ranging from anglicised Chandler to what it's now being described as: comedy-thriller, or thriller with comedy. It's very unlike the character that was being suggested when I first came in and it isn't the kind of character I would have wanted to do. I wanted something much more Chandleresque, but you need a very particular sort of writer to produce that kind of thing. And anyway that isn't what Thames bought. What they bought is comedy-thriller, so there are joke lines instead of Marlowe flip dialogue. Some of the ideas in it, like voice-over narrative, are Chandler, but the character now is much more happy-go-lucky. In fact, it's a bit of a contradiction with the books, where he has a serious drink problem behind him and a painfully broken marriage. Now we're having to suggest he has surmounted all this and can still be chirpy.'

It's certainly true that the darker side of Hazell's character only appears in attenuated form in the scripts. There are occasional references to his drinking, and one episode which deals with his marriage. But most of the problems belong to Hazell's clients, not to him. Kenneth Ware attempted when he first came on to the series to swing things more into line with the Chandleresque concept by making some modifications to the *Solomon* script.

Gordon and Terry didn't like this new version at all. They felt very strongly that it was a step back towards the kind of James Bond style that they had been trying to get away from. Terry's comments on the rewrite were frank:

TV: 'Gordon showed me the new thing. He didn't say he didn't like it or anything, he just said, what do you think? I got to page three and I said you're joking, what's this? I said, it's just not what he's about, all the lewd remarks. I said, if that's what you're going for, let them do it but scrub me off. And he said that was exactly how he felt. So one day it had been hot and I'd been training and I rushed out to Teddington, and Gordon was there with June and Ken. When I got there they were saying take this out and that out. And I just looked at Gordon and listened at that stage because I didn't know what they'd agreed on previously. They'd already been working three or four hours. So afterwards when Gordon asked me what did I feel about it, I said rubbish, it's diabolical. Mind you, I said, I think you've contributed to that, I don't think you were strong enough with them. He listened to my ideas and then he went back to them. I mean, he was the one who had to go back to the lion's den — I was at a distance telling him what to do.

You see, the politics are different from in football, they're a lot more subtle in these places. But at the end of the day, no matter what your subtleties are they've got to know what you think, so you might as well just go in and tell them. It cuts a lot of corners. So we did and we got it back on our lines again. It concerned me a lot at the time. I thought to myself, all the work we've done. I wouldn't have wanted people to go in and buy our books because they'd seen some other version of Hazell. It might have sold, but for the wrong reasons. That's not Thames' problem, I realise that. They've got their own problems. But what concerns me is that I'm not there to listen to what their problems are. If I did I might say, you've got a good point there, perhaps I'm wrong. Of course I'm prepared to be flexible, but you've got to have proper communication or you don't know what the other side's thinking. So I tried to be flexible until I saw that script and I thought it was miles off, there wasn't even any room for discussion.'

So Kenneth Ware's attempt to pull the conception of Hazell back towards what he had been informed was the original concept, an anglicised Marlowe, was not approved by Gordon and Terry. The Hazell that was beginning to emerge, though there were doubtless elements of Marlowe in him, also owed something to the traditional Dickensian cockney (remember that Gordon Williams himself referred to the Artful Dodger). There was also perhaps a touch of Alfie, as played by Michael Caine in the film of that name. But there continued to be some flexibility in the conception of the character, and modifications were produced by the introduction of new writers, and by the eventual decision on who to cast as Hazell.

One further aspect of the show which Kenneth Ware attempted to influence concerned the kinds of situation in which Hazell should find himself. From the start June Roberts was clear that she wanted to get away from strict realism:

JR: 'I wanted to say that the private detective in terms of his role in TV is pure fiction; he is not a real person, these stories are not real. They're entertaining stories, they're only believable because they hold your attention from beginning to end, but I saw no need for any character to be credible beyond the strength of the script.'

Kenneth Ware, however, had worked as writer and editor in the mainstream of the British television realist tradition. He believed that *Hazell* should be as real as possible. Thus Hazell as a character should develop as the series went along, should be affected by the things that happen to him as people are in real life:

KW: 'I worked on the original *Z Cars* and was involved in the setting up of *Softly, Softly*. Both these series purposely set out to allow the participants to grow as the series went along. For instance in *Z Cars* they were promoted in a real context, in terms of police procedure. Sgt. Watt became Inspector Watt at about the right time, if he'd been a good policeman, that he would have done in real life. I think the same sort of thing should happen in *Hazell*. The viewer should feel things happen to him. If the guy in episode 1 is the same as the guy in episode 13 then in a way nothing's happened to him.'

This conception of the series is reflected in some notes prepared for the writers on the kind of plots required:

1. They must consist of plausible actions of plausible people in plausible circumstances, bearing in mind that plausibility is largely a matter of style.
2. Must be technically sound in execution of crimes or actions and methods of detection.
3. Although plots should appear complex, suspenseful and mysterious they should have enough essential simplicity of structure to be explained simply when the time comes.
4. Final explanations should be accompanied by suspenseful action and preferably in short doses rather than all at once.
5. Solutions, once revealed, must seem to have been inevitable.
6. Ambiguous endings where the audience is left with something to guess would also, on occasion, be acceptable.
7. Most stories will probably evolve from tracing missing persons or retrieving missing objects or detecting why objects or people are missing.
8. Every client of Hazell must have a valid reason for not going to the police.

Not all these precepts, it is true, concern strict fidelity to real life. Some relate more to the principles of constructing suspenseful and entertaining plots. But the plots of Chandler's novels or of many 40s *film noir* certainly do not possess 'essential simplicity', as anyone who has seen or read *The Big Sleep* well knows.* As it turned out, the scripts of *Hazell* represent something of a compromise. Though in one sense they are all realistic, in that everyone has some 'plausible' motive for their actions and, to quote another note to writers, 'everything that happens to Hazell could happen to a man in a peculiar set of circumstances', the characters and situations that he encounters do vary quite a bit, from the mundane to the bizarre. But at the same time it's fair to say that for the most part the series does manage to get away from the kind of 'nitty gritty' realism of many of its precursors in the TV crime *genre* such as *Z Cars, The Sweeney* or *Public Eye,* though not going as far towards the creation of a stylised fantasy world as June Roberts would have liked.

Clearly any television programme is going to be a compromise, and no-one could be more aware of this than the people who worked on *Hazell,* many of whom made precisely this point to us. The compromise is negotiated not only between the different ideas of those involved (bearing in mind that in any case those 'ideas' have their source at a point beyond the individuals who propose them; thus conceptions of *Hazell* originated in its being made 'like' this programme, book or film, or 'unlike' that). It also has to be made between what those working on the show want it to be, and what the various structures within which they work will allow. An illustration of this point came in a further attempt by June Roberts to pull the series round to her way of thinking.

From the start June had wanted the series to contain strong roles for women. It's interesting that in Hollywood *film noir* there is a long list of forceful and active women characters, though June's wish to develop women's roles owed more to her feeling that there were simply far too few of them on television. Speaking after the series had finished recording she admitted her disappointment with how this aspect of it had turned out:

JR: 'The women's parts in this are as dull as they usually are. I think the exception, partly in the writing, partly in the performance, is Elizabeth Power, who plays Mrs Courtney in *Hazell Meets the First Eleven.* She's got a classic entrance, she's got a very strong personality,

* Both June Roberts and Kenneth Ware contested this point, maintaining that the plots of many 40s *film noirs* and of Chandler's novels are basically simple. We don't think they are — but in any case the *Hazell* plots are simpler still. Given the constraints of 51 minutes screen time, they are bound to be.

and that's the kind of woman I wanted to appear in episode after episode, a type of character who would really dominate the screen when she came on it. But if you look closely none of the women really participate in the stories in any way.

The concept of the part Vinnie (Hazell's girl friend) had was wonderful: ex-Rodean, rich, doing a most unlikely job (she's a debt collector) and with a very quirky off-beat character that you would need several episodes to understand. But apart from the description of her none of the writers knew what to do with her. She has a totally passive role all the way through. She's got a good entrance in episode 2 and some funny lines, she's got quite a good scene with Dornford, which is the only time in the whole series you see her doing anything. She's collecting a debt and upstaging Hazell, saying, this is how you do it, you poor emasculated fool, but doing it with charm and with femininity and with fun. After that she drops in and out, has a chat with him or has a kip with him but does nothing. And it doesn't matter how much talking you do to a writer in that area, unless they really understand the character they don't know how to use it.'

The obvious solution to this problem would have been to use women writers, and June believes this would have made an enormous difference. But this proved impossible; there simply wasn't enough time. Both because the earlier scripts took longer to write than anticipated and because the recording of most of the episodes was brought forward by 3 months, it became very difficult to experiment with the kind of women writers June would have wanted to use. In each case they were new to television and the shortage of time meant that there was great pressure not to take risks. In this case then, the inexorable dictates of studio schedules affected the kind of show that *Hazell* turned out to be.

What makes a 'good' script?

Since the series is built round Hazell's personality, clearly each script had to place him in situations that would allow that personality to be displayed. But there were other ingredients added to make the series both distinctive and entertaining.

Entertainment is, one might say, something which people in television find hard to define but easy to recognise. We shall not attempt to define it here in any general sense, but it is possible to indicate some of the characteristics which those involved with the *Hazell* scripts considered any good television writing should have, and some particular qualities that were looked for in scripts for this series. It wouldn't do to say that script writers have rules, since no-one, especially individualists such as writers tend to be, likes to be thought of as ruled, and they would undoubtedly say that you can do anything provided you can get away with it. Nevertheless there is a set of well-tried maxims, the custom and practice of the trade.

First of all, of course, one must observe the constraints imposed. We've already seen that there were limits on the amount of location filming and the number of sets, and on the amount of money each episode could cost. Writers were also encouraged to work in running characters (see below). Each episode had to run for exactly 51 minutes (making an hour-long show with the commercials) and had to divide neatly into 3 acts, with an appropriately suspenseful ending to each one. Each episode had to tell a complete story. And writers have to think about such details as the number of days over which the action occurs, what happens on which day and whether scenes are day or night. Such information will be necessary to preserve 'continuity' (e.g., Hazell would probably change his shirt if scene 16 were to take place a day after scene 15, but probably not if it were the same afternoon. The costume designer and wardrobe people will need to have this made clear in the script). Good 'professionals' can take this in their stride.

In terms of style, as opposed to simple technical requirements, one of the most important factors was pace. Crime series, unless possibly they are Agatha Christie-type whodunnits (and *Hazell* was never intended to be one of those), must move fast. In part this could be said to be a requirement of all television drama. Television drama doesn't have a captive audience stuck in their seats, as theatre or cinema have, so if there are longeurs people may switch over or off, and it works to extremely rigid time slots. But it's especially true of this *genre*. So, don't have long speeches. Try to start a scene in the middle and cut it off before the end. Thus don't show people entering a room, sitting down, beginning a conversation, then getting up and leaving. There's an illustration in the first episode, *Hazell Plays Solomon,* of this technique. Mrs Georgina Gunning, the rich American client, arrives at London Airport tired and irritable, and is met by Hazell and Gordon Gregory. In an early version of the script the scene reads:

GREGORY: You had a pleasant flight, I trust? (*he holds rear door open for her*).

GEORGINA: There is no way that eleven hours in an aeroplane can be pleasant, Mr. Gregory.

In a later version this becomes:
Hazell watches Gregory shaking hands with Georgina, then opening car door for her to get in.
GEORGINA: Pleasant? Eleven hours in the air?

Because 51 minutes is a very short time in which to tell a complete story involving perhaps as many as 20 characters no time can be wasted. In their first script of *Hazell Plays Solomon* Gordon and Terry had written a scene in which Hazell goes in search of the house where Georgina Gunning, the rich American, has hidden the Abreys' daughter. The scene contained a comic interchange between Hazell and a woman passer-by. This had to be cut, not because there was anything wrong with the writing but because there simply wasn't time for dialogue which wasn't essential to the plot.

Gordon and Terry also learnt to observe the old Hollywood scriptwriters' law of 'don't tell me, show me'. In part this is simply a question of leaving certain things which a novelist would describe at length to the set or costumer designer, actor or director to realise visually. Thus in the novel *Hazell Plays Solomon* there are several paragraphs describing the Abreys' flat. The script says merely 'cluttered and shabby'. But it's also a question of organising the action and dialogue to make the necessary points quickly and economically. A good example is to compare the openings of *Hazell Plays Solomon* as novel and as script for the first episode of the series. This is how the novel starts:

My name is James Hazell and I'm the biggest bastard who ever pushed your bell button.

No, that wasn't how I introduced myself to the creepy Clifford Abrey but it should have been, that warm July evening in the east end of London Town.

I had just given my newly-healed ankle a punishing work-out on seven flights of concrete stairs in a grey barrack block of flats called Herbert Morrison House in tatty old Bethnal Green.

If Abrey had known the truth about my visit he would have chucked me down the shaft of the wonky lift. Or at least he would have tried. But I didn't know myself, not then. If I had I would have done a quick disappearing act from the whole deal.

Baby capers are not my line . . .

Before I climbed that dump in the sky I had a drive round the district, just for old times' sake. I wasn't brought up in Bethnal Green but not too far away.

For all the changes the cemetery was still the area showpiece, the one place where the poor finally get a fair share of something.

Herbert Morrison House was a twenty-storey block, shabby and rain-streaked, the walls thick with spray-can messages, nicknames, gang slogans, incurable optimism about West Ham football team. I parked the car across the street, hoping the Abreys' flat would have a window on that side. It was a navy-blue two-door Triumph Stag which I had owned for two whole days. I'd chosen it with places like this in mind, where a flash job attracts every eager hand in the borough. The Stag would pass for ordinary — until you tried to pass it.

It took me a good ten minutes to climb those seven flights. It was only a month since they'd removed the last lot of plaster from my dud ankle and not much longer since I'd stopped trying to drink myself into the happy communism of the graveyard.

That ankle! It had been done eighteen months before, when some reluctant clients in Fulham had slammed a car door on it three or four times. Since then it had been broken and re-set twice by cheerful doctors. That bloody ankle! It cost me my career, my marriage and almost did for my sanity. I would have had it amputated only I was too attached to my right foot.

The first version of the script reads like this:

1. ext. street. day one

HAZELL: (VO) Tracking down the Abrey family was like a trip down memory lane, a warm July evening in the east end of London Town and I was thinking ain't life grand. I was earning at last, I had a new motor, new gear, and it was at least a month since I'd stopped trying to drink myself into the happy communism of the graveyard. Nothing could be finer in the state of semolina.
(pov [point of view] Hazell, we see high rise blocks)
Herbert Morrison House was your usual barrack block in the sky. (*stops car, gets out*). You don't have to be poor to live there but it helps.

2. ext. street. day
He locks car, crosses road to block with sign . . . 'Herbert Morrison House'. Still pov Hazell.

3. int. block. day
pov Hazell we see sign on lift door . . . 'out of order' . . .
HAZELL (VO): Well, everybody knows your working-class needs more exercise. (*starts up stairs*) It was only a month since they'd taken the plaster off (*rubs ankle*) that bleeding ankle, cost me my career, my marriage, almost did for my sanity. (*reaches landing, rubs ankle again*) I would have had it amputated but I was kind of sentimental about my foot.

pov Hazell he comes up stairs past three silent menacing youths, one black. He passes between them to hostile stares.

HAZELL: (VO) (*takes deep breaths*) I didn't know then why I was getting paid fifteen quid a day to track down the happy little Abrey family. (*he goes along balcony on seventh floor, comes to door numbered 57 rings bell*) If I had I would have done a quick disappearing act from the whole deal. Babies!

door opens. pov Hazell we see cautious face of Cliff Abrey.

Very little has been changed from the book. Even the three menacing youths are in the novel, a few pages further on. But here we see their attitude, expressed in their behaviour, rather than Hazell telling us of it. The main difference is that the action has been compressed. We don't see Hazell taking a drive round the area and of course we don't see him taking ten minutes to climb the stairs. Neither the car nor the tower block are given the kind of description they get in the novel. Television is much less discursive than a novel can afford to be.

But even this paring down of the novel didn't have enough pace, and in the final version of the script the voice-over narration has been cut by almost a quarter, dropping some of Hazell's wisecracks. (The fact that there are more explicit stage directions, particularly of the three youths, wouldn't of itself make the scene play longer.) So as shot the sequence reads like this:

1. ext. street. day one
In the traffic we see Hazell's blue Stag.
HAZELL: (VO) Tracking down the Abrey family was like a trip down Memory Lane. A warm July evening in the East End of London Town and I was thinking ain't life grand. Earning at last — a new motor, new gear and maybe even a new career. Nothing could be finer in the state of semolina.

1.a. ext. Robert Moore House. day
Hazell stops the car, carefully locks it and crosses the street towards a high-rise block of flats with the entrance sign: Robert Moore House

HAZELL: (VO) Robert Moore House was your usual barrack-block in the sky (*he goes into entrance*) (*the walls are covered by graffitti*) Twenty shabby storeys of spray-can philosophy and incurable optimism about West Ham football team.

2. int. R.M. House/foyer. day one
He approaches a set of lifts and sees pasted the notice: out of order. *He turns to stairs and starts to mount them.*

HAZELL: (VO) Oh, well — only seven floors (*rubs ankle*) Bleedin' ankle. I would have had it amputated but I was kind of sentimental about my foot.

3. int. R.M. House/landing day one
He turns onto landing and is confronted by three silent, hostile youths. Two of them — one white, one black — sit on bottom of next staircase. The third, black, stands leaning against the wall. Hazell stops, looks from face to face. None of them move. Hazell moves casually between and past and continues up stairs to the sound of their laughter.
We should be wondering about his apparent nonchalance in the face of their open hostility.

4. int. Abreys' landing. Day one
Hazell walking along landing. He stops at door number 57

HAZELL: (VO) Thing is, in this racket, people don't bung you a pony a day to sell sunshine and sweetness door to door . . . (*presses bell*) as it turned out I was probably the biggest bastard who ever pressed the Abrey's bell button . . .

One other thing is worth noting here, besides the tightening up and the change in Hazell's fee from £15 a day to £25 (doubtless to keep up with inflation): the first line of the novel has been put back into the script, though with a slight difference. Hazell is now not so much a bastard in general, but only one in this particular case, to the Abreys. Attempts to make him altogether tougher have eventually given way to a characterisation nearer to Gordon Williams' original formulation, that 'given any encouragement he is nice'.

Pace then, was vital in a *Hazell* script.* But it wasn't the only thing.

---

* Richard Harris thought that in television generally things had gone too far in this direction, that people were afraid to just let a scene play.

The script must not only move, but get somewhere, and so as we have seen attention was paid to getting the right kind of story. Disagreements as to whether Hazell should be placed in 'real' situations or whether it was fantasy were resolved in favour of plots that *could* happen (i.e., people had plausible motives and actions occured in a logical chain of events); but plots which at the same time were unusual — not the kind of thing one could imagine as likely to happen to a private eye every day, as the plots of *Z Cars* might be said to be the routine of a policeman's life. And within these plots the characters which Hazell meets are, as another note for writers puts it, 'realistically larger than life'. The gangsters Hazell runs into, for example, may have some of the characteristics of real gangsters (whatever those might be); but they are stylised versions of the real thing, their clothes and habits of speech more colourful than one can imagine them to be in life. The series never moved as far in the direction of stylisation as June Roberts might have liked, but *Hazell* is certainly a long way from the kind of realism which works by imitating the mundaneness and ordinariness of everyday life.

Besides the demand for pace, for unusual but plausible plots, for interesting 'characters', for a strong use of London locations and for the display of Hazell himself, one other feature was to be an essential ingredient of a good *Hazell* script. This was humour. Some notes for the writers specify what kind of humour:

Humour will stem from the following:
1. Incidental action.
2. Laconic voice-over
3. Eccentric characterisation.
4. Wise-cracking (as opposed to jokey) confrontations between Hazell and other characters.

There is a further note on the style of Hazell's voice-over comments:

Hazell's first person narrative is a stylised form of clever word play and original metaphorical slang. The only cockney aspect of it is his accent. Any cliché or proverb will have an unexpected twist in the punchline. His dialogue is spare, witty and laconic.

This does roughly describe the style of humour in the scripts, though in fact there is a certain amount of distinctively cockney wit and some rhyming slang. It's interesting to record that though humour is a notoriously subjective thing to discuss, a lot of effort went into trying to get it right. In the first episode, for example, there is a brief scene where Hazell is standing outside the offices of Dot Wilmington, from whom

64

he rents his own small office. He is speaking into the intercom, and in the first draft of the script announces himself as 'the man from ankle' (a reference to his recent injury). In the next draft this became: 'Quick, they're after me.' Then it was changed to: 'The bionic woman.' Still it wasn't right, and the line as eventually recorded is: '(AMERICAN ACCENT) James Hazell — business is my trouble.' The importance of humour in giving the series a distinctive mood which would appeal to the audience was to be a factor which influenced not only the type of writers employed but also the casting of the central role. It's a very urban kind of humour, hard-edged, aggressive, terse. It seems that there was one very particular reason for playing up the humorous side of Hazell. During production the BBC was believed to be setting up its own private eye series. The *Hazell* team therefore had to make their show different. This may also have had its effect in moderating the Chandler influence on *Hazell*.

The script editor

Almost all television drama series will employ a script editor (or story editor, as they are sometimes called). *Hazell* started life without one, because June Roberts had originally been a script editor herself and intended combining the role with that of producer. But when several new writers were brought in, a full-time script editor became necessary to work with them. In addition the difference of emphasis over what the series should be about, and the fact that besides Hazell himself several other regular characters were to appear, meant that someone had to assume responsiblity for making sure that all the scripts conformed to the pattern that had been set. Gordon Williams had originally seen his hero as 'one man alone against the big city'. But as ideas for the series developed Hazell became involved in relationships with others. He acquired a regular girl friend, Vinnie Rae, and brought with him from the books a cousin, Tel; a former colleague in the police, Detective-Inspector Minty; and his professional associates: Gordon Gregory, a solicitor, his secretary Diane, and Dot and Maureen, who give him office space and occasional jobs. The writers had to be briefed on how to handle all these characters.

Kenneth Ware, who initially took the job, explains what it entails:

KW: 'Basically you're responsible for picking the writers (though the producer would certainly be involved in their choice as well), briefing them and getting the script right when it comes in, in terms of the series as a whole. If you've got 5 writers on a series you're going to get 5 different styles and part of your job is to make it as even over-all as you possibly can. A good script editor should never have to do anything apart from pick the right writer and brief him correctly, because if you do that you're going to get the right script in. You're not going to have to change anything except the odd word here and there. Ideally you're working with a small team: on a series of 13 episodes preferably not more than 3. We've got more than that. On this series I was brought in late and there hadn't been an editor on it. Some scripts were already in and things weren't going quite right. You should really be involved from the moment a decision is made to start a series.'

A major task for the script editor is to ensure that the series has consistency, both in terms of style and in terms of the picture of the characters which is built up over the successive weeks of the series' transmission. Inevitably therefore the individuality of the writers is subordinated to the needs of the series. However many writers are actually employed, it must seem as far as possible that there is only one. Thus there had to be a unity of style for Hazell's voice-overs.

Kenneth Ware: 'Even with Gordon's scripts the voice-overs aren't consistent. The one he wrote with Terry Venables, the one he wrote on his own, the ones he wrote with Tony Hoare all have a different feel about them. This has to be straightened out so that it does at least sound like the same guy talking each time.'

There were also problems with flashbacks. Interestingly, films like *Double Indemnity* and *Farewell My Lovely* have quite complicated narrative structures making extensive use of flashbacks, and one or two of the early *Hazell* scripts had experimented with this technique. But they were later dropped.

Kenneth Ware: 'June cut those. I think Verity felt it too, that they weren't working. If you're going to use flashbacks at all they should be an integral part of all the scripts, not just used in a few.'

With the benefit of hindsight it is tempting to speculate that had the writers been instructed to construct more complex narrative patterns, to take from *film noir* more than the voice-over technique, then the highly stylised show that June Roberts planned might have been more easily achieved. As it was, the scripts she received were relatively straightforward in this respect; when, shortly before the series went into production, she opened discussions on what kind of visual style was to be attempted, she was faced with the problem of trying to graft a non-naturalistic 'look' onto material that, with the qualifications outlined in the previous section, was working within the tried and tested conventions of television drama.

Another example of the kind of work put in by the script editor to achieve consistency came in a script written by Richard Harris and entitled *Hazell And The Rubber-Heel Brigade*. In this instance it was a case of trying to get straight the facts about Hazell's background. In the course of this episode Hazell meets up with his ex-wife. Richard needed to know what facts about the marriage had been established, and got his reply from Kenneth Ware:

KW: 'Phoned Gordon Williams re Hazell's ex-wife and got the following info: her name is Jackie, it was a childless marriage that broke under strain of his being retired — on full pay — from the police and hitting the bottle. They were divorced and Jackie has remarried, has one child, and lives somewhere in Essex. Beyond that, and the fact that Hazell still feels genuine regret at the failure, you would have a free hand. Hope this helps!'

The script apparently met with some criticism from Gordon over the way the marriage had been handled, and Richard wrote to Gordon:

RH: 'As to Hazell's marital/job background. Again, I checked out that what I proposed to do was OK. And was told it was. I honestly believe my version of the break-up is as good as any. To change it now would totally screw up my script. The trouble is, nothing hard and fast has ever been set down. You must admit that even in your own script *Solomon*, on one page he's separated, on another he's divorced and his ex has got two kids. I don't see what I have chosen to use in any way alters Hazell's character.'

Not all the feed-back which writers can expect is limited to the technicalities of the characters' past histories. Gordon Williams, after writing the first script with Terry Venables and the next one on his own, had begun a collaboration with Tony Hoare, an experienced television writer who has done scripts for *The Sweeney*. After they had produced a number of scripts but while they were still engaged on others, they received a memo from June Roberts, who, clearly, still kept a very close watch on the progress of the writing:

JR: 'Dear Gordon and Tony,
    I've been re-reading the first three scripts and the current storylines and jotted down the following notes which I hope will be helpful.

CHAIRMAN JUNE'S LITTLE READ NOTES

1. Keep the language fresh. I'd prefer inventive expletives rather than conventional ones.
2. Keep the women as strong as Vinnie and Gloria. In television terms they can be just as interesting in a vertical position as in the predictably inevitable horizontal. Leave chauvinistic downtrodden stereotypes to *The Sweeney*.
3. *Charm* and humour are the only areas in which we can offer a style that makes us distinctive from the other two private eye series being set up, both of which will have a much more typically Chandleresque hero than we have and infinitely more violence.
4. Don't go overboard with filmed *dialogue* sequences.
5. Carry on with detailed story-lines before you start each script. They are invaluable.
6. Everyone is finding Gregory and Minty fairly easy to write for, which is a pity as Dot and Maureen are much more *original* characters. The more you can develop them the better. At the moment they're still smashing characters but lousy parts.
7. Cousin Tel is currently in one out of eight episodes. Is he worth keeping as a *running* character? Do you plan to use him again?
8. Keep your middle-classes interestingly and plausibly funny or ruthlessly clever. Let the fact that you're really a heavily biased left-wing inverted snob be our little secret.
9. I think you should give serious thought to the suggestion already made of a *Johnny Go Home* type of theme or a 'wall of silence' reaction to an attack (not killing) of an adolescent — or even
10. There is a 'Rag Trade Reggie Mancini'. I have to change his surname. Any suggestions? I also have to change Herbert Morrison House.
11. After episode 8 there is no reason why if you wanted to you couldn't change Hazell's home address. I'm not suggesting that you should — only that you can.
12. I like the camp 40s movies exchanges you've introduced in *Settles the Accounts*. I think it's a game we could pursue.
13. It's nearly Christmas — write faster!
14. Every morning when you get out of bed look in the mirror and say to yourself 'Every day in every way I'm getting better and better.' Then *get* better.'

Most of these remarks are self-explanatory, but some require a comment:

4. Dialogue sequences take more time to film and can anyway be done for the most part in the studio, so it's a waste of valuable film time to do them on location.

5. It's normal practice for a two or three page outline of the story to be submitted before actual writing begins.

6 & 7. Dot and Maureen are 'lousy parts' because though they appear in most episodes they don't have very much to do. This problem was never wholly solved. The difficulty is that the more times a running character appears in the series, the better the class of actor who can be offered the part. But it becomes very difficult for every writer to work all the running characters into a script and actually give them an active role in the story rather than a simple 'guest appearance'.

8. Despite this injunction some of what June called Gordon Williams, 'inverted snobbery' did creep back into the scripts. For example, the recorded version of *Hazell Plays Solomon* has a scene in which Hazell visits the 'cluttered and shabby' flat of the Abreys in Bethnal Green together with the successful and snooty Gordon Gregory. Hazell remarks in a voice-over: 'One hour of forcing the Gregorys of this country to live like the Abreys, and we'd have the biggest wave

Gordon Gregory (James Faulkner) meets the Abreys (Susan Littler, George Innes). Hazell on r.

of progress since children were rescued from the coal mines', though in fact this remark was lifte out of one of the Hazell novels by June Roberts herself. *Hazell Meets the First Eleven* also has a highly unflattering view of the wealthy middle-classes. But see the last page of this chapter for Gordon's own comment on June's remark.

9. This suggestion was never taken up; as the series turned out it possibly wasn't Hazell territory anyway.

10. The problem of names and places is described in the next chapter.

12. This game wasn't pursued with any consistency, despite June's initial enthusiasm for a show that could contain conscious echoes of Hollywood.

13. Gordon Williams and Tony Hoare comment on this: 'If we'd written any faster the typewriters would have been red hot.'

14. Gordon and Tony comment: 'We think June was joking.'

A rather different view of the script editor's function, at least of how it worked out in practice, was given to us by Peter Ransley. He talked to us while he was at work on the second of the scripts he wrote. The first, *Hazell Meets Mr Good-Eats,* was not subsequently recorded because the rescheduling of the studio dates meant that, in the end, only 10 out of the planned 13 episodes were done. But his second script, *Hazell Works For Nothing.* despite the difficulties he describes over the writing, was recorded. Peter Ransley possibly suffered from the fact of there being no script editor at all when he began. So when he spoke to us he wasn't too happy. We quote him at some length, however, not so much to show the particular difficulties encountered by *Hazell,* but because it shows how writers, who because of their working situation. away from the studio, and their particular place within the production, responsible for only the episode they are writing, are apt to feel a certain isolation:

PR: 'One of the problems is that you've got June's conception of the character, then you've got what's actually in the books, then you've got your own ideas about what you'd like to do with the character. And every time I talk about it on the phone he's different. The first time June rang me up [Peter had written for *Couples,* June's previous production] and I went over to see her and she said, read the books. So I did, the three of them, and I liked them so I said, yes, I'd like to do a script. So I produced the first one, which I think they were pleased with. I think they got progressively less pleased with it, but they bought it. But now the concept has changed. I think they liked my script because they could see it as an entity, as one thing that worked. But of course you're not doing one script, you're doing thirteen, and now they've got to say, how does that one script go with the other twelve?

So in between the first script and the second the character has changed. Different people have had different ideas, they've been casting and so on and a kind of consensus has emerged of what is wanted. Now to me this doesn't so much get communicated as leak through. First of all the idea was to make him as he was in the books, which is a bit chippy, kicking out at the middle classes, jokey, a very lively character. But then I'm told we're going to make Hazell more Chandleresque. I think I'd gathered that from talking to June previously, so my conception of it tallies with what I'm told. But one has the awful feeling that by the time I've finished the script it mightn't. [As it turned out Peter's suspicions weren't far wrong, since this move was to be reversed.]

That's why I think you need a telly writer in right from the start, to broadly prepare the whole 13 episodes and map things out. You see, another problem that's arisen on this one I'm doing now is that in the outline I put in Hazell's mother and father. His mother is in hospital and he's looking after Dad, and he gets involved through his mother in a case he doesn't want to get involved in. But yesterday Ken says to me on the phone try and keep Mum and Dad down and bring Tel in,

Hazell and Cousin Tel (Desmond McNamara)

because Tel is really working out as a nice character. I know their problems: if they can offer a part across 6 or 7 episodes they'll get a bigger name for Tel. [It's also the case that running characters save money in that they can use stock sets and need less rehearsal time.] But in this script I'm committed to an idea they've agreed to, involving Hazell's Mum and Dad. What's going to happen if I say, I must think about the series so I'll write Tel in? All my instincts tell me to ignore him because my job is to produce this script. I'll try and bring Tel in if I can, but what might happen if I do is that I might get mixed up, the whole thing gets diluted over too many characters and then the script doesn't work. And it's no use me saying to them then, well it doesn't work because of what you suggested. I think it's part of a writer's job to absorb the outside pressures and demands made on him; but only he knows what is actually happening within his particular script. He may be blind to something and make mistakes, but unless he's honest to himself I don't think a good script can be produced.'

Some of the writers we spoke to tended to rate what they called 'professionalism' very highly (though Gordon Williams called it 'the kiss of death'), and one aspect of that quality as they define it is the ability to put their own writing skills and ideas at the service of the series, to write according to a brief. But there is no doubt that there will always be tensions between the series format and the writer's own inclinations. A major task of the script editor must be to minimise, or at least manage, these tensions. For Kenneth Ware this was made especially difficult, first because he came late onto the production and was faced with a situation in which two drafts of the first script were already completed and yet an agreed concept of *Hazell* had still not been achieved. Secondly, the fact that he was himself involved in an attempt to redirect the series, in a way that some of the writers did not favour, made his position even harder. So, because *Hazell* was developing — for better or worse — into a series somewhat removed from the 'street-real' Raymond Chandler/Dashiel Hammett kind of show he thought it was going to be, Kenneth Ware asked to be released from his contract and left.

The job of script editor was then offered to Richard Harris. He had originally been asked to do one script, *Hazell And The Weekend Man*. This script was felt by June at the time (the autumn of 1976) to be the closest yet produced by someone not originally involved in Hazell's creation to what *Hazell* was really all about. Richard was then asked to do another script and eventually wrote three, the last two being *Hazell*

And The Rubber-Heel Brigade and *Hazell And The Walking Blur*. He accepted the job of script editor for specific reasons, though without great enthusiasm for the job itself:

RH: 'Too often you're regarded as a eunuch. I'm a writer, I write for a living and you get used to a particular routine, a particular set of problems. Suddenly you're a script editor and you go into an office and you're doing a job where sometimes you have to do things you don't particularly enjoy. You have to turn down writers' work or tell them it's not very good — not all the time, of course — but often enough, because that's why they're paying you. My problem with *Hazell* was that I had inherited almost all the required scripts. I thought they were very often wrong for the programme. (I would point out that had I been script editor, I would never have commissioned one of the stories I wrote myself. Maybe even two of them.) So, anyway, here I was having to criticise scripts with writers who had already been through the mill and who had been told that their scripts were okay. Some of them bared their teeth and frankly I was on their side . . . but it didn't stop me doing the job I had to do. What was frustrating for me was doing a job at half-cock, too often a scissors and paste affair. Then again, you see things happen to a script in production, like bad casting or bad direction or even sets that are totally opposed to the writers' thinking. And because you're a writer first and foremost you feel for the guy who's written the thing. But at the same time you have a loyalty to your show; there's nothing more destructive than people saying it's bloody awful — there are always a lot of those about. And there are all these egos at stake, and you're the guy who has to turn round and say, I don't like what you've just spent a month writing; and of course when you're young, especially, everything's precious.

The trouble with script editing is that the very name makes writers' hackles rise. They're usually young guys on the way through — like at the BBC there are script editors who know nothing about scripts and have no power so when you've finished dealing with them they've got to refer to the producer. Or, they're old guys who are over the hill and are working out their pension. Some extraordinary people become script editors. I've known girls, one moment they're typists, the next they're script editors. Well, that's not very flattering, is it? And it's easy for every script editor to get tarred with the same brush.

I took the job for the very simple reason that I'd done a tremendous amount of writing just prior to that, I'd done about 10 scripts in as many months. I was tired of the day-to-day business of writing. I have enormous financial pressure on me and I saw this as a way of changing gear slightly. This doesn't mean I took the job in any way saying, oh, well, I can whistle through this lot. But I thought it would be creatively treading water, and I wouldn't have to worry about meeting this bill or that. It seemed a good way of resting my writing brain and at the same time earning a living by doing the job to the best of my ability.'

Richard Harris' definition of the script editor's role overlapped to an extent with Kenneth Ware's, but provided some interesting expansions and differences of emphasis:

RH: 'You are responsible to your producer for the gathering of, in this case, 13 scripts. The way I see it is that the producer and the script editor talk at length and agree what the series is all about, as best they can. Whereupon, again in consultation with the producer (because that's where the buck stops) you approach the writers you think are the best for that particular job. Keeping it if possible to a small team; four, I think, is the most you should go for. You choose your writers and hopefully you get them. Often you don't because there are very few really good writers about and this means they're usually working. But let's assume you get your writers. Obviously then you brief each one on what the series is all about. You give them any formats there are, you generally talk about the characters and give them a foundation on which to operate. You say, what we want is a show with movement, or, don't be afraid to have long dialogue scenes if you want. Now if you've briefed your writers properly and you've chosen the right ones, when the scripts comes in the rewrites should be minimal.

The first thing you send them away for is ideas; or hopefully you give them ideas. A good script editor will toss ideas around. I always consider a script editor to be a working writer talking to another writer and working up an idea which the other writer will go away and develop. I will be quite happy to try and work up a plot for a writer to do. But some guys don't want to do that. There are no hard and fast ways of doing it but you will do a story line of some kind. Then when that comes in, it might be just a couple of paragraphs, you will say, make sure he does this here, don't forget to lead up to a climax there. Some writers will do a scene breakdown, where you can look at it much more closely. Then once you've cleared that you can unleash the writer, and hopefully in about a month back comes the script. And in theory then you say, bloody good, there are just a couple of points, do you want to talk about them over the phone or come in and have a chat about them? But sometimes even after all these processes you can get a script where something goes wrong. A scene is flabby, it doesn't go anywhere, or a character doesn't work too well.

The next step is the pre-production build-up when the director moves in and says certain things. He might say, I can't cope with this much film, or this doesn't really work. A fresh eye might discover things. If that happens you should always give your writer an opportunity to do the rewriting himself if he wants to. Sometimes they don't. If it's a minimal thing, say a scene in a park which could be set in Hazell's office, they might say, you do it. But whatever you do you send them a copy. Then you've got the read-through with the actors, where you get a closer timing on the script, and things can crop up here. And then again in rehearsals, someone might say, this scene just doesn't work. And the script editor's job is to come in and either explain the scene or put it right. Again, I would always phone the writer and say, do you want to do it? And then on recording day in the studio you're there, looking after the writer, sitting with him, acting as a go-between with him and the producer, buying him a drink and all that. Make him feel he's involved in the show. Some people don't come to the recording, they don't find it worth their while or they don't want to get involved in the hassle. But most do.'

A brief history of the scripts

We've already indicated that June Roberts was anxious to use new writers on the series, if at all possible.

JR: 'For all the risks you take with a new writer and for all the fact that thrillers are the hardest type of drama to write, the fact is that if you've done a lot of series writing before you have your own format and you just twist any new series into that, and I think new writers don't. They're much more open to suggestion, much more likely to give you something that's different.'

June therefore welcomed the chance of working with Gordon and Terry. The first script, *Hazell Plays Solomon,* went through many versions (7 at least), but June seemed to feel it was worth it and that the script eventually turned out well. June's enthusiasm for this kind of work was not altogether shared by the two script editors, Kenneth Ware and Richard Harris, who were more used to working with 'professionals'. Not that Richard was critical of Gordon; far from it.

RH: 'If you employ someone who's never written for television before to write eight scripts you're asking a lot. The guy will need firm guidance and assistance. I think Gordon has learned tremendously; that may sound patronising but it's not meant to be. There's a lot of learning to be done. It's bloody hard to do *one*, but to do as many as he's done is ridiculous. But he's marvellous.'

One reason why there were so many versions of *Solomon*, possibly, was that it was the first script to be written but the next to last to be recorded, and there was thus more time. It had to be the first written because it will be the first to be screened and therefore will introduce the character and fix certain things about him. How Hazell speaks and behaves in *Solomon* must to an extent set the pattern for later episodes. Nevertheless, in Richard Harris' opinion there were problems with the story:

RH: 'I couldn't accept Hazell's relationship with the woman, Toni Abrey. One minute he's there in the house, the next minute he's fucking her, the next minute he thinks he's in love with her. I suggested ways of adding dialogue to show some sort of relationship'.

The next script, *Hazell Pays A Debt*, was written by Gordon Williams on his own. The story is in fact the sub-plot of the novel of *Solomon*, about a gangster named O'Rourke who is out for revenge because he holds Hazell responsible for sending him to prison. The script had been enthusiastically received and officially accepted, but Richard Harris felt there were problems with it. However, by the time he was established as script editor the start of production was almost on him, and therefore only a limited amount of work was possible:

RH: 'I was never happy with it because it changed course too often and there were really three sub-plots, not one plot. I remember sitting down with Gordon and doing a solid day's work on it and getting it a little better, but only a little. We were talking about putting plasters on when I thought amputations were necessary. The only reason they weren't done was because of time'.

Hazell Pays A Debt was later to prove the most troublesome episode of all.

Before Richard Harris came on to the scene June had commissioned a script, *Hazell: Who Wants Tickets?*, from two young writers, Andrew Nicholds and Stan Hey, who had worked on *Time Out* magazine and who had not yet had anything produced on television. In this one Hazell becomes involved with a professional footballer and a ticket tout. Though June Roberts felt the story was very much Hazell 'material',

Gordon and Terry were not too keen on some aspects of the story line and eventually, because of an industrial dispute, to be described later, the series was cut down to only 10 episodes, and this script was dropped from production.

Kenneth Ware, feeling that more professionals should be involved, was made happier when Richard Harris was brought in to do *Hazell And The Weekend Man,* and, as we have seen, he subsequently wrote two more scripts. Gordon Williams, by this time, had teamed up with Tony Hoare, another professional with experience on *The Sweeney.* Their first collaboration was *Hazell Settles The Accounts,* which was generally felt to be very successful. It's interesting to note, though, that Gordon Williams felt that in the scripts he wrote with Tony Hoare *Hazell* becomes a little tougher; thus moving slightly towards the kinds of show which *Hazell* had been intended to get away from, and so confirming a little June Roberts' thoughts on the effect of using experienced writers, that they impose their own formats.

Nevertheless, this was only a slight shift, not a major change of direction, and Gordon and Tony were asked to produce four further scripts: *Hazell Goes To The Dogs, Hazell Meets The First Eleven, Hazell Stands In For Sam Stone* and *Hazell's Three-Star Night.* Again, because of the curtailment of the series, the last two were never recorded, though one may subsequently form the basis of a fourth Hazell novel.

Richard Harris (on the *First Eleven* script, in which Hazell becomes involved with the upper crust in Belgravia): 'Again, Gordon and I sat down. I thought it was bad in many areas. He took most of my points, we did a lot of jiggery-pokery, cutting down his excesses of hatred for the English upper-classes. [Gordon rejects such a description of his attitudes. As far as he's concerned *all* classes are fair game.] Gordon will always say, he's the bastard who cuts out all my jokes; but I'm the bastard who cuts out six bad jokes and leaves one good one. I think *The First Eleven* was much improved, but again it was a bit of a patchwork job because we were running out of time by then.'

As we have seen, Peter Ransley did two scripts, *Hazell Meets Mr Good-Eats* and *Hazell Works For Nothing,* only the second of which was recorded. Some difficulties arose in relation to *Hazell Works For Nothing.* The script had been liked by June and accepted, but when Richard Harris came to read it after he was appointed script editor he didn't like it very much, and in fact wanted not to use it. June disagreed

Belgravia: Hazell Meets The First Eleven

with his assessment, but did agree he should rewrite two or three scenes. Some of what he rewrote Peter in turn didn't like and it was changed back to the original. However, in the script as eventually recorded one scene which had appeared in Peter Ransley's first draft was cut because the script was a bit too long, and another scene was recast. Peter said that the script as performed was 95% as he wrote it. But it's worth noting as a general point, which would apply to other scripts in the series, and perhaps more so than in the case of *Hazell Works For Nothing*, that the appearance of a writer's name on the credits at the end of a show need not necessarily mean that s/he is individually responsible for every single word spoken.

Two further scripts were to be commissioned. Quite early on, in the summer of 1976, Willis Hall wrote one called *Hazell: Putting The Boot In*. This ran into problems, partly because of the fact that it didn't conform strictly to the plot structure format for the series. The rule was that the audience should have no privileged information. It knows only what Hazell knows and follows the story through him. Willis Hall's script had scenes in which Hazell did not appear. This problem, though tricky, was eventually solved, but this script was never used because of the curtailment of the series from 13 to 10 episodes.

Then, late in the day, it became clear that another script would be required (this was before the decision to cut back the series to 10 episodes, which was not taken until half had already been recorded, in the summer of 1977). Shortage of time at this point made further experiments with new television writers too much of a gamble, and Richard Harris therefore brought in Trevor Preston, who has done a lot of writing for series such as *Special Branch* and *The Sweeney*. And so once again the series took a small step towards what it had been intended to get away from. Trevor Preston's script, *Hazell And The Maltese Vulture*, despite the echo in the title of Humphrey Bogart, has one or two *Sweeney* touches, such as a fight with a gang of crooks in a garage, shot on film. The episode is still recognisably *Hazell*, and its use of low-key lighting brings it nearer than some other episodes to the kind of visual stylisation June Roberts had wanted. All the same, despite the fact that it undoubtedly works well in its own terms, *The Maltese Vulture* tends to bear out June's feelings about using writers who have worked extensively on other series: that they inevitably bring something of those other series with them.

The scripts; conclusions

It is clear that the scripts are a crucial factor in determining what kind of series *Hazell* should be. It seems worth pausing, therefore, to consider some of the things the writers had to say about their work. As we have already said in the Introduction, we do not propose to offer an analysis of the programme as such. But something needs to be said about what kind of drama *Hazell* is, and why it is what it is. This is not to imply that the writers, even together with the producer and script editors, are entirely responsible for giving *Hazell* its distinctive characteristics. But in an essentially narrative medium such as television drama, those whose job it is to provide the plot structures and characterisation have a decisive influence on the shape of the series as a whole. Those who come after, the actors, directors, designers and so on, must inevitably see their role as interpreters, always bearing in mind that such interpretation can significantly affect the nature of the final product.

First of all it has always to be remembered that *Hazell* is entertainment, pure and simple (though to adapt Oscar Wilde, one could say that entertainment on television is rarely pure and never simple). Many of those who worked on *Hazell* would probably ask what is wrong with that. Yet almost all the writers we spoke to, and some of the actors and directors too, had a rather ambiguous attitude towards the kind of work they were doing. The primary purpose of a series such as *Hazell* (and one must remember that this doesn't necessarily apply to all television drama, even on a supposedly 'commercial' system like ITV) is to appeal to as large an audience as possible. We think that the writers respected the material they were working with. Certainly we found very little of that cynicism one suspects must surround some television productions.* But virtually without exception, though for different reasons perhaps, they preferred other kinds of writing. Possibly the most positive about it was Stan Hey, who thought that *Hazell* was both interesting in itself and also useful training for when he was in a position to choose his own projects:

SH: 'I think basically we were desperate enough for work to say yes to anything within reason. There was no point in being snobby about it and saying, this isn't an original piece of work, we're just hacking out somebody else's character. We had to say yes. But having said that, I think it's a help having so many things given, so that you can concentrate on constructing a really good story and making the dialogue interesting. There's a lot of satisfaction in doing original work, but at our stage, when we haven't had anything original produced, this is very useful. Perhaps in ten or fifteen years time, if we're still writing, we can afford to say no, I'm not doing that, it's someone else's conception. But at this stage for a new writer it's great to have lists of things beside you. Like which football team does Hazell support? West Ham — so we can write gags about West Ham (which isn't difficult). Certainly having to write to a style is good discipline. The tendency when you're doing something original is to overwrite, and to value everything too highly. It's all sacrosanct, and if someone says that line is no good you say, I've written that, it's mine, you can't take it away. But with this sort of thing you're less sensitive about possessing a line. We've enjoyed it so far and I think in terms of constructing a sound watertight story and getting the character right we'll get a lot of satisfaction from it.'

Stan Hey's partner, Andrew Nickolds, made the point to us that

*On the other hand there were few illusions either. Richard Harris remarked that when as a script editor he made cuts in a script it was rarely for 'artistic' reasons. It was more likely to be in order to save an extra set. 'It all too often comes down to carpentry.'

many of the best writers in television worked on series that were primarily conceived in terms of entertainment, and he also saw *Hazell* as good and necessary experience; but again with the implication that he hoped to 'progress' on to something else eventually. Peter Ransley wished to reject the kind of critical categorisation which goes on whereby only single plays are taken seriously:

PR: 'I think one of the things that is wrong with television is that you have a split between series and single plays so that in people's heads there is the idea that single plays by and large don't get the ratings and that series, if they're on at 9 o'clock and are plugged and have a name actor and reasonably successful scripts *will* get ratings. But you can get very good work in series which is critically neglected and you can get in a single play some of the most appalling work. There's a kind of labelling going on whereby the audiences believe all series are good and all single plays bad, and critics think all series are bad and all single plays good — or at least they carry that kind of expectation with them to the viewing.'

Yet he admitted that he wanted to write more single plays, and indeed that he would like to do more work in the theatre than he does. But financially he found this very difficult. 'Series are what there is to be written and what people will pay you to write.'

Richard Harris too, though he sees himself more as a television writer (but one who has written for the theatre too), has reservations

RH: 'Where the danger lies is in getting caught up in series writing and never doing original plays. And the result is you get onto a treadmill. In TV there is definitely something called the series writer; certain guys would never write for series. You can't imagine David Mercer doing it. The danger is to be multi-talented, the jack of all trades. I don't mean to sound conceited, but people know they can phone me and ask me to do any sort of show. I think I earn my money because nine times out of ten I produce a good script for the show they want. But it's very easy to go for a whole year and end up thinking, Christ, what have I done for myself? I call myself a writer and yet I've not really flexed my muscles. This doesn't mean I don't think series writing isn't hard. I think it's extremely hard and I think there are some very good series episodes written. But I suppose ego enters into it and you really want to be judged by your one-off efforts. I'd far rather be called a good TV dramatist than a good TV series writer. It feels inferior and it's treated as such.'

For Gordon Williams and Terry Venables it's a slightly different situation, and for them it's a case not of different kinds of television writing but of a choice between television and books. For Terry books are better partly because he feels he has more control over them, partly because books have more status for him:

TV: 'I prefer books. There's much more satisfaction in it. Initially, I think, we all do things for the satisfaction of it. The financial side of it comes afterwards. At the end of the day you've got to have a certain amount; we all want to be financially sound. But firstly I would do something for the satisfaction and that's why I want to do the books; because when you feel that book and look at it, you think, bloody hell, that's terrific. Television is like a pop song compared to a masterpiece, an opera song, something like that. I think a television script gets a bit mutilated, it goes away from you, you haven't got much control over it. It's nice to see it on the screen but I would get more kick out of going on the tube and seeing someone reading the book. I've not seen that yet — I'm not in the tube! But if you see someone reading the book I would think that's a great thing.'

Gordon Williams too prefers books, though for rather different reasons:

GW: 'Basically I like writing books. It was a hard enough job to get out of journalism — not that there's anything wrong with journalism, it's just that I wanted to write books. But it's quite nice to come to the studio and get around. You have a much more active social life. You can write books for ten years and meet literally two people: your editor and your publisher. But I'm very conscious of the fact that time is going by; when it boils down to it, the TV script is going to be finished in 51 minutes and then the news comes on. It's not the same as having a hard-back book there on the shelf.'

In his opinion, also, the economic pressures militate against television writing being of the same quality as books:

GW: 'A script fee is not adequate for the time it would take you to write a novel. Although novels don't pay very well either, you are gambling that this one might be a best-seller. It might go on for ten years and so you put six months into it. Whereas with a script you're getting £1,200-£1,400 for it and though with repeats it could make double that eventually, it's never going to make more than that. Therefore it would not be wise to spend a year writing the perfect Chekovian script because it might be great television but you would be starving to death. So you have to compromise. I think that unless you are into a sort of James Joyce kind of writing, really going into the interior of the human mind, which is possibly the best fiction, then you're really describing a film which is already in your head. My theory is that in a sense if you are talking about hack writing you are not in fact mining into your own knowledge, you are proving your mental facility at repeating a formula, and this is the sub-culture of our time. That is, private detectives always behave in this manner, cowboys always act like this. Your skill at earning a living as a script-writer in the hack sense would be how quickly you can encapsulate it and get it down. Almost like those really popular songs which are not so much written down, they're discovered.'

For Gordon Williams, then, television series writing can never achieve the same quality as great literature, and certainly no-one would have claimed that *Hazell* is trying to. The object of the script writers, producer and script editors was to produce material that would conform to the technical and aesthetic requirements of television drama (thus the scripts must not only be the right length and so on but also have coherent plots, consistent characters, etc.); and which would also hold an audience through its entertaining display of character, location, humour, narrative pace. It's interesting, however, that though most of the writers felt that they were, or would be, engaged on writing that was more important to them than *Hazell*, no-one suggested to us that popular forms such as the crime series offered opportunities to express, albeit in a different way, the things they might want to write about in their books or single plays. We don't therefore conclude that they weren't aware of such opportunities, or indeed that they never took them. Generally speaking, though, the writers appeared to assume a distinct separation between 'entertainment' and 'serious' drama or fiction.

But as we've suggested we don't think there is any such thing as 'mere' entertainment. It always takes particular forms. What form is *Hazell*, and why does it take this form? It should be clear by now that *Hazell* owes much to the crime novel, the television crime series and the movies, particularly to the Hollywood *film noir* of the 40s. But the distinctive mix of these influences which was eventually achieved can be ascribed, we think, at least in part to the characteristics of the writers involved. One has to say, first of all, that individual personalities are important here. None of the Hazell scripts would be the way they are if they had not been written by the people who *did* write them. What they wrote is obviously influenced by their particular psychology and their experiences. For example, Peter Ransley describes where he got his ideas from:

PR: 'I have a great big file upstairs, which I label "ideas", originally enough. And I shove in any old clippings or odd thoughts that I feel I might want to write about. And if nothing presents itself to me I get the file out and go through everything. Or I go up to the library and root around there to see if that produces anything. And I go on long walks and finish up in the pub. There's one I usually go to on the Chiswick High Road, and there's a lot of blokes in there who work for Wimpy's, the restaurant people. That gave me the idea for *Hazell Meets Mr Good-Eats,* in which there's a Colonel Sanders type character. The second script, *Hazell Works For Nothing,* is about a man who's on the run for a robbery he didn't commit, a case of mistaken identity. That might stem a bit from the Peter Hain case, with him fighting the charge because he's articulate and middle-class, but me wondering about the number of people who haven't got that degree of media exposure and might be in jail now.

Another idea I put up was on industrial espionage. I used to work in industry and I know a little bit about what goes on. It seemed to me an interesting subject and the kind of thing a private detective might get involved in. Then there was another idea about dogs, which doesn't sound very fruitful, but they liked it. I was also involved in the dog business in a remote way, the breeding of dogs and so on. It's a very competitive business, with a bit of crookedness going on in it. Over a beery lunch it sounded like a good idea, but eventually June said she didn't like it after all, and I didn't blame her.'

So Peter Ransley's own experience and the kind of things that interest him obviously influenced his choice of material. But it also seems to us that *Hazell* owes something to the social background of the writers on the series. Hazell himself, as Gordon Williams describes him, has left his working-class background but 'it has not left him'. In a sense the same might be said of the writers. As far as we are able to say almost all of them come from working-class or lower middle-class origins. The fact of being writers has inevitably, though to a varying extent, removed them from these origins. Hazell, by virtue of his job, moves through the whole range of the social structure, from the underworld of pimps, prostitutes and thieves, through the respectable working-class (the Abreys, for example), the not so respectable (Cousin Tel) and up into the middle-classes in their various orders (bank clerks,

84

tax inspectors, successful solicitors). In *Hazell Meets The First Eleven* he touches the fringes of the upper-classes. His girl friend too, Vinnie Rae, is Roedean-educated. It is tempting to see the private detective as a kind of alter-ego of the writer, mirroring the writer's own comparative classlessness and the isolation that can sometimes go with it. This, however, would be too facile, since not all writers write about private detectives and not all the *Hazell* writers would feel they have cut themselves off from their backgrounds.

What one can argue, we think, is that Hazell's attitudes to people are very much affected by his feelings about the social class to which they belong. So to Gordon Gregory, who is smoothly middle-class, Hazell is alternately ironic and aggressive. To Cousin Tel he is affectionately indulgent and sharply moralistic. To Minty, the policeman, he displays all the traditional working-class suspicion of the police (despite, or perhaps because of, his former membership of the Force). We wouldn't wish to claim that Hazell's social attitudes can simply be equated with those of his creators, but it seems unlikely that such a creation would have come from a group of writers educated at public schools and Oxbridge.

It's also worth remarking that Hazell is not only isolated from his social background but also works alone. The writer's situation in television is also a comparatively lonely one. Everyone else works predominantly in the studio; writers work at home, only occasionally coming into contact with those who will realise their scripts. And there is a sense in which, as a friend who had read the novels pointed out, Hazell too is a writer, telling us stories in his own words through the device of the first-person narration. Again, one cannot stretch the point too far. Not all television drama is about first-person narrators who work alone.

To pursue this line of enquiry, on the extent to which the cultural and social situation of those responsible for the programme determines what kind of product results from their efforts, would take us further into an analysis of the show than we can go in this context. To do it justice would require not only a detailed examination of the 15 completed scripts but also a close look at the 10 recorded episodes, besides more exhaustive interviews with the writers than we were able to achieve. It would also require information on other series; unfortunately none exists. But it seems to us a productive line for further research. We have included these brief comments here, together with previous remarks on Gordon Williams 'inverted left-wing snobbery' (a term he rejects — he describes his politics as being 'well to the left of Genghis Khan') and June Roberts' comment on the failure of *Hazell* to provide strong roles for women, in order to indicate that while our main concern has been with the industrial, economic, institutional and aesthetic determinants of the programme, we do not therefore suppose that television programmes can be understood without reference to the social and cultural situation of those who make them.

5 The Programme Liaison Officer

The script editor has other responsibilities besides getting the scripts 'right'. Firstly, a synopsis of each episode has to be prepared, partly for publicity purposes, including the *TV Times*, and partly for the benefit of Thames' Advertising Sales Department. The latter has to make sure that the commercials don't clash with the programmes and that Thames aren't showing, for example, a commercial for British Airways immediately after a programme featuring an air crash. In this respect care is also taken with the actors who appear, so that an actor cast in *Hazell* as, say, a child molester doesn't also appear in the first commercial break selling ice-creams to tiny tots.

A further task of the script editor is to make a list of anything in a script which might cause legal or other problems. This list is sent, together with the script, to Thames' programme liaison officer, John Bedells. He explains his function:

JB: 'The main job is trying to ensure that we're not going to be open to libel actions, so I check on the names of people if they're in some way identified in the script. There might be all sorts of people named Hamilton, but if there are no particular descriptive attributes given in the script this doesn't matter. However, if it's a chap called Sir Percy Hamilton I can look it up in *Debrett* to see if there really is such a person. It's not only people but places and companies. Writers are always giving fictional names like the Acme Paper Hat Co., thinking that there can't possibly be such a firm, and there always is. I spend at least a few hours a week in Companies House and in the Business Names Registry in the City, looking up names and often finding them and then having to invent new ones which I can clear.'

Of course what is said in a script about a person or company may not be libellous, but people are often quick to take offence, especially if the offender is a company with large financial resources. So no risks are taken. In *Hazell Pays A Debt* there was originally a reference to a 'Florida Club'. Since there proved to be such a club the name was changed to 'Club Tampico'. In *Hazell Meets The First Eleven* there is a character called Charles Courtney, a member of the Stock Exchange.

This name had to be checked against the list of members of the Exchange and also in *Who's Who*, to ensure there was no such person.

While we're on the subject of references to real persons or things, it's worth recording that it's company policy that no programme should contain any recognisable brand names unless the script specifically requires it. Thus although Hazell is seen smoking cigarettes and drinking whisky the labels on the packets and bottles have been carefully disguised by the stage manager so that they cannot be identified with any particular brand. It costs a lot to advertise on Thames so the company isn't going to give it away free. It also cuts out the possibility of such advertising being obtained through bribery.

Some things can't be so easily disguised, such as cars. It's laid down in the books that Hazell drives a British Leyland Stag. Thames thought

Hazell and his Stag

in this case the publicity might be worth something to British Leyland and they were able to negotiate the free loan of a Stag for the duration of the series. In response to their request to know how the car would be used, June Roberts wrote to the company thanking them: 'The Stag is

Hazell's only possession and he adores it. It never lets him down and he frequently extols its virtues.'

As well as *Who's Who, Debrett* and other reference works on the eminent, John Bedells has a complete set of phone directories for the British Isles.

JB: 'For example if it's a Mr Fitzherbert of Leatherhead I look in the Leatherhead directory. If there are lots of Fitzherberts there, or if there are none, there's no problem. But if there's just one I will consider changing the name. Or, what's been done occasionally, I will ring him and ask if he has any objection. Usually they don't. With addresses I've got *Kelly's Directory*, the *A to Z*. That sort of thing. When it's essential to name a street we try to make sure the number of the house we use doesn't exist in that street. But there have been difficulties. We had a case where they used a number that was higher than the highest number in the street and we got a bitter letter of complaint from somebody who had lived in that number when it existed. It had been pulled down.'

Although it is this kind of work which takes up most of his time, John Bedells is best known in the company as 'the censor'. It's not the term he prefers to use himself. He works in liaison with the Independent Broadcasting Authority (hence his official title), interpreting to the programme-makers the views of the IBA on the content of programmes and advising the IBA in advance when there are likely to be problems in any Thames productions. It is the IBA, under the terms of the IBA Act, which is legally responsible for all ITV programmes and which under the Act is enjoined to ensure that its various provisions are complied with. As we have seen, the IBA is involved in the drawing up of the ITV schedules. It continues to be involved both during and after the production of the programmes.

One of the major areas of the IBA's concern, the preservation of political 'impartiality', did not have much relevance to *Hazell*. Of more concern was what the IBA in its *Guide to Independent Television and Independent Local Radio* calls 'the unholy trinity of sex, violence and bad language'. The IBA is required by law to ensure that nothing is included in ITV programmes which 'offends against good taste or decency or is likely to encourage or incite to crime or lead to disorder or to be offensive to public feeling'. The IBA are sent scripts and synopses so that they can raise in advance any questions they may have. At the same time John Bedells talks to the programme-makers about any difficulties he foresees. But, he says, there are no hard and fast rules:

JB: 'The Act is a very vague thing. It says that companies must avoid bad taste or offensive material, but it doesn't say what this is. It leaves it to our judgement to assess what the traffic will bear. I regard myself as a sort of interpreter of customs and moral attitudes. We don't have any list of swear words or sexual pecularities or anything, we have to look at the thing as a whole and say, in this context would that be offensive?'

The IBA has what it calls its Family Viewing Policy, which prohibits the screening of anything deemed to be harmful to children before 9 in the evening.

JB: 'There are going to be enormous numbers of children watching after 9 o'clock. But because a line has to be drawn somewhere we say it's the responsibility of the adults to judge whether their children should be watching television at that time.'

Hazell, of course, was scheduled after 9, so it didn't have to be suitable for children.

Nevertheless it ran into some problems over its use of language. There might not be an actual list of prohibited words, but it's clear that certain expressions are, to all intents and purposes, banned:

JB: 'There are some words I wouldn't want used at any time, some of the four letter ones. Although one or two of them have been used on television one has to think very hard whether their use could possibly be justified. It's the language that causes most complaint about television. I think the reason is that people can easily recognise it. And there is a very deep-rooted objection among many people to blasphemy, so I always try to persuade the producers not to use "Jesus" or "Christ". "God" is no problem, though I say if it is used it should only be on occasions of great stress. "Bloody" is used all the time but people start counting it, so I try and cut down the number of times it's used.'

So the expression 'Jesus' was cut from the script of *Hazell Settles The Accounts,* and John Bedells also objected to some other language. Hazell, it will be remembered from Gordon Williams' outline, is fond of the expression 'Kinnell!' This neatly disguised variant of a phrase in fairly common usage, it was hoped, would be acceptable as a compromise between the speech that a man like Hazell would actually use and what was permissable on television. Unfortunately it was not (though it does actually occur in at least one episode). John Bedells took further exception to the use of 'Balls' and 'Piss off' in another script. In a note to June Roberts he commented: 'If for 9 p.m. please substitute less offensive expletives.' [It should be said that in addition to the Family Viewing Policy there is another cut-off point at 10.30 p.m. after which it is assumed that even more children will be in bed.] June contested this judgement in a reply: 'The expressions "Balls" and "Piss off" . . . are both expletives that when used specifically for a *comic* effect I feel in certain instances I shall accept and don't believe will be offensive in a programme of this kind in this slot.'

Violence was not a major problem on *Hazell*. Although it is a crime series there is comparatively little physical violence and Hazell himself is responsible for only one death (for which he feels genuine remorse). But this is an issue on which the IBA are very sensitive. They have produced a *Code on Violence*; it's too long to quote in full, but certain sections are relevant to *Hazell*:

All concerned in the making of programmes for Independent Television have to act within a series of constraints. They must take into account the degree of public concern about particular issues, the boundaries of public taste, the limits of the law and any available information from research about the short or longer-term social consequences of their actions . . . Ideally a Code should give a clear guide to behaviour based on reliable knowledge of the consequences of different decisions. Unfortunately no Code of this kind can be provided. There are few relevant facts and few reliable findings derived from generally accepted research studies. Nevertheless, it must be recognised that this is an area of public concern which extends to factual as well as fictional programmes. People fear that violence on the television screen may be harmful, either to the in- dividual viewer (particularly if the viewer is a child) or to society as a whole . . . Dramatic truth may occasionally demand the portrayal of a sadistic character, but there can be no defence of violence shown solely for its own sake, or of the gratuitous exploitation of sadistic or other perverted practices. Ingenious and unfamiliar methods of inflicting pain or injury — particularly if capable of easy imitation — should not be shown without the most careful consideration . . . This Code cannot provide universal rules. The programme-maker must carry responsibility for his own decisions. In so sensitive an area risks require special justification. If in doubt cut.

It is perhaps a little disingenuous of the IBA to say that 'the programme-maker must carry responsibility for his (sic) own decisions.'

It's precisely because the programme-maker is not, ultimately, given this responsibility that friction arises. This is not the place for a debate on censorship, but the particular circumstances in which censorship operated on *Hazell* do throw some light on the general situation. Many programme-makers undoubtedly feel that the IBA and those who work closely with it are often over-cautious and, perhaps more important, that their decisions are often arbitrary and accompanied by little in the way of justification. For the programme-maker the problem is partly one of wanting the freedom to be responsible for their own decisions, and partly, if this is not allowed, of not knowing just where the line is being drawn and why. The IBA, on the other hand, maintains that it is bound by the Act and that its interpretation of the Act must not stray too far from the standards of the majority. If it did there would soon be calls for more public interference in television, which would not be to the liking of the programme-makers.

John Bedells believes that his job is to offer a perspective on questions of taste and morality which is that of the 'average viewer' rather than that of the television professional, and that his background is of some help in achieving this:

JB: 'This is a second career for me. I was in the Navy and retired in 1960. Then I was on the administrative side with Rediffusion [the company from which Thames was born]. I went into the programme side in 1962. I was a departmental manager, the right hand man of the departmental controller, the one that does the paper work, sees to schedules, fixes locations and things like that; first in the Drama Department, then in Scripts and Film Administration. (Interestingly, the present manager in the Drama Department is also an ex-Navy man.) I did time in the Features Department, then for six or seven years I was manager in the Education and Religion Department, which I liked best of all, partly because I think it's an older man's job. Then this job came up and the previous liaison officer said have you thought of John Bedells, he's a JP and has a knowledge of what goes on in nearly all departments. And I was concerned with quite a number of organisations outside, such as the church, which brought me into touch with people. So I had some experience of the views of ordinary men and women about television, which I think is lacked by many people in this profession. When you get into television it becomes a sort of closed shop and you tend not to know what people outside are thinking.'

No-one could deny that people in television are unrepresentative of the general population in respect of their lifestyles and general views about such things as sexual morality. The problem is whether the best way to deal with this situation is to erect a buffer in the form of the IBA between them and the people they make programmes for. It's inevitable that in such a situation the IBA will seek to find some sort of consensus which it can apply, and equally inevitable that it will fail, since such a consensus no longer exists in our soceity, if it ever did. The result is that the IBA is not liberal enough for most programme-makers and some of the audience and too liberal for others.

It's not surprising, then, that there were one or two differences of opinion over violence in *Hazell*, as there were over language. *Hazell Settles The Accounts* has a fight between Hazell and a couple of crooks, in the course of which Hazell uses a corkscrew. To be precise, the script specifies that 'Hazell's hand closes on the corkscrew and suddenly with shocking speed and viciousness he brings it down on Graves' hand — a knife would have impaled his hand to the bar.' The IBA Code, remember, specifically forbids 'ingenious and unfamiliar methods of inflicting pain or injury'. Accordingly John Bedells wrote a memo to June Roberts:

JB: 'The corkscrew stab is probably too sickening. Please ensure that scenes of such violence are *most* carefully handled. There is strong reaction to them at present.'

June defended the scene:

JR: 'The one alteration I feel I can't make is Hazell slamming a corkscrew down on someone's hand. Impaling the guy with a knife *would* be too violent but all Hazell does is bruise him and the implement could look fairly innocuous. If *Gangsters* (a BBC crime series) can show a woman stabbing a gentleman in the groin with a heroin-filled hypodermic, I don't think this will have the shock impact you anticipate.' (In fact as shot the scene *does* have quite a shock effect.)

Generally, Bedells had this to say about violence:

JB: 'It depends on how it's done. Gratuitous violence is going to be offensive. But if the event calls for violence . . . There is violence in society, it's a part of everyone's life in some way or another. And violence isn't always a physical thing; there's a great deal of mental and verbal violence, which people don't recognise as being the same sort of thing but which is often more damaging. So it's got to be taken on its merits. But the old argument that you can always switch off if you don't like it doesn't really hold up, because it's not as easy as all that to switch off when other people are watching. And you've got to remember that people have paid to see this. If you are going to give them things that are going to distress them so much that they are going to switch off then they are not getting value for their licence fee.'

Hazell, despite the fact that there is a fair amount of sexual activity in the series, didn't have any real problems with the third member of the 'holy trinity'. In *Hazell And The Maltese Vulture* there is a short blue-movie sequence (seen at some distance, in black and white) and Verity Lambert sat in on the recording to advise where the dividing line should be drawn between the necessary amount of realism and the requirements of 'good taste'. But this was an exception. As with language and violence John Bedells claims there are no definite rules:

JB: 'In the appropriate place there's nothing wrong with nudity, though it is more worrying in light entertainment situation comedy where it goes out at 7 or 8 o'clock. It's perfectly all right to have Benny Hill doing jokes about nudist colonies where one's not going to see anything. But there was a seduction scene in *Man About The House* which I thought went a bit far. I heard it caused a great deal of disgust among some who had children watching. It wasn't nude or anything, but there was a lot of blouse unbuttoning and skirt loosening. I mean, sex is fine, in its right place, but always the debate goes on about when and how.

Another situation comedy has become controversial; it's a spin-off from *Man About The House*. He's set up with his girl friend but he isn't married to her. The Controller of Light Entertainment said he thought it was perfectly charming and all right to go out at 7.15. But in my view it wasn't because the whole thing is a running gag about how virile he is and it shows children a family set-up where the normal conventions aren't observed. And then they get puzzled, you know, and ask awkward questions of their parents. I know we're in a broad-minded age and we're adult and know how to treat these things, but with children at a young age one should show them that the family unit is between a man and a woman who are married and that children are brought up in the protection of a married couple.'

What this doesn't account for, unfortunately, is the reaction of children who aren't 'brought up in the protection of a married couple'. However, it would be unfair to John Bedells to suggest that his judgements are always less enlightened than those of the programme-makers. In a scene in *Hazell Meets The First Eleven* Hazell is at a posh party where he has assumed the character of a rough cockney barrow-boy who has made good. While talking to his host he notices a black model girl walk past and remarks: 'Who's the schwarzer?' Vinnie, Hazell's girl friend, replies: 'James never calls a spade a spade.'

John Bedells: 'There are times when you can use the work 'spade' although it's an offensive one to blacks. But this struck me as a rather cheap remark. A couple of rough blokes could call someone a filthy spade and you'd be all right using it because everyone knows that they're foul-mouthed anyway and you're supposed to take offence at what they say. But she is supposed to be a decent girl who treats people reasonably politely. To make a joke like that I would have thought is not in character.'

In this case June agreed and the remark was cut.

What happens if he cannot get a producer to agree with his opinions?

JB: 'It's not mandatory. If a producer says no, I won't cut that, and I feel very strongly about it, well, one of us may eventually give way and compromise. But if we can't agree I've got direct access to Jeremy Isaacs, who's responsible for all the programmes we make. And I can say to him, I have advised that this shouldn't happen and I can't get agreement. If that fails I can apply to the IBA and tell them the same. Obviously I won't tell tales on the Director of Programmes at Thames, but I might ring up our contact at the IBA and say, I've got a feeling that you're going to be worried about something that is happening here and which they're determined to do. We'll give you the information, as much of it as we can, and you can come in on the act in plenty of time before it hits the screen.

I tend to start off by saying, and I think June knows this really, you must cut this, knowing quite well that she's going to come back and say I can't. Then we do a bit of horsetrading. The main thing is, you've got to get on with producers; it's no use getting their backs up. I suppose I've done that to June once or twice; she's a determined young lady. But it's as well to be able to get on with all sorts of people and to know how they like to be talked to about these things. You want to be conciliatory, to be comradely, but you have to know when to say no, this has got to stop.'

Lastly, we asked John Bedells what kind of feedback he got on his decisions.

JB: 'Well, if there's a big mistake and Jeremy Isaacs gets a lot of letters he'll send some to me, either to answer if they're small fry, or to draft replies for him. And sometimes the IBA pass on letters of complaint, either when they're 100% in sympathy with what we've done or feel they haven't enough information to defend it. But they're very reasonable, they're not always on the look-out for us making mistakes. They like to be told early enough when difficulties are likely to be encountered and then, if they've had the chance to give us some advice they'll back us as hard as they can. But if they're not really kept in the picture they can be resentful, naturally. And when that happens they usually chuck the letters over to us to answer, or we get rude letters from them.'

Censorship, we found, was not a major issue on *Hazell*; doubtless if one were studying a current affairs programme more substantial questions might be raised. With *Hazell* it was a series of minor and, to the programme-makers, niggling points. Perhaps with drama the real question concerns not so much these points, nor even the occasional programme that is made but not shown (though there are such programmes, even if not recently at Thames), but the programmes that never get made at all. This would take us outside the scope of this enquiry.

6 Casting

Thames has a Casting Department which is responsible for casting not only drama productions but schools and children's programmes, light entertainment and so on. It has two main functions: to assist producers and directors in their choice of actors for roles, and to negotiate contracts with the artists, or more precisely with their agents. The Head of Casting is Liz Sadler, who will cast some shows herself, though most will be assigned to other casting directors within her department. There's some tendency to specialise:

LS: 'You try as much as possible to put the right casting director onto the right project. And if there's a show we've done 2 or 3 series of I will normally change the casting director, because you can get in a bit of a rut since you've got basically the same type of characters coming up in each one. A new person will come to it fresh and have different ideas. It's a good thing we don't all think the same otherwise you would just go on seeing the same people on the box all the time.'

Before casting begins the producer will have consulted with the Casting Department on the budget for artists. The producer will indicate roughly what sort of performer s/he is going for, whether it will be star names or unknowns, and then the Casting Department will draw up a budget within the appropriate range, working out the cost of rehearsal fees, production fees, overtime, national insurance, etc., for the whole cast. If it's more than the producer feels will be available, then of course the Casting Department will have to lower its sights and work out a smaller budget. One part of the department's expertise is knowing exactly the going rate for any particular artist.

The work of the department isn't confined to seeking performers for specific roles. They get a lot of requests from agents and from artists directly asking for interviews or inviting casting directors to performances.

LS: 'We go to the theatre a lot. You have to, just to keep up to date with all the new talent there is around. There's an awful lot, especially in the fringe theatre and lunch-time theatre. It's not always easy to get to lunch-time theatre being out here at Teddington, but between us we do cover an enormous amount. You see a lot of stuff which if you had a choice you wouldn't necessarily go to, but you have to try and see virtually everything. We don't cover the provincial reps as much as we'd like to, but we get there when we can because there's a great deal of interesting work going on there, more so often than in the West End. One's always looking out for people generally, but of course you do have the project you're working on currently in your mind.'

Theatre is the major, indeed virtually the only, source of new actors, though a fortunate few might go straight into television from drama school. More established actors, however, may do very little besides television.

It is usually the director who will have the major say in casting, though in most cases the producer will be involved too, but in the case of the title role for *Hazell* directors were hardly involved at all. But the casting director plays a crucial part.

LS: 'Directors do rely a lot on casting directors because we know more artists than they do and therefore we can suggest people to them who they don't know. It's very gratifying when you've seen a particular actor on lots of things and you're just waiting for the right part to come along to give them a break and then you get a director who's prepared to take a chance.'

Several of the directors on *Hazell* acknowledged the help they got. Don Leaver, who directed *Hazell And The Weekend Man*, the first episode to be recorded, had this to say:

DL: 'Quite frankly, though I would love to pretend to you that after I finish at the studio I go rushing off to the theatre every night, I don't. When you've got a family life and a home to go to you don't want to spend every evening in a theatre. So this is the value of a Casting Department: people's opinions who you can trust and who do in fact cover everything. The major work of a good Casting Department isn't done in casting sessions, it's done out on the fringe and watching T V. I do watch quite a lot of television but you'd end up with square eyes if you saw it all.'

Directors can also get assistance from *Spotlight*, the casting directory which contains photos and career details of hundreds of actors and actresses. But this is only useful as a reminder. It can't tell you if they can act.

Don Leaver: 'In any case not everyone is in it and even if they are, if you haven't seen them they are just a face. You can ring their agents. But though I know two or three agents who would be very honest and whose opinions one could trust, there are a lot whom one couldn't trust at all; they're so keen to get their clients work. They may indeed believe in their clients, but even so . . . I think casting is a much under-rated department. As a director you're never stuck for a name for a part, but your thinking tends to become tired if you don't have anyone to bounce your ideas up against.'

Brian Farnham, who directed the last episode recorded, *Hazell And The Walking Blur*, went straight from *Hazell* to directing a play for the BBC, where there is no Casting Department.

BF: 'At the BBC you're on your own. I had to cast thirty parts, a lot of them small one and two liners. It would have been nice to have had a casting director and said to them, find me six people who have just come out of drama school, and let's cast them because they'll be cheap and it means I'll be meeting new people.'

The title role

From the moment the decision was taken, very early on, to tell the story of each episode through Hazell himself, to have him on screen virtually all the time and commenting on the action through voice-over narration, the question of who should play the role became a crucial one; in some ways the most crucial the producer had to make. As June Roberts said, 50 minutes solid of someone performing in front of you could be boring unless they're a strong and attractive personality. This in itself would have made the casting decision hard enough. But several other factors complicated it further.

To start with, it wasn't a part which could be written round whatever actor was cast. The character already existed in a fairly definite form (despite later modifications) in the three books, which everyone involved in casting had read. They all therefore began with a relatively fixed idea of what they were looking for. Nor was the role a very straightforward one.

JR: 'It's a very complex part. If it were pure comedy it would be easy to cast. If it were the ex-alcoholic cynical ex-policeman with a broken marriage and grievance against the world it would be easy to cast. But I need someone who can marry both extremes of that personality and make you believe in both.'

There was also the problem that Hazell is supposed to be in his middle-thirties. June Roberts was anxious that the series should be fresh and different and therefore that the actor playing the title role should not be identified in the public's mind with any other roles.

JR: 'We're trying to find somebody who hasn't been overexposed. But at 33 or 34 most actors who've shown a great deal of promise and have stood out have got a series of their own or are very well established. So you're looking for someone who by accident simply hasn't been discovered or whose strength is in supporting character parts and who hasn't been felt strong enough to carry a series.'

A further requirement was an actor with a genuine cockney accent.

JR: 'I would much rather we get a genuine cockney, not so much just for the accent but also because the face and the whole sort of look of a genuine cockney is, I think, distinctive. And also it's a big enough job to carry the whole series without having to master another accent as well.'

Besides having a genuine accent, the actor would also need what June called 'an interesting voice' which during the voice-over narration could hold the audience even while the actor was not present on screen. One more requirement, not much talked about but at the back of people's minds none the less, was that since the show would be in production for many months it would help if the leading role was filled by someone they could all get along with.

The three people centrally concerned with casting Hazell himself were Liz Sadler, June Roberts and Verity Lambert. Each had a number of ideas for the part, but there was no-one who seemed to all three to be absolutely right. The decision on the casting of the leading part is basically the producer's, but, we asked Verity Lambert, what happens if she disagrees with the choice?

VL: 'It happens much less often than you might think, because everyone is looking for the same things. But ultimately I carry the can and if a producer wants to cast someone that I'm really and truly convinced is wrong then I would say no. Because in the end if the casting turns out to be wrong then it's my fault.'

Things never got to this pass, but there were to be differences of opinion before a decision acceptable to both June and Verity was reached. The first person June thought of for the part was Nicholas Ball, who had been in an episode of *Couples.*

JR: 'The reason was that he was the only actor I knew who physically fitted the description in the books. I had one or two reservations about him, in terms of how much humour he would bring to the character, and how much charisma. But he was always there very strongly as someone who physically fitted the bill and had something and was a new face.' Verity also thought that Nick Ball was a definite possibility, though she thought he might be a little young for the part, in terms of looks. Since no-one was quite sure they decided to look around a bit more. In fact they looked around a good deal; June and Liz Sadler eventually drew up a list of 47 actors who were possibles.

JR: 'They were people whose work I knew, or they looked right in *Spotlight*, or they'd been recommended by people who knew their work. I saw them, Liz Sadler saw them, in some cases Verity did too and as soon as he joined us Kenneth Ware was present also. What happens is, someone will come in, you describe the series, describe the character and you find out what they've done before. Basically you're looking at their appearance, you're listening to their voice, and you're assessing their personality and what you think it will add to the part. In a lot of cases we were able to say just from one meeting, no, that person's wrong. But we might put them on another short list for one of the subsidiary characters if we think they're right for it.'

Eventually the 47 were whittled down to four. Besides Nick Ball there were Billy Murray, John Leyton and John Nettles. Though all along Nick Ball had been a strong possibility for June, she also came to feel that John Nettles was a serious contender. 'His sort of throw-away humour, even in the strained atmosphere of an interview, impressed me.' Verity, still having doubts about Nick Ball looking too young, was inclined to favour Billy Murray. Everyone thought that John Leyton should be kept on the list. But the more people discussed it the less certain they became. The only way to make a decision, it seemed, was to do some camera tests. This for Thames was a very unusual step; in fact Liz Sadler can't remember the company having done it before. Because of the shortage of studio space such tests are quite difficult to arrange, and thus holding the tests was an indication of the difficulties experienced in making a final decision.

Nick Ball describes how he came to be on the short list and what happened at the tests:

NB: 'I heard about *Hazell* around April 1976, through Colin Bucksey, who had directed my episode of *Couples*. Then I saw June in the restaurant at Thames and she told me she was looking for the male lead. So I said, why aren't I on the list? And she said, you are. It was convenient I'd worked with June in *Couples;* that character was another Londoner, and roughish. It was quite a nice part. The programmes were like monologues virtually, good for actors because you do it all yourself, with four cameras on you and the director picking shots. I think she also saw some of *The Crezz,* and the character in that was in an upper bracket from Hazell, but East End made good. So that's how it happened; I'd been around doing those sorts of part. Agents can often find out for you what's going on, and when it comes down to the nitty-gritty of negotiating a deal there's a lot of stuff you wouldn't want to do in person and where you need an agent's experience. But as for getting the job, you have to do that yourself; all an agent can do is help you get in the running.

So when the test came up I'd read the book of *Solomon,* and they sent me the script of it, having marked out the pages they were going to do in the test. I got a rough idea of the part, and I talked to Colin about it, who'd read the other two books. When I got there I was the last of the day. I got a brief word with the director who was doing the test (Don Leaver). And then I did it. It's a completely blank set, just a white backcloth and a couple of bits of furniture. They'd got a couple of actors in too. One of the scenes was with a girl because they wanted to see Hazell with a girl. It's a very cold situation to go into, without any rehearsal.

Apparently my use of language gave them problems. I don't believe you can get an actor to speak parrot fashion. You have to bend the words to make them fit. Being a test anyway it's very loose and you're floundering about trying to make the words seem right. June said to me afterwards, do you normally do that, change the words? I said, it's quite likely, it's a possibility. I've got to put into it what I feel I can put into it and if that means changing the words . . . She was happier when we agreed that if there were problems like that we would talk them through and I'd have to say why I wanted to make changes. Which is very good, because it makes you think, now why do I want that change?'

Nick's changes in the script during the camera tests were indeed a problem for June; not because the script is in itself sacrosanct but because she thought the changes were for the worse, that Nick wasn't getting the best out of the humour and that he showed 'instincts that were not right'. Only some considerable time later did she come to feel happier about this aspect of his playing.

The idea of having the tests was that they would make people's minds up once and for all. Unfortunately they merely changed people's preferences around without immediately producing a unanimous decision. Repeated viewings of the tests and discussion of them did lead to one quick decision, that Billy Murray was not right for the part. (It should be said at this point that in none of the cases of the actors tested was their acting competence in question. All four were very good actors or they wouldn't have got as far as the test. The final decision was made on the grounds not of who was the 'best' actor but of who was most suited to the particular part.) That still left three. John Leyton had given an excellent performance in the studio, all agreed. Yet somehow when the tapes were re-run he didn't strike people as what they were looking for. On screen, as opposed to on the studio floor, he didn't seem to be Hazell. That left Nick Ball and John Nettles. June's worries about Nick's playing of the comedy led her increasingly to prefer John Nettles. But not everyone agreed with her. By this time several other people were being consulted, including Terry Venables.

TV: 'I thought Nick Ball looked right. I'd heard there was a certain criticism of his handling of the humour, which was important. But he looked quite good to me. With John Nettles I thought he was terrific in the scene with Minty, spot on. But he was too tough in the scene with the girl, like he was George Raft or James Cagney. Whereas I didn't think Nick was tough enough with Minty, but was very good with the girl.'

Verity, on the other hand, though impressed with John Nettles' performance, and continuing a little worried about Nick's age (she inclined to see Hazell as someone who had been through it a bit, whereas June thought his boyishness would be an asset), was disturbed by a resemblance she saw between John Nettles and John Thaw, who stars as Jack Regan in *The Sweeney*. This was an important factor if *Hazell* was to retain its difference from other TV crime series. June didn't think the resemblance as strong as Verity, though acknowledging that it might be noticeable to some.

The indecision lasted for some weeks. Clearly everyone had to be as sure as they could possibly be about a choice which could affect the success of the whole series. But a decision couldn't be too long delayed since the 'possibles' might sign up for other commitments, and there would be much preparation to be done, in choosing costumes and so on, before the series entered the studio. In the end Verity and June decided on Nick Ball. Gordon and Terry, who had the right to be consulted, also went for Nick. June still felt that John Nettles would have been good in the part, but 'I cast Nick thinking that there were areas that worried me but that he had always been in my head from the beginning. It was my first instinct, so I followed it through.' For Verity too: 'In the end we just had to go by our instincts.'

We talked to Nick shortly after he had been given the part:

NB: 'It's going to be very hard work because of the way they're shooting it. I'm in every shot for 6 months' filming, which is a lot. And it's going to be quite tough, some of it, so I'll have to get fit, that sort of nonsense. And there are the disparate things in the character that have got to be worked out; I think that's quite good but you've got to feel your way round a character that has these two sides to him. It's also unfortunate that we can't do a pilot, an establishing feature-length show. [This had been the intention at one point, but production was brought forward from April to January, which meant there wasn't enough time.] And I think it's also unfortunate that there won't be that much of it on film.

There's a lot riding on it, it's more than me making however many pounds a week it is and having my name up in lights. I can have my name up in lights for 6 months, but then it's goodbye if it's not good enough. Or it can be a very good break and I can go on to bigger things. So it's important that I have some control over it. I think that's an actor's continual problem, to try and wrest some control over what he's doing. Not to get away from, but to get involved in it. It's the same in theatre. I was involved in the fringe, in a company that was a kind of collective, and that's the ideal. The cinema is the other extreme. To become as involved as you can in the various elements of the product that you make (and it is indeed a product) is very important. Actors have a lot riding on it, it's their reputation as much as anyone else's.'

A contract was then negotiated between the Casting Department and Nick's agent. The fee takes into account what he has been paid for previous productions, the fact that he will be 'carrying' the series and that he will be tied up over several months. At the same time, written into the contract are the terms for a possible second series. At an increased fee the company have an option on his services, but are obliged to take up that option by November 1977. There are also clauses for repeats and overseas sales.

Nick Ball, for all June's determination to find a genuine cockney, actually comes from Hastings. But his general background seems in

Nicholas Ball as Hazell

many ways suited to the part of Hazell. He left school at 15 without any GCEs and spent 5 years or so doing odd jobs before he had any thoughts about acting. Then appearing with an old friend of his in an amateur production of *The Hollow Crown* revived the taste for acting he had had at school, and he decided to go to drama school in Bristol.

NB: 'This was extraordinary, a new world to me. I'd never been involved in anything academic, and there were quite a few academics there who'd done a university course first. And there were others who were shuffling people like me, virtually not read a book at all — well, I had but not like they had.'

Since then he's done quite a lot of television work, a little bit of rep, some fringe and a film, but most of it has been modern acting rather than the classical parts which constitute a lot of British actors' training.

It seems only fair to Nick Ball to report at this point that despite the reservations there were about him at the start, no-one subsequently felt that they had made a wrong decision (granted, of course, that they couldn't know how the others might have actually turned out). When all the episodes were finally recorded June Roberts commented:

JR: 'I think Nick got off to a very difficult start in that he'd never carried a series before, and also it took him a long time to see the character the same way I saw it. I was looking for someone to be light and funny, a sort of pragmatic coward who could handle himself if he had to but who didn't really like to get into trouble; and with a lot of charm. I think Nick saw him as a very macho hero and latched onto the fact that there was a violent streak in him which once he did let go he couldn't control. I think Nick could have gone in that direction if the scripts had been twisted round to that. [And at the end Nick still felt quite strongly that the series should have had more 'action' and would have benefited from being done on film, which would have allowed that.) But by the time we'd done about 4 episodes and his experience and confidence grew we got a lot of the other dimensions as well, and by the end of the series I think he was really quite strong and I was very impressed by the way he grew into the part. We'd probably both like to go back and do the first 4 episodes again so as to get into them the kind of pace and energy and charm that he brought into the later ones.'

Verity too felt that they'd made the right decision and that by the time they got to the later episodes Nick was very good in the part. Nor did she think the earlier uncertainty was his fault:

VL: 'The directors too were fighting to find out just what the style was. It's one of those things that can happen when you're starting a new series, that it can take a little while before people hit on the way to do it.'

The smaller roles

Hazell had both a large number of running characters, appearing in more than one episode, and parts of varying size, some quite large, in single episodes. Sheila Trezise was the casting director for the whole

106

series. For each part she would draw up a list, sometimes as many as 12 people, in consultation with June and, in the case of the one-off parts, with the director of that episode. Interviews would then be arranged. At these, normally attended by Sheila and the director and sometimes by June as well, the actor or actress was first given a resume of the series and a description of the part s/he would play. Then they are asked for a brief account of their recent acting experience. Those up for a longer part will be asked to read a scene or two, and after they have gone Sheila and the director will talk over their reactions. Sheila will feed in information about any roles she has seen them in, and both she and the director will assess whether the individual is a good performer and whether they seem right for the part, in terms of physical appearance and personality. Sometimes a name will be noted as a possible for another part.

Many of the parts in *Hazell* were quite small, with an appearance on the screen lasting only a minute or so. In such conditions it's inevitable that those responsible for casting will look for someone who will make the right visual impression, will have a certain kind of face or be the right 'type', and much of the discussion at casting sessions revolves round this. If Sheila Trezise or the director had seen a previous performance this would obviously count for a lot, for or against. But the smaller the part the greater seemed the tendency to typecast. This could, and in one or two cases possibly did, lead to the casting of people who turned out to be not particularly good actors. But in general the chronic underemployment in the acting profession means that television, with its higher rates of pay than the theatre, can attract artists of high acting ability into even quite tiny parts.

One effect of this, however, is a sense of frustration amongst some performers. In order to get the best possible people some of the running characters were deliberately built up into larger parts. Minty, for example, appears in virtually every episode, and in several scenes in most of them. This enabled June to cast an actor of the stature of Roddy McMillan, who wouldn't have been interested in a couple of lines in 2 or 3 episodes. But some of the regular actors and actresses felt that their parts gave them too little to do. For James Faulkner, who plays Gordon Gregory, what he was doing 'wasn't really acting'. Despite his relatively frequent appearances, he still felt that he had no time to do more than create an immediate impression. His performance, he felt, had to be fairly unsubtle, going for the strongest and most obvious effects. Nor was there much opportunity to develop the character from

Detective-Inspector Minty (Roddy McMillan)

episode to episode since he had to be recognisably the same Gordon Gregory as in the previous episode and the time he was on screen was only enough to achieve that and no more. This is a problem for directors too, in that they are taking over characters who are already fixed. There's really no time on the screen to extend and develop them. Thus for the running characters, James Faulkner felt, direction tended to be just a question of getting the physical things right, like where to move. The economics of acting meant that people were glad to get such parts, but they didn't feel they were being stretched much. Obviously such a situation is characteristic of television generally, not just of *Hazell*, though possibly exacerbated in this series. Because of the dominance of the central character, and the fact that *Hazell* has so many running characters (7 in all), those playing these parts felt a little more squeezed than they might have done. Brian Farnham was certainly aware of the problem on his episode, *Hazell And The Walking Blur:*

BF: 'You've got lovely people like Maggie Riley who's playing Maureen and who's really got nothing to do. She was really there just as a

Hazell and Gordon Gregory (James Faulkner) in Gregory's office

reactor, to react to other people, and one found every scene she was in ending up with a close up of her. I've been as guilty of that as anybody. She does it so beautifully anyway, but I'm sure it happens in every episode. I think there is a possible way round that, if there's a second series. There's absolutely no reason why a whole episode shouldn't be built round one of the running characters. Take Fiona Mollison, who plays Gregory's secretary Diane. She had nothing to do in my episode, but she did it beautifully. There's no reason why something shouldn't happen to her because of some client of Gregory's.'

We asked Barbara Young, who played Dot Wilmington, to comment on the experience of playing a running character in the series, especially in the light of June Roberts' comments about the failure to create strong roles for women.

BY: 'It's difficult to play a lady sitting behind a desk who doesn't actually get involved in any action, but who just has a bantering style of relationship with the hero. You can supply a bit yourself, you can dress it right and act it right. But people used to ask me, what do you do in this episode and I used to say, well, nothing really. I turned down the part twice, because I didn't think they could do much with it. But I took it because I was quite interested in the whole lesbian thing between the two women. I thought I could play the part like a fella, which would be quite funny, if this lady who looked quite dainty really did everything to Nick which a gentleman would do to a lady, including patting his bum. Hazell can look like a little boy and that could be his charm. But I have a feeling that might be one element they remove in the next series because they find it difficult to cope with that.

I think the *Hazell* situation is fairly typical. I was talking to another actress from a different series and I said, that's nice, you've got plenty of work. She said, yes. I said, is it interesting? She said, no. I said, where do they put you? She said, in the kitchen. She said, where do they put you? I said, in the office. And that's what they always do, you're always behind a sink or a desk. What they never do is involve you in the action. They try, but their minds seize up, they really can't think of anything else to do with you.'

7 Finding a Style

At the beginning of December, exactly a month before rehearsals for the first episode were due to start, June Roberts called a meeting. Besides June, 11 people attended: Kenneth Ware, Don Leaver, his production assistant Liz Cadley, Sheila Trezise (casting director), Dave Ferris and Bill Palmer (the two designers on the series), Denver Thornton (location manager), Bob Dawson (scene master), Peter Howell (senior cameraman), Del Randall (technical supervisor) and Aubrey Proderick (make-up). Normally on a series of this kind these people would not meet each other in this way, but would tend to liaise with one another through the producer. The innovation appears to have been much appreciated by those who were present.

The immediate purpose of the meeting was to discuss the possibilities of giving *Hazell* a distinctive visual style. June explained that what she had in mind was some kind of equivalent to the look of 40s *film noir*. A

low key lighting producing heavy shadows in Crossfire (RKO, 1947)

series made for colour television could not simply reproduce the low key lighting with its resultant heavy, deep shadows which those movies, made in black and white, had employed. But *Hazell,* since it was not to be a piece of straightforward naturalism, could experiment in ways of producing somewhat similar effects by different means.

One problem in finding and sticking to a consistent style for a whole series has already been touched on in reference to the difficulty of keeping the same team for all the episodes. The fact that *Hazell* would not be able to keep the same lighting crew and would have several lighting directors working on it meant that a radically unusual lighting style could not be sustained across the whole series, Inevitably each lighting director would bring his own ideas to the episode of which he was in charge, and the same would be true of directors. No amount of consultation with the producer, it seems, would completely iron out the variations that would occur.

The idea was floated, therefore, that *Hazell* could be shot through special filters placed over the camera lenses. Once a certain kind of filter had been decided on it could be used for every episode and so each one would come out looking the same. The technical people present (that is, Del Randall and Peter Howell), raised a couple of objections to this, however. Firstly, the IBA sets certain technical standards for all television transmissions. If Thames were to put out a programme which did not conform to these standards it could be in trouble, and it would be the technical people who would be to blame. Filters would tend to reduce the brightness of the picture, possibly to below a level acceptable to the IBA. And there would be the additional problem that the engineers responsible for actual transmission might, on that account, compensate electronically for what they might see as the 'poor' colour quality, thus negating the production team's carefully achieved effects.

Secondly there was the danger that the automatic gain controls built into domestic receivers might do the same.* The colour monitors used in the control room of a television studio are of far greater quality than those on which the audience receives its programmes. Thus what might appear very effective in the studio might look merely rather gloomy in the living room unless the picture on each set were boosted electronically. But if it were, this might simply cancel out what it was hoped to achieve.

However, June was determined to see what could be done in the way of

* This is a device which endeavours to keep the signal strength at a pre-set optimum level, whatever the brightness of the signal received.

visual stylisation, and she therefore arranged for some studio tests to be made. These took place 3 weeks after the meeting, in one of the studios at Teddington. Present were June, Don Leaver (who was to direct the first episode) and a number of technicians. During the tests a third method of achieving the intended effect, besides lighting and filters, was suggested. This was that the picture quality could be altered electronically by the vision control operator. But again this had to be ruled out, for the same reason as made stylised lighting impossible; that each episode would very likely have a different racks operator, and it would be impossible to get them all to produce the same effect. And again it might run into trouble with the IBA.

The difficulty with the filters was in getting an effect which was strong enough to be noticed *as* an effect yet not so strong that it would simply look peculiar. (One has to remember that because this kind of thing is so rarely done in television, the audience is not used to it and, at least this is what television professionals believe, will not accept it as readily as they might do in the cinema.) Several filters were tried, all in a yellowish colour range. The intention was, as far as one could tell, to find a look that would not be 'natural' and which would look elegant and stylish; though it's hard to describe in words exactly what was sought. People seemed to know what they were looking for, but they weren't necessarily articulating it verbally.

First of all some shots were made of some empty stock sets, and then some actors, including Nick Ball, were introduced, wearing the kind of make-up normal for studio drama work. Scenes were played with and without filters, with both day and night lighting. June and Don found one filter they thought possible, but generally the technicians remained sceptical, feeling that the tests confirmed their earlier misgivings. In addition, they were worried that on a black and white receiver the filters would register merely as a muddy picture. There was also the problem that there would be difficulty in matching up such pictures with the film inserts of the location sequences (and similar filters over the film cameras would not necessarily have produced the same result). A further point was raised by Del Randall:

DR: 'The ambient light in every home is different, and so whereas a lot of people might watch with a centre light with a 150 watt bulb in it, other people might have subdued lighting. This makes quite a difference to the amount of light coming off the screen. These are the sorts of things that we have to try and keep an eye on as technical supervisors; we have to think about what the viewer is going to see. The monitors we're watching in the gallery are in ideal conditions (i.e., with very little ambient light) and thus capable of coping with variations in contrast far greater than a home television set.' Filters would cut down the amount of light and what might be acceptable on the gallery monitors might not be to the viewer at home. Of course the viewer could use the manual contrast and brightness controls to compensate for that, but it certainly wouldn't be acceptable to the IBA if people had to start adjusting their sets when *Hazell* came on.

There were two further objections to the filters, this time aesthetic rather than technical. One was that many people thought they would give the show a 'period' quality; a kind of 'thirtyish' look, many felt. Since *Hazell* is in fact contemporary, this wouldn't be right. Secondly, and this was an objection raised by Verity Lambert, although the filter gave very pretty pictures it tended to slow down the action. June felt that wouldn't have mattered if the scripts had been given even more pace than they had already. But by this time a certain style had been set for the scripts which would have been very hard to alter.

In the end a combination of technical and aesthetic objections defeated the experiment, and the filters were abandoned. It wouldn't be fair to blame this on the technicians, who were not implacably hostile. One of them remarked, for instance, that despite what others were saying, there would not necessarily have been audience resistance, since in his opinion the audience would accept non-naturalistic colour just so long as the flesh tones were realistic. It was only if people's faces started looking funny colours that viewers would start fiddling with their sets and phoning up the companies to complain.* Part of the problem is that the technical staff, in the nature of their jobs, are bound to think first about getting an acceptable standard of picture. If they don't they will hear about it from the IBA. From their point of view aesthetic requirements must take second place. And of course the nature of the production system is such that they are usually only brought in at a very late state. By the time the experiments took place *Hazell* was only 2 weeks away from the start of production. The scripts were, for the most part, written. June had taken the unusual step of holding a meeting to

---

*This, however, was part of the problem, as Del Randall saw it: 'When the filters were put in the designers were saying, it's great, look at that wallpaper. But they forgot about the person sitting at a desk either looking jaundiced or as though they'd just come off a holiday. So we went against the filter for that reason.' In other words, it was difficult to get flesh tones right with the filter.

discuss the programme's style, but even so this had been comparatively late in the day. To have held it earlier would have been impossible because no-one could have known which technical people would have been assigned to *Hazell* before that date. So the system makes it all but impossible for everyone who will be involved to get together right at the beginning to discuss an integrated approach to the series, an approach which would have allowed the technicians, writers and so on to have decided from the outset on a style that would have married form and content. As it was, not only were there technical objections, but in the opinion of some the scripts didn't go in quite the direction that was being sought in the visual style. One lighting director remarked that he felt the scripts were rather lighter in tone than would justify the search for an equivalent to *film noir*, the world of which is rather more angst-ridden than that of *Hazell*.

The studio tests also involved some experiments with the techniques to be used with the voice-overs. There was a feeling that it might be necessary to signal these to the audience in some way. So some trial runs were made with various kinds of echo effect. Visual signalling was also tried. Voice-overs were done with a mix to Nick Ball's face and a

Hazell: a shot from the title sequence

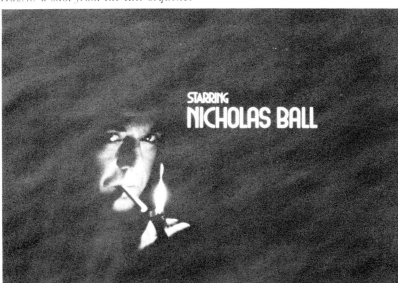

mix back into the action, and mix to him and then a cut back. There was also the possibility of using different lenses to indicate his withdrawal from the scene during the voice-over. But as it turned out none of these devices were found necessary, and in the programmes as they were finally made the voice-overs have natural sound and no special visual effect. Sometimes the camera shows Hazell looking at what he is commenting on, sometimes it shows just the scene with his voice come from off-screen. The consensus of opinion was that the audience would have no problem in accepting the voice-over convention and that that there was no need for any elaborate visual or auditory effects.

The upshot of all the discussions about visual style was that it should be left to the designers and, to a certain extent, the lighting directors, to achieve the desired effects. The sets, as we shall see, were generally in a muted range of colours, often shades of brown, except where the scripts specifically called for something more garish. And in some scenes, for example a number in *Hazell And The Maltese Vulture,* the lighting is deliberately dark, approaching, as near as is possible in colour television, the Hollywood style of the 40s. But in general the influence of Hollywood on the actual look of *Hazell* is vestigial compared to what at one time in the development of the programme it might have been. This discussion of style was interestingly prefigured in early talks about titles and music. The opening titles and the slides which mark the beginning and end of the separate parts of each episode (showing, in black and white, Hazell's face picked out in low-key lighting) are the clearest sign of this influence in purely visual terms. As far as the scripts are concerned, as we have seen, the influence is perceptible but muted.

8 Music and Titles

Virtually every television show (with the possible exception of the weather forecast) has an opening title sequence, and music usually accompanies this sequence as well as being used incidentally elsewhere. The function of such sequences is clear enough. They must serve to identify each programme and differentiate it from the others, and must provide an enticement to the viewer to keep watching.

Television producers are well aware of the need to get their show off to a good start, and since the title sequence will be the only one to be shown more than once in the series particular care is taken in its production. Music too needs a lot of thought. A good theme tune can help to fix the programme in the audience's minds. (Indeed with some shows one suspects that people enjoy listening to the theme music more than actually watching the show.)

As well as an opening sequence there will be closing credits. It seems to be generally conceded in television that the audience never watch them, but of course they're very important to the people whose names appear — so much so that it seems credits have been steadily getting longer as more and more of the production team get their names on the show. For *Hazell*, credits on screen were given to the main actors and actresses, the film cameraman and editor, sound recordist and dubbing mixer, theme music, lyrics and singer, writer, script editor, designers, producer and director, as well as a credit: 'based on books by Gordon Williams and Terry Venables'.

Music

In early June 1976 a discussion took place between June, Gordon, Terry and Verity about the music and the title sequence for the series. Gordon didn't want the music to be old-fashioned or 'touristy' — he wanted a modern 'big city' sound, and neither Gordon nor Terry were keen on having a theme song, which June was also worried about because it would be expensive and she would therefore have to get special permission. This, however, she must have done because it was finally decided to approach Ray Davies of *The Kinks* rock band to do a song for the opening and closing credits. Both Gordon and Terry liked his song 'Dead End Street', which they thought was the right sort of sound for the series and in addition, as a Londoner, Ray Davies seemed an appropriate choice. June contacted him in early October 1976. She later wrote him the following letter:

JR: 'There seems to be some confusion about the amount of music required for *Hazell*. I'm not thinking in terms of an album. *Rock Follies* was a television musical with half-a-dozen specially written songs for each episode. All we are talking about is one song that can be played over opening and closing titles, which eventually could possibly be released as a single.

One section of the song I would like to be an instrumental *only,* so that I can try and use it as background to the voice-over sections. I need approximately 1 minute of this, composed in such a way that I can fade in or out easily at any point.

We are talking in terms of a song lasting approximately 3 minutes — 30 seconds of lyric followed by 1 minute instrumental followed by up to 1 minute and 15 seconds of lyric. All I require in addition to that is 7 seconds of music to cover the end/beginning of parts captions.

Any other information about the character of Hazell which will help you I feel sure you will get from reading the scripts that I've sent you. It's important to remember that the series is as much about London as it is about Hazell.'

June was prepared to pay the bulk of the money allocated for music for the title song because she thought that it was very important. This meant however, that for incidental music she would have to use library music, which is especially produced for this purpose and therefore has all the rights cleared. These records are classified according to style. Thus on a programme like *Hazell,* on which rock music was considered to be most appropriate, records 'in the style of Led Zeppelin' or 'The Soft Machine' would be selected. If a commercially released record is wanted, as was the case in the cafe sequence in *Hazell And The Maltese Vulture* then all the foreign rights have to be cleared (as well as the British ones) and that can be difficult. In that particular instance an early '60s single was used on the recording day, only to discover later that they couldn't clear the rights and so it had to be changed in the dubbing session.

June wrote Ray Davies again on 22 November reminding him that his deadline had passed and that shooting of the title sequence was booked for early December. It is impossible for the graphics designer and director to draw up a story board and shoot the sequence without the music being ready in some form.

Ray Davies finally said that he couldn't do the music and therefore the shooting dates were cancelled. By the end of December June had managed to get Andy McKay (who wrote the music for *Rock Follies*) to compose and Judy Raines to write the lyrics. The new deadline for the music was the end of January, at which point it was hoped to be able to record it. It was also intended to try out Nick's singing but this idea was dropped, June preferring to have a woman singer. By this time June had decided that she wanted very short opening titles of only 20 seconds and slightly shorter closing credits of 1 minute 15 seconds. Judy Raines geared the lyrics she wrote (which were done before the music) towards a twelve bar blues arrangement, which bothered June slightly in that she wanted the music to be fairly light and upbeat as the series had a lot of comedy. Judy felt that that was not necessarily a contradiction and the music as it now exists proves that she was right in that it is a fairly bouncy example of twelve bar blues.

Andy produced a tape of his music played on a piano to which the graphics designer could work (in the meantime) and finally everybody entered the recording studio on 9 March 1977 — some months later than June would ideally have liked.

There is a full recording studio in the Teddington building which also doubles, if necessary, as a dubbing theatre. One problem that would have occurred if Ray Davies had done the music was that he wanted to record the music at his own private recording studio and that might possibly have created difficulties if Thames had wanted to insist on their sound supervisor being present. As it was the music was recorded at Teddington with 3 technicians — sound supervisor, tape operator (grams) and floor manager. There were 5 instrumentalists including Andy McKay on saxophone and bass, drums, piano and guitar. All the musicians had worked on *Rock Follies*. Maggie Bell was chosen to be the singer.

Title sequence

A series like *Hazell* will have a graphic designer appointed to it for the whole run — in this case it was Bernard Allum. He was responsible for devising the credit sequence, choosing or designing the type-face and also producing any action props that need making such as cheque books, etc. (Thames are careful not to use the cheques of any particular bank). The only thing he won't draw are large signs such as those placed outside buildings — this will be done by a sign writer. Much the most important task for Bernard was to devise the title sequence.

Bernard's first task was to read a couple of the scripts — he didn't read the books as he could have done because he felt that he was a visual person (i.e., he didn't read much) and would rather work on the basis of people's stray comments and his general sense of what something is about. At the meeting in early June 1976, when the music was discussed by June, Gordon and others, ideas for titles were also thrown up. Various suggestions were made, such as the series having a gimmick (Gordon used the example of Kojak's lollipop) or of making the titles entirely in black and white. There was also a strong sense at the meeting that London should be the main theme of the title sequence and suggestions were made of showing Hazell in a traffic jam or walking down Oxford Street or of a montage sequence of London. Bernard wasn't at this meeting but according to him June's final brief to him was that she wanted the titles to say 'London' in a visual sense and to combine this with a silhouette of Nick in order to suggest the idea of a private eye being somebody working in the shadows. June had apparently seen a Humphrey Bogart movie which had used silhouettes in the title sequence and she had been quite impressed by them.

Having been given that brief Bernard's first job was to draw a story-board which he could then show to the producer to indicate the type of end product he envisaged. It is at this stage that the producer will say whether or not to go ahead. June liked the idea and so Bernard proceeded with his design. Alistair Reid was brought in to direct the live action so the next step was to discuss the sequence with him. He and Bernard decided that the only way to do it in live action form (as opposed to animation) was to rent a film studio for a day. The television studio couldn't be used because the optical effects required can only be produced on film.

In order to obtain the silhouette effect they wanted they had the studio dressed in white and Nick in black. They also dyed his hair black and blacked his face and hands. The whole sequence was shot on high contrast black and white film. A difficult problem for Bernard, and the reason for the title sequence being produced so late (a number of the programmes were fully edited before the credit sequence was placed on to them) was that he couldn't work until he could hear the music. They couldn't shoot the film without having the music to synchronise with and cue to, and in the event finally had to make do with the composer's original piano tape of the music, which was far from ideal.

For the live action Bernard and Alistair filmed Nick walking across the floor in front of the camera, sitting in a chair and just turning his head. Against this last movement they tried tracking and zooming the camera in and out. By the end of filming they had a series of sequences of Nick moving in silhouette against a stark white background.

At the end of the day Nick cleaned himself up for a shot (this time not in silhouette) of him lighting a cigarette. This shot was to be used at the end of the opening credits and as the slide which marks the beginning and end of each part of the show. It was shot on colour film and in total darkness — the light source was provided by the Zippo lighter Nick uses in the shot. The lack of any other lighting at all both creates the shadows on his face and the intense black that surrounds him.

The following night Bernard went out in a camera car with Alistair, the location manager, the PA, the cameraman and focus puller to shoot the night lights which are used as the background on the credit sequence. Unlike the film work on the rest of the series, 35mm was used, possibly because the rostrum camera that was to be used later was 35mm but also because in animation the registration (the marrying of different prints) is critical enough to require the double claw of the larger format camera (most 16mm cameras have a single claw to transport the film across the shutter which means that there is a tendency for the film to pull to one side slightly). Eastmancolor film was used. The team drove around London and every time some interesting light effects were seen they would stop the car and shoot: neon signs, relections of lights on the river, fish and chip shop lights, traffic lights and general views from the car were taken.

Having done that Bernard viewed the rushes and for the black and white silhouette sequences of Hazell ordered high contrast matrix and masters prints of the film. The former provides a silhouette of Hazell against a white background and the latter is a reverse of that so that you see Hazell in white against a black background. The reason for this is that on the opening title sequence Hazell is in silhouette against a background of flashing lights but in the final credit sequence the lights are placed on his body (which had to be white if one was to see the lights). Having ordered that, Bernard created the flashing light sequence by running 20 different sequences of lights on to one negative in order to obtain the busy and confused effect he wanted.

STARRING
NICHOLAS BALL

In the sequence as it appears Bernard intercut a shot of Hazell in silhouette walking across the screen against a background which alternates between the flashing lights and the title *Hazell* which is gradually revealed by his movement. The type-face that Bernard used for the series was one that he designed and copyrighted a year before (financially a good deal as far as he was concerned!). As explained in the section on music he only had 20 seconds for the first sequence (which he personally felt was too short) and the fairly standard 1 minutes 15 seconds for the end credits.

What Bernard eventually produced succeeded in combining the idea of London as being one of the stars of the programme with the *film noir* idea — ideas which are present in the programme as made but less so than originally intended. Gordon Williams liked the credits, but remarked that if Bernard had read the scripts he would have seen that Hazell is struggling all the way through the series to give up smoking. The use of cigarettes in the title sequence glamorises smoking in a way that Gordon felt was unfortunate.

9 Design, Costume Design, Makeup

This chapter deals with the work of those people who had particular responsibility for the visual appearance of the show: designers, costume designers, make-up and lighting directors.

Design

Two designers were assigned to *Hazell* — Dave Ferris and Bill Palmer — and they worked on all the episodes bar the last one, whch was done by Gordon Toms. The reason for the change at the end was that it was felt that there was too much work involved for the two of them on a series such as this, which had a 2-week turn-round, and therefore halfway through the series it was agreed that a freelance designer should come in to help. However, as a result of the PAs' dispute, discussed below, the situation suddenly changed and so in the end only the last episode was designed by somebody else.

Television designers often come from stage design, which was the case for Dave Ferris who, after having been to art school, worked for a period in the theatre before joining Thames. Designers will be brought in at a very early stage, especially in a programme like *Hazell* where there was an attempt to produce something that *looked* rather different. So the designers attended the early screenings of *Double Indemnity* and *The Big Sleep* which June had set up and they discussed at some length, after reading the novels, what June wanted in terms of sets. One problem that emerged was the number of sets that the scripts required; some of the scripts were coming through with too many sets for the studio space that was eventually allocated. Ideally, the production team would have liked (and were originally promised) the largest studio — Studio 1 — for all the episodes. But because of scheduling problems they ended up being initially allocated Studio 1 for 2 episodes only and so the 2 most complex scripts (in terms of sets) were chosen for those dates. (Another effect of the PAs' dispute on *Hazell* was that as a result of the consequent re-scheduling, Studio 1 became available for the last 3 episodes.) Space in Studio 2 was severely limited with sets virtually on top of each other and little room for camera movement. The production team was very annoyed (and the designers incensed) when they discovered on one occasion that Studio 1 was being used for the *Benny Hill Show* despite it having very few sets. Apparently stars can exercise power over such matters! It seemed a strange scheduling decision, especially since the prop crew and the designers had been in the studio until 12 the previous night trying to cram all the sets into Studio 2.

As related elsewhere it was decided that it was not technically possible either to light the series in a particular way or to use special filters in order to achieve the visual effect that June originally wanted. A third method of achieving stylisation was therefore adopted in which the designers were to use a limited range of colours in order to achieve a more sombre effect. It was thought that this might at least simulate some of the effects of filters without altering the colour of the artists' faces. Bill Palmer said that they used warm or neutral colours like cream and brown for most of the sets, e.g., Hazell's office. (In fact the stairs outside his office are the one set that do relate to *film noir* type sets in that the shadows cast by the balustrades on the wall are very clear and distinct.) An additional reason for using neutral colours, according to Bill, was that the schedule was tight, there was no time or space for experimentation. In general, people seemed very pleased with the sets though Verity Lambert did say that she felt the result of using neutral colours was that the programme looked too 'tasteful' — like a BBC2 classic serial was her description — and that was precisely the effect that they didn't want to achieve. She also felt that Hazell's flat looked too elegant although she did admit that seen in the studio, the furniture had looked suitably vulgar. There is an undoubted problem here in that most people feel colour television generally has the effect of making everything look nice and pretty — it is extremely difficult to achieve dirty and dingy effects.

On certain sets very garish colours were used. For example in *Hazell Settles the Accounts* 'decadent' colours (reds and golds) were chosen for the prostitute's room, and in the sauna parlour scene in *Hazell And The Walking Blur* strong red colouring was achieved through the use of lighting on white walls.

According to Bill, both he and Dave were surprised by the tight scheduling of *Hazell* — they thought that there would be 1 month per episode, and that is certainly what they felt they required if they were to attempt anything very new or original. As it was there was a 2-week

shadows on the stairs: Crossfire (RKO, 1947) and the landing outside Hazell's office

turn-round. They therefore divided the episodes between themselves, because the shortest time in which they can read the scripts, draw the designs and have the sets built is 28 days. The timetable runs as follows.

The drawings have to be given to the set builders 20 days before the production enters the studio which, on a 28-day schedule, leaves only 8 days for reading, sketching, discussing the problems with the director, producer and lighting director, and drawing the plans. An example of the kind of discussion that takes place with the director was the problem that Brian Farnham faced in shooting the scene in the banqueting hall in *Hazell And The Walking Blur*. This set had to have a low ceiling of wooden beams (because that looked real) and the design was based on the actual look of the interior of the hall outside which the exteriors were shot. The problem was that the ceiling made it very difficult to get the cameras, lights and sound booms in for close-ups. Therefore Brian asked the designers to have the sets built so that the ceiling could be lifted off once the long shots had been taken.

Having discussed the designs with the people who are most directly involved with the sets the designer will draw accurate plans and elevations of the sets and a number of copies will be made. One set of drawings will be cut up and made into a 3-dimensional model. The director and lighting director will then be able to use the models in order to obtain a more precise sense of where they will be able to place their cameras and lights. The actual set building for *Hazell* was not done at Teddington although there are large carpenters shops on site. Apparently the more complex and large sets are built there but Thames have an annual contract with the firm of Watts and Corry in Manchester who are contracted for so many hours work in the year. The plans and elevations will go there and they will construct and paint all the sets. This is done remarkably quickly but construction is aided by the fact that standard sizes are used for the flats which will therefore be repainted many times before they wear out. This may seem surprising given how different in size and proportion all the rooms look on the screen but one must remember that rooms are built on a modular basis so that there are possibilities for enormous variation. Once the sets have all been painted they will be erected in Manchester and Dave or Bill will travel up to see and check them. If there is anything wrong they will be corrected before being packed up and sent down to London.

Once the drawings are finished and have been sent to Manchester the designer then has to find the props he requries. He will, of course know approximately the type of furniture he wants, which he will discuss with the buyer, who is employed full-time by Thames to hire props. The buyer will have an expert knowledge of the specialisms of the different prop companies and will deal with all the administrative and financial work involved in the hiring. Dave or Bill would therefore discuss their requirements and decide which firms should be visited and go with the buyer to choose the exact pieces they would like. It can happen that some pieces of furniture will be extremely expensive and then the designer will consult the buyer as to whether it is possible to have it and keep within budget. It is the buyer's responsibility to advise them and to keep within the budget.

The stock sets are slightly different to the others in a number of ways. Firstly they were generally designed by Bill and Dave together and one presumes that they were able to spend more time on them as some of them were drawn in late 1976 some weeks before the first episode. The models for them are more strongly built, using balsa wood (because

128

they have to last through the whole series) and the sets themselves also look as though they are more substantially built. Certainly a set like Hazell's office with its curved gabled window was specially constructed and not made out of standard flats. Dave Ferris described the designing of Hazell's and Dot's offices as follows:

DF: 'So now we're basically down to designing the interior of Dot's office, trying to get an idea of how Dot thinks mentally, what sort of

Dot's office

lesbian relationship she has with Maureen, and what her business is. It's no use inventing some fictitious business without knowing the ins and outs of how that building is run or how the office is run — whether she has people visiting her, what sort of files she would have, whether she would have filing cabinets or whether they would all be bound up in brown envelopes, etc. At the moment there seems to be some vagueness about the type of business she is running so we're trying to sort that out. We're trying to play with a staircase in this set so that whenever Hazell is arriving he's coming up this flight of bloody stairs to get to his office

designer's sketch for Hazell's office

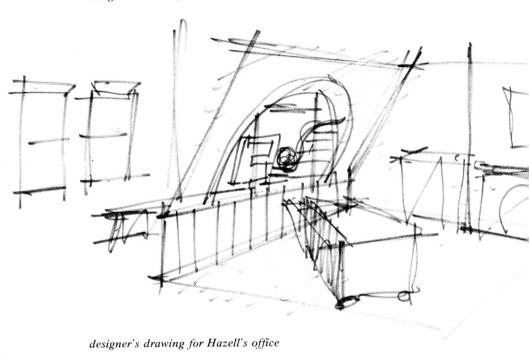

designer's drawing for Hazell's office

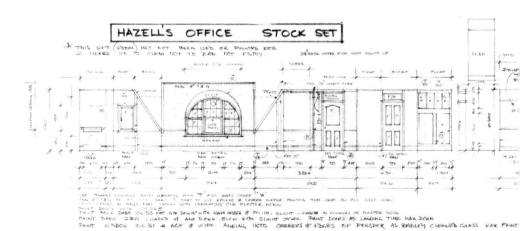

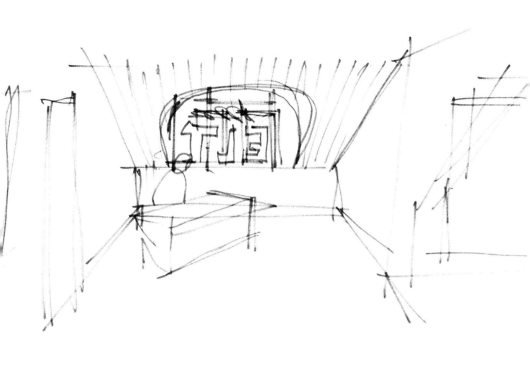

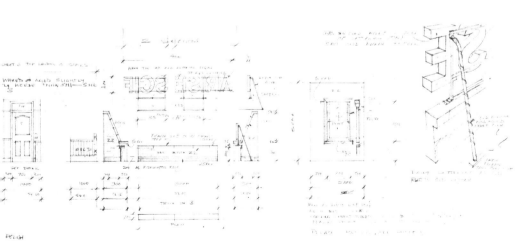

131

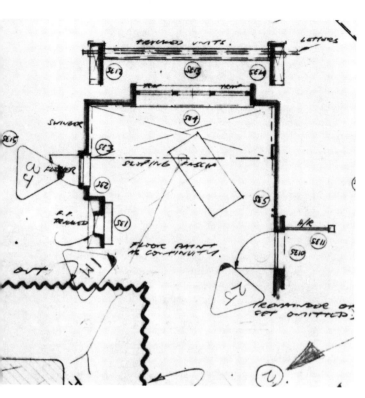

Hazell's office laid out on the floor plan

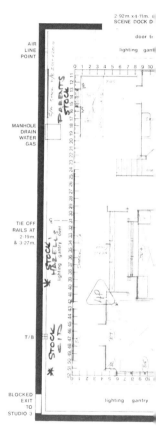

floor plan for Studio 2 of sets for Hazell Pays A Debt

132

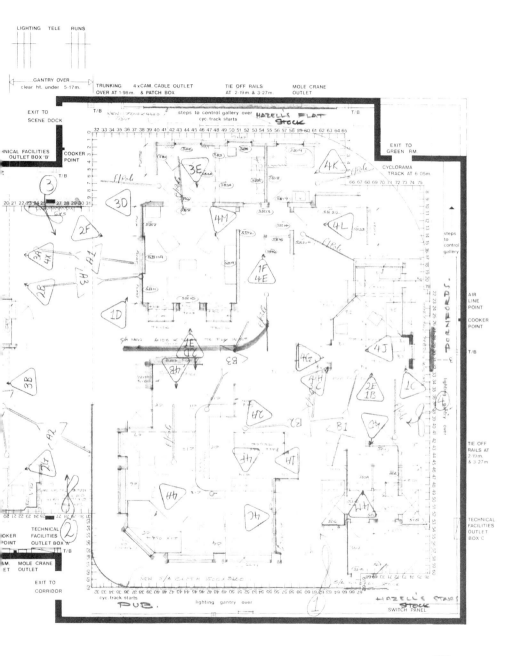

designer's model of Hazell's office

Hazell (Nicholas Ball) and Dot (Barbara Young) in Hazell's office

continuity picture of Hazell's office

135

designer's sketch for 'Chez Bert's' in Hazell Settles The Accounts

designer's model for 'Chez Bert's'

136

continuity picture of 'Chez Bert's'

Nicholas Ball and Pamela Stephenson ('Gloria'), on the set of 'Chez Bert's'

designer's sketch of Hazell's flat

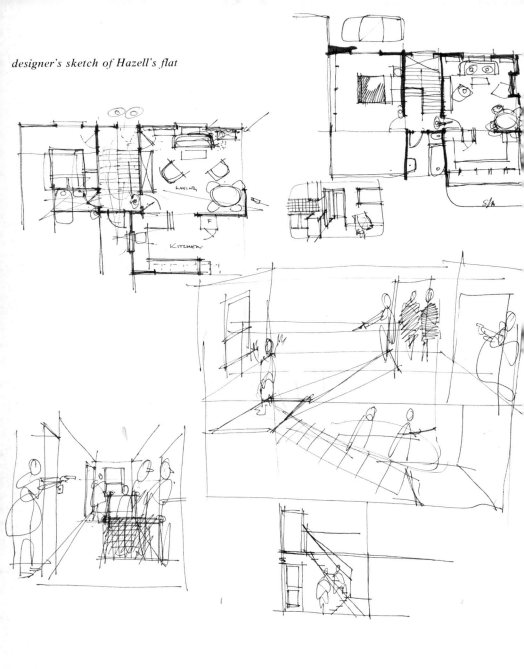

138

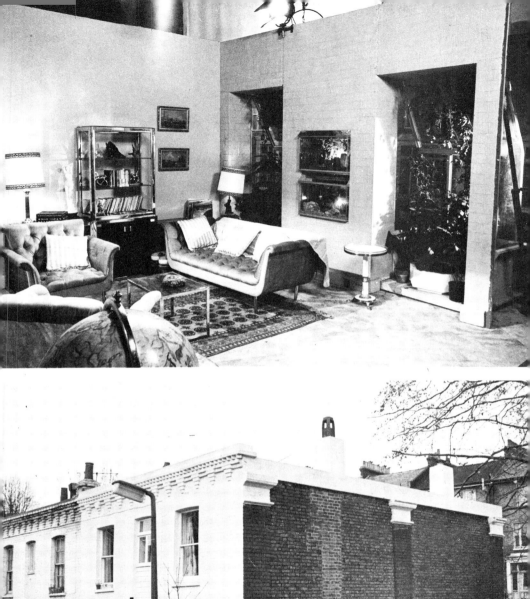

and every time he has to pass theirs. His office is at the top and is a dingy little bugger of a place, sort of Mickey Spillane type of feel about it. We're worried about how to light it.'

It is evident from what Dave said that he can only hope that each director will want to shoot Hazell walking up these stairs in each episode — there is no saying that they will do that unless June agreed with Dave and insisted that all directors had to include such a scene. What is additionally interesting about his comments is that apart from what he assumes to be unproblematic, i.e., the fact that Dot and Maureen's relationship is a lesbian one (which is only vaguely hinted at in the scripts), he is as much concerned about motivation as Gordon and Richard Harris. Once again the basic impulse is to make the programme look 'real' — an impulse which runs counter to some of the more original intentions of the programme. Thus the designers clearly went to an enormous amount of trouble to put in as much detail as possible (to the extent that on one set of *Hazell And The Walking Blur* there was so much furniture that the cameras couldn't get in and some of it had to be taken out). To include so much detail must assume (and perhaps make it almost inevitable) that the lighting director will illuminate the whole of the set, thus effectively shutting off the possibility of *film noir*-type, low-key, lighting.

Designers will also work with the location manager in choosing locations and will obtain permission to enter and photograph the interiors of any buildings which are chosen as exteriors, in order to match the proportions of their sets as closely as possible with the exteriors. They will also have to help organise any props and vehicles needed for location work. Thus in addition to designing sets they will spend a good deal of time looking for locations, attending location work, going to rehearsals and will be working in the studio full-time the 3 days that are spent erecting scenery and rehearsing and recording the episode.

One other task the designer will fulfil when out with the location manager is to take photographs of the surrounding buildings and skyline. Most sets require either a cyclorama or a backcloth to suggest a world outside the windows. The former is simply an enormous curtain usually of a neutral grey type of colour which provides a surface that can be lit to provide a plain background. On a series like *Hazell* backdrops were mostly used outside the windows of the sets. These were usually huge paintings of London buildings and skylines and, despite the fact that they are hardly seen and very little use is made of them (with exceptions like the scene outside Hazell's office window, which has a neon sign) a good deal of trouble is taken to produce them. From the photographs taken, the designer will choose the most suitable and they will be copied by scenic artists employed at Teddington.

A glance at the budget for an episode of *Hazell* indicates very clearly the importance of design within the production as a whole; about half of all above the line costs goes on sets and props. It would be extremely interesting to know to what extent this sense of its importance, as felt by professional programme-makers, is shared by the audience. Does the audience notice the trouble and expense? It has been suggested, for example, that the showing of old Hollywood movies on television, with their traditionally lavish sets and costumes, has raised the expectations of the audience in relation to standards of design for television drama, though it is by no means clear how such an assertion could be proved. What is certain, however, is that despite some people's feeling that television, compared to the cinema, is largely an affair of talking heads, the settings which those heads are placed in are given a high priority in production. One of the designers himself placed the priority so high as to say that designers in a sense direct the show because how they build their sets determines where the director can put the cameras and what s/he will want them to look at. But we don't think it likely many directors would assent to this.

Costume design and make-up

With costume design as with everything else June tried to get people involved early, but in this case it wasn't possible. She had decided to use Frank Van Raay because she had worked with him before and had liked what he'd done. But Frank was tied up on another show and couldn't start on *Hazell* till the end of October, just a couple of months before the show went into the studio. At that time Frank met June and Nick Ball for lunch to discuss what kind of clothes Hazell should wear.

FVR: 'The general idea was that he should be sharp, very fashionable in a way — not dressed in jeans or anything like that: he buys suits, good shirts. What we tried to avoid was what you always see in TV detective series, where the hero wears safari-style leather jackets like in *Van Der Valk*. The funny thing is we came back to that in the end sometimes, because there's action in the series and when you know you're going out for a fight you don't put your suit on.'

Frank and Nick went to quite a lot of trouble to find what they wanted. For example Nick was keen to get some tab-collared shirts. It took a long time before he and Frank eventually came across some in a shop in the King's Road, because they weren't fashionable at the time, though Nick hoped he could help make them so. On a contemporary series such as *Hazell* almost all the clothes would be bought rather than made. Frank would prefer to make them since this would ensure getting exactly what he wanted, but there simply isn't time. Accordingly all the main actors in the series had a complete wardrobe bought for them. Nick's was bought well in advance to give him time to wear the clothes in before he had to appear in them on screen.

With those characters appearing in a single episode Frank will first talk to the actors at the initial read-through. He may ask them if they have any suitable clothes of their own. If they have he will ask them to use them since this not only saves the company money (though the actor will get an allowance) but also means that the person will be more at ease than if wearing new clothes. However some performers are suspected of claiming they've got nothing but an old pair of jeans, thus ensuring a new outfit for themselves. Actors can keep the clothes bought for them on payment to the company of a proportion of the price. Shortage of storage space makes it uneconomic for the company to build up a wardrobe of costumes. Most people appearing in *Hazell* did get some new clothes out of it, though to one actor whose part required him to wear drag they perhaps weren't of much use.

In Frank's opinion costume design for television is more difficult than for the theatre (which he has also worked in). Firstly, greater realism is required: 'you have to go into backgrounds more, characters' social lives, where they come from, what their parents are like.' This is because costumes on television will be seen much more than on the stage. Another major problem is colour. Certain colours, in particular blue, are avoided as far as possible because they show up too brightly on screen. And on *Hazell* a design decision had been taken to use muted colours except in special circumstances. Hazell himself is thus dressed mostly in a range of browns and greys.

For Hazell's clothes Frank took the comparatively unusual step of going down to the East End and taking some pictures of what people were actually wearing. Since he was going to be working on the show for a long time, and since Hazell himself would virtually never be off screen, he wanted to be sure of getting it right. It was also important to Nick that he had clothes that would do something for him. Frank remarked that Nick was playing a much bigger and more important part than any he had played before and when an actor finds himself in such a situation he is apt to fall back on how he looks outside, whether he feels he is visually making an impression. So one function of costume design is to help give the artists that confidence.

June Roberts took a close interest in the costumes, as indeed she appeared to do in everything. At one point a problem arose about the kind of costumes Frank had selected for Vinnie, Hazell's girl friend. June accordingly wrote him a memo:

JR: 'Please can I ask for you to rethink Vinnie's wardrobe. I know and am sympathetic to the problems that you are having in finding the right costumes for her but on at least two occasions I think she has been depicted on the screen in an extremely unflattering light. I would like to abandon the fur coat, the hats and the green trouser suit. When you are next buying for Vinnie please would you let me come along so that I can see for myself what the problems are and okay before the purchase what seems best to suit her. It is crucial that we project an image for her which is classy, sexy and really makes an impact.

I think you are on exactly the right lines for Diane (Gregory's secretary), who looked very good indeed in *First Eleven*. I'd like to know before we get into the studio what all the women are wearing, particularly the guest artists playing glamour-roles.

With Hazell I would like him to wear at least once in every episode the tan suede jacket with black polo-neck sweater and a dark suit *with* tie and clip. I'd prefer him not to wear an open-neck shirt with his suits. I'd also like to know prior to filming and studio what else he will change into. I thought generally the costumes on *First Eleven* were smashing.'

As this memo suggests, normally the costume designer's work would only receive inspection when the artists appeared on the set wearing the clothes he had provided, by which time it's usually too late for any changes. The designer thus bears a heavy responsibility to get things right and though he will confer with the producer and director before each episode there is rarely time for either of them to actually participate in picking the clothes. Yet it's a vital area; the wrong clothes can easily spoil an actor's performance or a whole scene.

As far as the women's parts were concerned, it appears to have been the policy to have at least one well-dressed lady in each episode to add a touch of class (in more sense than one, perhaps). We accompanied Frank on one shopping expedition with the actress who was to play such a part, that of Ingrid in *Hazell And The Walking Blur*. We went first to Brown's, a fashionable and fairly expensive clothes shop in Sloane Street. Katharine Schofield, who was playing the part, needed a couple of dresses. Frank had used this shop before and, not surprisingly, they were pleased to see him. Katharine tried on half a dozen things before she found something which she felt good in and which satisfied Frank's idea of how the character should look. She seemed very anxious to get clothes that accentuated what she felt were her good features and did the best by her. Actors and actresses generally will tend to be very well aware of how they look on screen: it's their living, after all. The main requirement was for an evening dress that would look glamorous but not tarty and eventually a black dress was decided on, fairly classical in design. Frank also felt the colour would fit in with the overall design of the series. In all, the two dresses bought cost nearly £200, though Frank thought he had got a bargain as both were reduced in a sale. Then we all went down the road to the Chelsea Cobbler in the King's Road, where Katharine got a couple of pairs of shoes for around £40. To us it seemed a lot since we could hardly imagine that many people would even notice the shoes of an actress who was to be on screen for perhaps 5 minutes in all, but it's another example of the kind of attention that is paid to detail.

Once the clothes have been chosen Frank's other area of responsibility is to ensure continuity on costumes, though in practice he largely delegated this job to Mandy Harper, his assistant. The main thing is to make sure that the performers are wearing the right clothes for the scene — that, to use a crude example, Ingrid isn't wearing her evening dress in a day-time scene.

Costume design needs to be done in co-ordination with make-up. On *Hazell* make-up was usually straightforward, requiring none of the elaborate wigs, for example, that might be needed on a period show. As such it's basically a question of putting on some colour and outlining of the facial features to counteract the flattening and deadening effects of the very strong lighting needed for the colour television cameras. The artists will be consulted at the read-through on any problems that might occur — some are sensitive to certain kinds of make-up, for example. Some actresses like to do their own, or at least help with it, and may have ideas about what kind of make-up they look best in. Sally Thorpe, who did the make-up on several of the episodes, did have one rather more elaborate job in *Hazell And The Walking Blur*, where Hazell's client becomes engaged, while drunk, to a lady who turns out

144

to be a gentleman in drag. The problem here was to make up the actor to look sufficiently convincing to have taken in the client, but not so convincing that the audience would not suspect something odd. Sally had to use a heavier base than normal to cover the actor's beard and she also had to pluck his eyebrows. She had bought an acryllic wig — to have had one specially made would have cost as much as £150, and though such an expense would not be unusual in a period show, in this case it was hardly justified, especially since a slightly cheap effect was just what was needed. The whole make-up took about an hour to apply, but fortunately she wasn't faced with the problem make-up people often get, of being required to change an actor's make-up rapidly between one scene and the next. There was, however, a continuity problem, in that the actor had appeared in a film sequence before his studio scene, and this had been shot several days previously. So during filming Sally had taken some Polaroid snaps which she consulted later in the studio.

Sally, like Frank, occasionally got memos from June, such as this one:

JR: 'Please would you ensure that unless a situation is very formal that Celia Gregory (Vinnie) always appears with her hair loose and in its own natural style. I would like her make-up to be kept as soft and flattering as possible. This was very effectively achieved in *First Eleven*. Also I would like Fiona Mollison (Diane) to have her hair down most of the time but am happy to vary the style and occasionally have it up for one scene. It is essential that both these characters always look as good as they possibly can.'

Frank remarked to us that on other shows he had once or twice had problems with the hair styles that had been chosen: 'then you do something like put a hat or a scarf on it.'

10 Lighting

At Teddington there are 9 lighting directors. Administratively they are part of the Engineering Department, but they work closely with the designers and are far more involved in the detailed preparations for a show than other personnel of engineering such as the camera section, and in some IT V companies they come under the same department as design, wardrobe and make-up. Because of the administrative arrangements at Thames it is very difficult for a producer to get a single lighting director assigned to a whole series. The producer may request this, but in practice will have to end up taking who is available. Thus on *Hazell* there were 4 lighting directors on 10 episodes recorded. This inevitably created some problems in achieving an overall consistency in the styles of lighting used.

Lighting in a television studio has to fulfil two functions. First, there has to be enough light for the cameras to record an image. Second, lighting is one of the most important means of creating a style or a mood. Achieving the first is not a problem, though one should remember that in general television requires more light than film, since its definition is poorer and people will not normally be watching in a darkened room. It is to the need to create the right aesthetic effect, in accordance with the interpretation of the script made by the producer, director and others, that the lighting director pays most attention.

When we talked to Bill Lee, who lit several episodes, he made the point that there were two aspects to this. One was that the set had to be lit for the mood of the scene; this involved not just getting the light 'realistic' in the sense of making it seem like day-time or night, and making the light appear to come from visible sources such as windows or lamps, but also of producing the right 'feel' for the scene — garish, cheerful, gloomy or whatever. The other important task was to get the actors' faces right. He himself was particularly interested in this side of it, and admitted that his views on portraiture might be somewhat traditional, in that he was a great believer in lighting women's faces 'beautifully'. Lighting, he claimed, could make far more difference to a woman's face on screen than make-up. The two extremes to avoid were

146

'steep light', which comes from above and throws harsh shadows, and frontal light, which removes them completely. Modelling of the facial contours, especially of the cheekbones, needs an angled light for the best effects. For men he likes to get a more rugged effect through the use of side lighting and a balance of hard and soft light. These comments should be seen in relation to the deliberate attempt on *Hazell* to use costumes and make-up, especially hair styles, in order to inject a certain amount of glamour (an old-fashioned term, perhaps, which does however suggest a certain continuity with the Hollywood lighting tradition).

Bill Lee contrasted the atmospheric use of lighting in *Hazell* with that on another Thames series he worked on, *London Belongs To Me*. In the latter the lighting directors had studied photographs of the 30s by Henri Cartier-Bresson and Bill Brandt, who had used high-speed Leicas for their work and shot with available source light, producing pictures with soft shadows. This the lighting directors had attempted to reproduce. With *Hazell* the lighting style was the reverse. A decision had been made to go for the clean-cut and polished style usually associated with Hollywood (though to be strictly accurate one would have to note that this is only one style of Hollywood lighting).

The normal sequence of events on *Hazell* was for the lighting director to get a script some 8 weeks before recording. There will then be meetings with the director and designer to discuss their requirements. He will also attend the technical meeting always held the day before rehearsals start. Bill Lee said that he then liked to go to a rehearsal 3 days before the production enters the studio, when 'blocking' (i.e., arranging the actors' moves) will be completed but while the director is still open to suggestions. After that he will plot all his lighting set ups on his floor plan, marking the angles which every single light will have in relation to the set, the performers and the cameras. Then at the lighting run, a couple of days before going into the studio, he will walk through every scene with the cast and the director to check his plans.

The last episode to be recorded, *Hazell And The Walking Blur*, was directed by Brian Farnham and lit by Ken Tester-Brown. As they walked round during the lighting run Brian pointed out that in an early scene he had deliberately placed Hazell against a window in a hotel room so that his face was partly in shadow. He therefore didn't want his face picked out with a key light. Brian was consciously going for subdued, even low-key, light in several scenes. Thus in another scene, set in a banqueting hall, he wanted a sort of subterranean effect. Brian

the 'dirty frosted-glass' look in the cabbies' shelter

the 'subterranean' look of the banqueting set

had previously visited such a place in the West End to shoot some still photographs which the episode required, and had noted the absence of windows and the rather gloomy lighting, and this was what he wanted to reproduce. In another scene, set in a taxi-drivers' shelter, he wanted to match some exteriors they had shot on film of such a shelter, and which they had done in the late afternoon. So the studio set had to be lit similarly and also had to catch the look of the place — what Brian called a 'dirty, frosted-glass look'. In another scene Hazell is with Minty in a police interview room. Brian wanted very low lighting, precisely directed to fall only on the actors' faces, so that if they moved back in their sets they would go into shadow — a deliberate attempt to recreate a Hollywood 40s style interrogation sequence. Brian, like some of the

picking out the actors' faces: Robert Mitchum in Out Of The Past *(RKO. 1947) and Roddy McMillan, Diana Rowan and Nicholas Ball in* The Walking Blur

other directors, felt that many lighting directors tended to use too much light, so he was giving very careful instructions about what he wanted.

The danger of course was that this 'moody' kind of lighting would be at variance with the sharp, clean look which had been decided on as the overall lighting style. Possibly in the end it was a bit, which only illustrates once again the difficulty of achieving consistency. The producer, who is the one person in a position to impose it, was not normally present at the lighting runs; by the time the cast were on the set and everyone could actually see what the lighting looked like there was very little time to make major changes.

On studio days the lighting director divides his time between the floor and the lighting control room adjacent to the gallery where the technical supervisor and vision mixer sit. In the lighting control room there is a range of monitors on which the lighting director can see what effect he's getting. The lights are all controlled from up there on an elaborate console. On this you can pre-set each lighting set up, with the correct lights switched on at the correct level of brightness. The console can 'remember' up to 99 different set ups, and for each shot the operator will punch up the relevant button, the lights having previously been moved into position by the electricians. (They are worked by electric motors which power them along a grid system in the studio roof.) The lighting director then needs only to make fine adjustments, which he does by going down onto the studio floor and with a long pole moving the metal flaps ('flags') around each light to alter slightly the direction or intensity. We wondered why he didn't simply sit upstairs and relay instructions to someone on the floor, but Ken Tester-Brown said the kind of adjustments he needed to do were so fine that it was hard to explain over the inter-com and it was easier to pop down and do it himself.

One of the most difficult aspects of lighting on a show like *Hazell* is the problem of balancing up the studio lighting with that on the film inserts. On filming there is a separate lighting cameraman, who in all likelihood will never meet the lighting director. This lack of liaison means that the lighting cameraman on the film sequences will probably go for a fairly bland look rather than anything very strongly stylised, for fear that he should produce something totally out of keeping with what will happen in the studio. The situation would be different if the location scenes were done with an Outside Broadcast (OB) Unit, using video cameras, since then the lighting director of the studio scenes would be in charge. But such units weren't used on *Hazell*, partly because of the supposed advantages of film over tape, already discussed, and partly because O B units involve a lot of setting up and are too bulky for convenient shooting in locations such as Soho. And as yet there are very few hand-held video cameras in professional use in this country.

To us as outsiders it seems strange that, given the immense amount of trouble taken to ensure a unified style both across episodes and within them, the system of working dictates that so many people should be involved in lighting one series. But a combination of company agreements with the unions (themselves to some extent perhaps the legacy of days when film and video were more separate than they are now) and administrative arrangements make it harder to achieve a consistent style in lighting than perhaps in any other area. In the end June Roberts seemed quite pleased with the degree of consistency she had managed to achieve. But there's a certain irony in the fact that she described the look they were going for as 'moody', which doesn't sound quite the same as Bill Lee's ideas on a 'clean-cut and polished' style. Viewers can judge for themselves which description comes closest; our suspicion is that some episodes are nearer to one and some to the other.

11 In the Studio

This chapter outlines the work of those people whose role is performed either largely or completely during actual production in the studio.

Technical supervisor

Del Randall was a technical supervisor on some episodes of *Hazell* but was also Thames studio supervisor for the whole series.

DR: 'I've got two roles with this series: I'm technical supervisor and studio supervisor. The studio supervisor is what some people call the super-tech. There are 2 technical supervisors who are also studio supervisors at Teddington and 6 other technical supervisors. As a studio supervisor I am given a series and I have to be the liaison man for June to contact regarding all the technical and operation aspects of the whole series. A technical supervisor does a similar job on a one-off episode. Sometimes I'm wearing both hats, I'm working on an episode and also involved in the whole series, but basically we're there to advise when necessary on technical and operational aspects of the programme'.

So when the producer wishes to know something about cameras or whatever, the first person she will go to is the technical supervisor, not to the relevant department. This doesn't mean that the super-tech is completely conversant with all the different areas of work because each is highly specialised but they do have a pretty good idea of the problems that each area does come up against. And if they themselves require any detailed information they know who to go to.

Del Randall: 'That happens before we get into the studio. In the studio we're in the control room and we are there as the reference point and liaison point for production and all the technical areas, the VTR and tele-cine as well as the technical people on the floor. As technical supervisors we normally get involved at the production planning meeting . . . We are in fact in charge, or responsible for the crew, and when it gets into the studio we are the senior man there as far as the operational and technical aspect of the show goes. Thus we sit in the main control room on studio days.'

We asked Del why it was he was the studio supervisor for the whole series — a job which is largely administrative and doesn't involve being in the studio at all — but technical supervisor for only some of the episodes:

DR: 'Because one has other productions to do as well, and as there are only 2 of us in the more senior position of studio supervisors, and all our time is taken up on the larger series — smaller programmes tend to run themselves a little easier from this point of view — the other guys wouldn't get any of the good work at all, would they? I mean I could quite easily arrange it so that I did work on each one but it's hardly fair to the other guys to be doing *Magpie* each day of the week whilst we're doing drama and the big light entertainment shows.'

We asked him when he first heard of *Hazell*.

DR: 'One would have heard of it through the advanced schedules. We hear of it as a name — a working title — and then you do a bit of follow up work and find out who's producing. Then you contact them and try and work out what, for example, the weight of the series is going to be. *Hazell* — Drama, that's all the advanced schedules said. It's up to us then to try and find out from the producer what the scripts are, what the weight is regarding sets — are they likely to be very heavy sets that need a lot of dressing; are they going to need heavy technical equipment, e.g., the mole crane (the big heavy crane used for cameras] — so that we get some idea of the crewing requirements.'

Thus in fact the technical supervisor needs to contact not only the producer but also the designers. Again, as so many other people had said, Del really appreciated what is plainly unusual in the setting up of most television series — the initial discussion where June brought together all the different departments to discuss matters of common interest. Del said that he gleaned lots of information from that meeting so that by the time the series came on to the studio floor he knew that it was going to be a relatively lightweight show. We asked him what made the sets 'heavy'?

DR: 'Two or three storeys, large staircases, large ornate settings that need a hell of a lot of dressing, all contribute to make sets heavy. Also big stuff that you are going to need big camera mountings on. The only one in *Hazell* is the staircase coming down out of the offices, but that sort of thing can go on a lot more if it's a big drama, the *Romance* series that we did for instance — they were very large composite sets and you were required to have fork lift trucks in to get the cameras up.'

More significantly, especially in the case of this series and its original conception, Del is concerned with any unusual technical requests. Questions concerning the weight and size of sets will be raised but they will be fairly easily coped with and anyhow what is possible is finally determined by the size of the studio that has been scheduled for the different episodes of the series. Of particular interest in the case of *Hazell* was the question of the visual style.

DR: 'So the little technical aspect that cropped up in that meeting was the use of colour filters — we discussed it at some length there and then we had an experimental session. Now if one just lets the designers go ahead without the technical men there they tend to go over the top to a degree that we end up with pictures of poor technical quality — I mean that might be right for what they want but technically be unacceptable. One has to keep up certain standards — the IBA require picture quality standards and if you drop below them then Thames is answerable to the IBA and it can get a bit nasty. And so I was putting forward views at that meeting — in fact quite strongly to one of the designers at one stage because he was saying, oh why can't we have dark sets and so on. The answer is because it never looks right at home and I had to explain to him why. Otherwise they would have gone ahead with sets of completely the wrong colour, because it is in their heads, in their minds. They thought it would look OK but once it becomes an electronic signal it goes bad and looks wrong.'

We asked Del if, after these experiments, the programme then proceeded quite normally technically:

DR: 'Pretty straight really. I mean they decided at that stage to go for certain colour wallpapers and certain sorts of paint and woodwork which would give them that effect. Of course on top of that each lighting director comes in for each episode with a slightly different idea, so again one has problems — this is where there's no technical continuity where I think there should be, in fact. This is a problem that I find and it's very difficult to know how to deal with it because each lighting director comes in with his own idea of lighting a particular set. One even gets it in *Rainbow,* of all things. Each lighting director comes in to light this tiny little kid's presentation set (it's a thing for toddlers) and they all light it in different ways. What I would like to see, and doesn't happen and we don't seem to be able to follow it through in this direction, is that for instance in Hazell's office there's a stock lighting set up for every episode.'

So the two studio supervisors at Thames are responsible for the total production output of Teddington. They would tend to keep their eye on all aspects of the production side of a programme (rather than the engineering side which they wouldn't necessarily know everything about) including such things as the building of the sets. If any problems should crop up then essentially he considers himself to be an ombudsman or a troubleshooter. All the technical supervisors at Teddington came up from the operational side of television, having been cameramen, boom operators, vision controllers, etc.

When in the studio the technical supervisor will sit in the production control room along with the director, P A, vision mixer, producer and designer. If there are any technical problems he will handle them. When a recording tape is running out he will contact the V T R operator and ensure that a new one will be lined up while the director is rehearsing a scene in the studio so as not to waste valuable time. If the director wishes anything technical to be changed or wants to see some film or hear a 'voice over', that will be arranged through the technical supervisor. The technical supervisor will also arrange tea breaks and any technical work that needs to take place in them.

DR: 'There's all these little things to joggle and juggle around with, things that we try and keep away from the directors so that these silly little problems don't detract from the director, whose first concern is obviously the show.'

The technical supervisor will rarely go onto the studio floor himself. If there are any problems then the floor managers will usually deal with it in the first instance. But if there is any trouble then the technical supervisor may have to go down and call a meeting of the people involved. Additionally if there is a safety hazard he will have to investigate that. He will walk around the technical areas such as the V T R room, the vision control room or the sound control room, but more for personal contact than to deal with problems. They can just as easily be handled usually over the intercom. Once the show gets going they are very much tied to the director, however:

DR: ' . . . especially on a series like this where you have freelance directors coming in just to do one show and going out again. I mean most of them on *Hazell* have worked here before, but we also go and make ourselves known, to make them feel at home and explain the sort of facilities we've got here, because in each studio the facilities vary slightly and the mode of working is different depending on the studios.'

The job is clearly not an easy one to describe because it mainly involves the organisation and smooth running of the technical side of the whole operation without being directly responsible for any one aspect of how the programme will look.

DR: 'If the director wants to go over time he has to ask me, I have to go and ask the crews if they will. I've got total responsibility for agreeing to overtime, etc., in the studio, and as to how the studio schedule is used. It's the sort of job, particularly when the show gets as far as the studio, and subject to nothing going wrong, which is purely liaison. If you're working with a bunch of professionals around you then I suppose you're in control of everything. If you have professionals around you your job's easy. It's when things go wrong that the buck stops with you.'

Floor manager

The Floor Manager's job is to be the director's right hand man, rather like the first assistant director on a film crew and to be the organiser on the studio floor on behalf of the director when s/he is upstairs in the control room. He wears a pair of radio headphones (as opposed to the line headphones that camera and boom operators will wear) and carries a walkie-talkie. This gives him mobility on the studio floor, which is necessary if he is to represent the director to all the different people working there. Whilst the director is in the control room (the 'gallery') co-ordinating lighting, sound and cameras through the microphone system there has to be someone down on the studio floor who knows the show, who knows the artists personally and who will ensure that the production runs smoothly. The floor manager then is the physical embodiment of the disembodied voice of the director.

Basically floor managers come from two backgrounds: either they have worked in the theatre (as a stage manager possibly) or they start as floor assistants and then work their way up. At the BBC floor managers come from either source and the corporation has a training scheme for the job. We don't know about other companies but Thames doesn't have such a scheme and the company therefore requires a person to start as a floor assistant and to be assigned to a floor manager for quite a long period of time, learning what the job involves.

The hierarchy of the job is constructed on the basis of 3 posts — floor assistant, assistant floor manager and floor manager. The original job title of floor assistants, call-boys, reflected the fact that it was then an all male job. When a girl was appointed at the beginning of 1977 the title was no longer appropriate. (Incidentally all floor managers at Thames are male but John Lopes, the floor manager we interviewed, thought that 50% of the BBC's floor managers were female). Floor assistants are not allowed to wear headphones because they are members of NATTKE and only ACTT members are allowed to wear them (which is, therefore, the union that the floor managers belong to). The only exception to this is when the scene crew are operating roller captions for the end credits. The floor assistant will operate as a caption puller and will then wear headphones. Basically a floor assistant will only be required on a very heavy show and will do all the running around jobs in support of the assistant floor manager. Such assistance will include things like doing a relay cue.

John Lopes: 'For instance, if you can imagine a three walled set with a door in the wall further from you, you simply haven't the time to go round the back of the set to cue another artist especially if it is a simultaneous cue. Your assistant will ensure that he stands in a position where he can see the artist at the back of the set whilst staying in your eyeline and will thereby relay the cue I will receive from the director.'

The floor assistant will check that the artists have arrived on time, check that they've gone to make-up and costumes, call them on to the set a few minutes before they're needed. He will also collect slides and captions from graphics, take the slides over to tele-cine (see p 213 below) and will bring the captions on to the floor.

John Lopes, as the first floor manager to work on *Hazell*, was informed by his head of department that he would be working on it approximately 3 weeks before the first read through. His first job is to get hold of a reading copy of the script and his first contact with the show is the read-through. If possible he should attend the technical meeting the day before the first read-through but that is often difficult and he will ask somebody to attend for him if he can't make it. The reason that it is often not possible for him to attend is that a floor

157

manager works on an episode for exactly the 2 weeks it is in rehearsal and in the studio. The second day of the studio session marks the last day of his involvement with that episode. However that is the day the technical meeting for the next episode takes place. John Lopes describes what he does on the first day of rehearsals:

JL: 'During the read-through I memorise artists' names, especially their first names. So by the end of the read-through I know their names and I go up to them and introduce myself and make sure that if there's any little problem which no-one else can help them with they should come to me and I try to smooth the path for the director as much as possible. The rest of the rehearsal period I spend anticipating studio problems; I watch where the director stands during rehearsals because that's a good indicator of where he's going to put a camera sooner or later. It's suprising how much one can observe by just sitting and watching the director and the artists moving about. It means you must have a plan with you and keep relating what they are doing to the planned positions in the studio — you've got to imagine the walls there, imagine the lights, imagine the boom and that's the only way that you can anticipate problems.'

So, over the 2 weeks of the rehearsals the floor manager is there every day with the exception of the 3 filming days. This is because there is a union demarcation line over this matter and the location manager rather than the floor manager operates as the first assistant director on a film location. If a location is covered by an electronic camera, however, when an outside broadcast unit is used rather than film, then the floor manager is there. Thus the floor manager is like a lighting director in this respect — both of them will only go on location if an O B unit is used. This splitting of jobs can create problems over continuity, as Peter Piddick, another floor manager, pointed out, but the 3 free days can be used by the floor managers to do jobs such as going to see the designers to ensure that he has received and understood any set modifications that the director may have made. In rehearsals he is watching everything, memorising moves and marking his plan. Apparently most directors leave the planning of the sound booms and where they should be placed to the floor manager. Interestingly this detail (and it's an important one) is not dealt with by the sound people because that would be to leave the decisions until too late. Thus a floor manager will find himself noting whether the director places characters further than 10 feet away from each other because if he does then the floor manager will have to mark up a second boom and operator in order to cover the dialogue.

John Lopes: 'It's too late on the studio day for the sound supervisor and his crew to decide how sound is going to be covered; it's very much like the camera — it's too late on the day for the senior cameraman and the director to decide where all the cameras should go. If we did things that way, which is really a film technique, we simply wouldn't be able to cope with the tight studio schedule.'

A couple of days prior to the technical run the floor manager copies the director's camera plan and has enough copies printed so that when the camera and sound technicians come they each have a copy of the ground plan. (The lighting director will have made his own plan for use by his section.) Thus he will do the final camera plan and will also put down the furniture and the boom positions.

The work that the floor manager has to do on the first studio day will depend on the director's method of working. With one exception, the directors on *Hazell* worked on the principle of 'rehearse the first day and record the second', and we describe below what the floor manager will be doing under that system. Most importantly he will be attempting to work ahead of the director rather than simply following him as he will have been doing in rehearsals.

John Lopes: 'I'm making sure that the next set that he's coming to is ready from a scene point of view. I've made sure that the scene boys have got the doors and the walls in the correct position. I have to do this because these days we build and strike sets quite a lot in the process of making the programme and also because directors tend to shoot in a 360 degree fashion, which is a more film-like technique. In addition to making quite sure that the next set is ready I'm making notes about cues and I'm watching again for any slight change from what we did in rehearsal, so that when the director goes upstairs I'm confident, I'm competent and I'm with the latest change. Otherwise, it's very embarassing for him to have to repeat to me what we changed on the floor.'

As far as the boom operators are concerned John has given them a camera plan with the operators' positions marked on it and will also have marked them in a different coloured crayon for each operator. This way their positions are colour-coded and they don't have to search for their next position. The floor manager will have had to check not only camera positions and any movement in them but also set design and whether there were to be any ceilings or other potential impediments for the boom. One thing he cannot be prepared for, of course, is the creation of shadows by the boom. However, nobody can be sure of this in advance and it is in fact one of the main things that people seem to be looking for when in the studio. The slightest hint of boom shadow during the recording of a scene will require that the whole thing is done again.

JL: 'No, I can't anticipate shadows, I've no idea where the lighting director is going to place his lamps. But I can anticipate the problems, and so will the director. The director, better than I, will anticipate all the problems of lighting someone, say, in the corner of a room. With my experience of being a boom operator what I can do to help is to remind the director that it might be difficult for sound to get at the artist in a particular place.'

John Lopes is an unusual floor manager at Thames in that before he became one he had been an assistant cameraman, a camerman, a boom operator and a vision mixer, which meant that he had a good knowledge and personal experience both of technical problems on the floor for the operators and also of what conditions can be like in the control room. The floor manager keeps in close contact with the director in the control room but doesn't bother him/her with trivial problems:

JL: ' . . . because the director is under a terrible amount of pressure in the gallery and if the director does begin to unreasonably scream and shout it doesn't upset me because I expect him to behave abnormally in the gallery. He's under an enormous amount of pressure.'

It is clear when observing a studio in action that a floor manager's job can be very tricky. A whole range of demands and requests are being made upon him often simultaneously and he has to respond to all of them. It is not unusual to have a director speaking to him over his headphones whilst he is talking to somebody else and attempting to organise the set so that a recording can begin. Nor is it unusual for a director, exasperated by somebody's slowness or interference, to hurl something abusive over the intercom and for the floor manager to translate it into a very calm and polite request. John Lopes' experience of the gallery plus his professional pride would never allow him to shout back at the director.

Not only the director but also lighting and sound can speak to the floor manager. The headphone contact system in the studio works as follows. The sound control room is in direct contact with the boom operator(s) and the director/PA with the cameramen and floor manager — these are two mutually exclusive lines. However both control rooms can speak to anybody on the floor with headphones on merely by flicking a switch. Similarly the lighting control room can speak to anybody on the floor but primarily they are speaking to boom operators and to the make-up artists in the cubicles. The lighting charge hand, however, who is their main person on the floor (when the lighting director is in the control room) does not wear headphones and he has to communicate with the lighting director either through a telephone that is on the wall or by asking the floor manager to relay a message to the lighting control room through the technical supervisor in the main control room. Messages from the floor can only go to the relevant control room in the first instance — if a boom operator wished to speak to the director, for example, that has to be relayed through sound control. This description makes the situation appear more complicated than it is, but we mention these details because efficient communication between the 80-odd people working in the very large space which is a TV studio is very complex, and if anybody can be said to be the non-controlling pivot to the process it is the floor manager. All the different control rooms can speak to him and he will be required to channel a good deal of information through to non-headphone wearers on the floor. Similarly if they wish to speak to someone in a control room they are likely to go through him and he through the technical supervisor.

Directors vary in their methods of working. On recording days some will be rushing down from the gallery to the floor every few minutes, while others will largely stay in the gallery, thus leaving the floor manager to generally run things down below. In this case the floor manager will ask everybody to be quiet for the recording, cue the performers and generally ensure that everything runs smoothly. We noted one day that an actor was late (on the first of the 2 days) and Peter Piddick, floor manager for that episode, had to stand in and read his lines. We asked if that was a normal sort of request to make of a floor manager.

John Lopes: 'It's quite normal for a floor manager to be expected to stand in and read-in if necessary — the mistake can be made by the

floor manager who gives the calls for the artists for the next day. I've
made this mistake before now — I've anticipated a director to work at
say a rate of 9 pages an hour and he's beaten me to it for some reason.
It's embarrasing and I stand in but fortunately it's only for a few
minutes. So now I err in the other direction — I over-anticipate.'

On that particular occasion the artist was simply late but it is the floor
manager's responsibility to call the artists for a particular time and also
to ask the director on their behalf if they can go when they have finished
their sections. Thus he is very much responsible for the movement of
the actors and actresses:

JL: ' . . . it is most important that I liaise with the director. Even though
an artist may appear to have been finished with, on paper, the director
may need him for some extra sound recording or shot which he may
have in mind and which he may not have put down on the script. It
always makes sense to check with the director that someone is
completely finished with, not only from the point of view of good
manners but also the director may want to say a personal goodbye to
that actor.'

At the end of the second day the floor manager's work on a show will
end. This means that theoretically it is possible for a floor manager to
be assigned to every episode of a series. Although it is the policy of the
head of the department to do this, in the case of *Hazell* that wasn't
possible and therefore several people worked on it. This could have
been due to holiday schedules, the limited number of senior floor
managers available or a personality clash.

How much does the job vary on other kinds of programmes?

JL: 'I think, and I am sure that my colleagues would agree, that the
approach for a light entertainment show, certainly from a floor
manager's point of view, is very different — it's a very relaxed informal
atmosphere. The whole nature of light entertainment is different. I
think it requires a different sort of personality if it is to be handled
really well. Of course any of the experienced floor managers can cope
with any sort of show, but we're now talking about the very best. And I
think that if you're going to get the very best then you need an extrovert
with a great personality and a good wit. He is going to do the greatest
justice to a light entertainment show. It's a vastly different proposition
working with light entertainment as opposed to drama. I prefer drama
— practically all my experience has been in drama and I feel at home
with it. The techniques are different; in light entertainment you're

handling the singers, dancers, musicians, comedians. Situation comedy is the closest you come to drama and even then, in situation comedy you only have a small number of sets — you don't have to rehearse quite as long as you do on drama. There is also the question of warming up (i.e., putting the studio audience in the mood). We had a very exceptional floor manager, who is actually now a producer, who did his own warm-ups — he was great, he was sensational, he could have had a one-man show quite happily. He was great on the ad-lib, but he's very much an exception in every sense of the word. Having an audience really makes it so different and if you can keep your audience happy, smiling, relaxed, laughing with the occasional witticism then you're really contributing to the well-being of the show.'

Stage manager

Like the floor manager the stage manager is engaged by the head of the floor managers' section. Generally speaking they are likely to be women (all of them are at Thames), which possibly reflects the fact that most come from the theatre where this is also true. The head of floor managers will issue a contract to a stage manager approximately one week before the first read through and then she will go and make herself known to the director and the designer and discuss the episode with them in terms of the props to be used. She will take away a reading copy of the script from the director, and a set of plans of the studio floor and a set of elevations of the sets, from the designer. From the former she will draw up a list of action props and order them to be bought if they are not stock props. Action props consist of small objects used by the actors such as a packet of cigarettes, a lighter, a bag of chips, a gun, etc. If Hazell, for example, regularly used a particular cigarette lighter then that would be a stock prop which would be stored. This list will be discussed with the director and designer and then the stage manager will requisition them because the actual ordering and buying is done by the prop-buyer.

From the plans and elevations she will know what the precise layout of the studio is going to be and it will be her responsibility to mark up the floor of the rehearsal room accordingly. Each set will be marked on the floor with coloured tape — a different colour for each set. The extremeties of the set, the walls, will be laid out in relation to each other just as they will be laid out in the studio (sometimes of course sets will have to overlap if the rehearsal room floor isn't as big as the studio floor). On the day of the first read-through the designer will check over the markings to ensure that they are accurate and that there haven't been any mistakes or misreadings of the plan.

For the rehearsals the stage manager will have to order a set of rehearsal props — only the most essential props will be used, e.g., a settee, a set of chairs, a bed and a number of upright wooden poles on bases with hinged wooden flags on them. These will be used to represent the doors. On the first day of rehearsals on Don Leaver's episode (the first to be recorded) he was upset because Thames had not been able to get a full set of rehearsal props for him and he found it very difficult to begin rehearsing.

The stage manager will also be responsible for obtaining anything such as a tape recorder if it is required; on *Hazell* one was needed to play back the 'voice-overs', so that the performers could judge how long they had to engage in stage business while it was playing.

Once rehearsals have started the stage manager will follow each scene very carefully (like the floor manager) making notes on the director's plan of the artists' movements and the precise placing of all the props. Additionally, when the artists have finally put the script down then she will act as prompter and will stand in for them if they are missing for any reason. She will co-ordinate all the props and necessary equipment for the rehearsals and she will liaise between the director and the designer. Because the designers will be busy buying props and checking the scenery they will spend very little time at rehearsals. Therefore if there are any problems such as the director deciding that he would prefer a different size sideboard or whatever then the stage manager will let the designer know.

Meanwhile the stage manager will type out a comprehensive list of all the props to be used in each scene together with the setting for each prop which, once it is approved by the designer, she will be give to the prop which, once it is approved by the designer, she will give to the crew will consist of three or four prop men each of whom will be assigned the responsibility of dressing one or two sets. The props are stored in a lockable wire cage and each set will be dressed at the commencement of the studio rehearsal according to the designers' specifications. The dressing of the action props will be done by the crew during the show; this is especially necessary when the action prop is a consumable

The most difficult props of all are the live ones. In the first episode, *Hazell And The Weekend Man*, the designers had the bright idea of making Hazell's office seem even more real by hiring a flock of pigeons and setting them free outside his window. They were sedated so that they wouldn't just fly away; as a result they wouldn't fly at all. They simply walked around and most of the time can be seen on the screen doing this despite the efforts of their trainer to coax them into flight. Needless to say they were not re-engaged for other episodes!

Before the artists and crew move on to the next set the stage manager will check that the set is fully dressed and everything is in the correct position. And then she will ensure that the action props are at hand and ready for use. In order to ensure continuity of dressing in the stock sets (such as Hazell's and Dot's offices,) the designers arranged for colour photographs to be taken of each set and if necessary, from a number of angles. These are continuity photos and the stage manager will refer to them to ensure that they are copied exactly. Thus there should be no continuity problem. John Lopes mentioned that to his surprise a continuity detail was missed on an episode of *London Belongs To Me*. One of the principals apparently pointed out that a coat hook which was clearly visible on the back of a door in episode 1 was missing on episode 3. The photograph was checked and it was pointed out to the designer who was as astonished as everybody else.

Unlike the floor manager the stage manager also goes out on location for the filming sessions where she will be mainly concerned with action props: for example, in *Hazell And The Walking Blur* Hazell eats a bag of chips in the Stag. The presence of the stage manager on location makes the continuity of props between filming and studio work much easier to handle.

Vision mixer

The vision mixer sits in the main control room between the technical supervisor and the director and punches up each shot as required by him/her. In front of him is a console with a set of switches that allows him to cut between any of the 4 cameras and other facilities such as captions, tele-cine and tele-slide machines. The console also controls the special effects generator and permits the mixer to fade, mix and wipe shots vertically and horizontally (as opposed to simply cutting between them) and also to key in and reverse negatives and positives, etc. As explained below(p226)because of time-code editing it is now possible to do these things at the editing stage, but that is a very recent development.

Because the vision mixer is in the same room he can hear the P A calling the shots to the camera and sound crews, but he will not be listening to her because if he was taking notice of her instructions he would be too late in his cutting. The vision mixer has the script in front of him with all the shots listed but he will be looking more intently at the monitors and anticipating the next shot. The vision mixer will also be watching for details such as the possibility of an artist rising in a scene slightly earlier or later than they did in rehearsal (and actors may play a scene slightly differently each time) because then the vision mixer has to anticipate in order to cut at the new point. Thus the vision mixer has to watch both the script and the monitors and he has to be well ahead of what the artists are saying. Due to historical accident, all the vision mixers at Thames are male whilst in other IT V companies they are always women.

On a series such as *Hazell,* the main intention is to try and make the cut as unobtrusive as possible, and to that end the vision mixer will try and disguise the cut to make the programme flow. The intent is that the audience is too involved in the action to notice how the shots are put together. Good technique is invisible.

In the past, people became vision mixers by coming from floor crews. In fact, originally vision mixers were attached to a crew even though they worked in the control room. But that is no longer the case and it is quite possible nowadays for vision mixers not to have been tech-ops. Why this should have happened is not exactly clear but undoubtedly the nature of this particular job has changed quite dramatically — as it will do again when time-code editing becomes the standard way of editing a programme. When shows were still going out live, as opposed to being recorded, a vision mixer's job was extremely demanding and exhausting. On a live show they cannot afford to allow their mind to wander for a second. On recorded shows their level of concentration has to be first class. But with stop-taking there are obviously rest periods. A large number of people in television actually bemoan the fact that the days of live television are virtually over (though there are still the sports programmes, news and election programmes) and say how much they preferred and were excited by the tensions involved in going live. Vision mixers are no exception to this but it was John Lopes who described the situation in a way that summed up what most people said:

JL: 'But television people must surely be competitive by nature; I mean we enjoy the dare, we're dream-makers — it's really a dream factory, a television studio, isn't it — and we enjoy the challenge and the team work involved in making a programme. Can you just imagine a team working flat out all day long for a live show, dress run after dress run and all pulling it together on the night? It's the same excitement that you must have in the theatre today when you perform live in front of an audience. If it's a tricky show with lots of tricky effects with people changing as quickly as possible and dashing into position, there's always that chance of a camera going down and having to quickly re-arrange your plans and switch to an alternative camera. There are few shows where one can do that now. There must be some people who prefer the present system but I would prefer to do a live drama because of the sheer excitement of it, the euphoria of going through something live. Of course you're terrified at the time, but what a high you reach.'

Vision mixers don't simply follow instructions; they may occasionally make suggestions to the director about cutting. But increasingly, because of the new editing technology, the director can afford to make the cutting loose, knowing that it will be possible to tighten things up at the editing stage. On the other hand, of course, since only what the vision mixer selects from the 4 shots available to him at any one time will actually be recorded, it is his finger on the button which ultimately decides what material the director will have to work with at the editing stage.

Camera operator

Camera operators normally begin as official technical operators, who operate technical equipment, either cameras or sound. Once somebody becomes an official technical operator, however, it doesn't necessarily mean that they immediately become a cameraman (as far as we know, at the moment Thames have no women camera operators) or a boom operator. They can be a trainee or assistant for a long time. In the case of the cameras this involves pulling the cables around for the cameraman when he's using the standard 'Vinten' dolly or tracking the 'Mole' crane or low-angle dolly when they are being used instead. This latter was using a number of episodes of *Hazell* and whenever you see an extreme low angled shot it will have been taken by using that particular dolly. Because the camerman has to sit on it it is the responsibility of his assistant to push him around.

Hazell used the 4 cameras that are standard in the Thames studios, and there is a strict hierarchy: i.e., there are first, second, third and fourth camera operators. If there are any particularly difficult shots to take which involve a complex movement of the camera and some fast reframing and focussing then the director will ensure that the PA who is allotting the shots will give those to the first cameraman. This is something that will be discussed at the technical run-through.

The cameras are fitted with standard zoom lenses which offer a large range of focal lengths (as opposed to the old camera which had 'turret' lenses — on the front of the camera there was a revolving turret which had 3 or 4 lenses with different focal lengths and if the cameraman wished to get a close-up he would rotate the turret and select a lens). There is, however, an extensive range of other lenses and filters in the studio if special effects are required. Although the cameras are for colour, the operators' viewfinder is in black and white as are most of the monitors on the studio floor (and the few colour ones are apparently not carefully lined up for colour).

Each camera operator has a set of cards (made out by the PA) which list and detail each one of their shots. These are attached to the cameras and they will work from these cards rather than from the script. They are in contact with the director and the PA through headsets. It tends to be a one-way channel of communication, with the PA calling out the shot numbers to each cameraman just in advance of a cut to his camera. But from time-to-time cameramen will make suggestions about shots to the director if they think some improvement can be made. The usual style of shooting in the studio, cutting between 3 or 4 cameras during a sequence, normally allows for any reframing that may be necessary to be accomplished in plenty of time during a cut-away to another camera. But in a complicated scene some quite rapid adjustments may be necessary and the very cramped space of most studio sets means that considerable experience is required to operate the bulky cameras.

Sound

In the studio during recording there will normally be 7 people working on the sound, 5 of these operating the sound booms on the floor and 2 in the sound control room, adjacent to the central control gallery. The boom operators have two main worries. One is that they have to get their booms in the right place for the kind of sound required. This will depend on what sort of shot is on-screen. Thus if a character is seen in close-up the sound must seem to be coming from a position close to the viewer. If it's a long shot the sound must seem to be coming from a distance. If there are 2 characters at a distance from each other (say, more than 10 feet), 2 booms with separate mikes will have to be used if the cameras are cutting between close-ups of them.

Because the cameras will almost always be shooting approximately at eye level (this being the 'natural' way of seeing people) the booms will usually be positioned above the actors' heads. The other thing the boom operator has to think about is keeping the boom not only out of the camera's line of vision but out of the way of throwing shadows from the lights (mostly positioned overhead) onto the set or, still worse, onto the actors' faces. This is quite tricky work because the boom operator can only tell *exactly* where his boom is when it or its shadow shows up on one of the monitors placed over the studio floor. The knack, it seems, is to watch during the rehearsal of a shot how each camera is framing the picture (by using the monitors) and then to find a spot on the wall of the set where the boom won't be in shot, and to place the boom in that spot next time. Unfortunately, a slight reframing by a cameraman can easily bring the boom back in shot. The fact that it's not actually all that unusual to see a boom creeping into shot when you're watching television is an indication (assuming all boom operators are equally skilled) of the difficulties of the job.

The boom operators have a direct link to the sound control room, from where the sound controller can issue instructions. Up there the sound is recorded both married to the picture on the videotape and on a separate track. This separation will allow the director at the editing stage to alter the relation of sound and picture if so desired. During *Hazell* a tape recorder was also needed to relay down to the studio floor Hazell's passages of voice-over during the scenes which contained them, so that the actors could time their actions to the voice. The voice-over and any other kind of sound which has to be played during recording is the responsibility of the gram operator. The other person upstairs, the sound controller, will be mainly concerned with getting the right quality of sound — correcting tone and balance. He will also check through the sound quality of the film inserts; thus on one sequence in *Hazell Plays Solomon* shot near a river, the sound of the water was found to be so loud as to almost drown out the actors' voices and this had to be corrected at the dubbing stage. At this stage too most of the effects (doors slamming, radios playing, etc.) and the music would be put on to the sound track. The voice-overs (recorded well before so that they would be available during rehearsals and on the studio floor) were sometimes dubbed on in the studio but were normally left till the final sound dub.

As we've seen, voice-overs were to be one of the distinctive features of *Hazell,* serving the purpose both of linking the show stylistically to Hollywood and Raymond Chandler and of placing the character of Hazell himself squarely at the centre of the action. It was therefore important to get them right, in terms of scripting and performance. So a lot of trouble was taken over recording them in the studio and sometimes, though Nick had already done them, they were re-done while the show was being taped. One worry was that they might have the effect of stopping the action and since pace was a prime concern this couldn't be allowed to occur. The director had to make sure that plenty was happening on the screen and that the action didn't just freeze while Nick spoke his lines. Apart from this, as far as we could tell, sound recording posed no unusual problems.

12 Production Assistants and Directors

The production assistant

The duties of a production assistant (PA) are multifarious. As Liz Cadley, who worked on several episodes of *Hazell*, said, basically their role and function is that of a liaison officer. (Interestingly technical supervisors and floor managers similarly described their jobs.) The PA operates as the middle person between director and people in other departments, thereby relieving him or her of almost all administrative duties. Although the director will meet regularly with the producer, script editor and designers, with whom s/he will have to discuss very detailed matters, the PA will both answer all the questions that different departments will raise (if she can) and will also organise a whole range of aspects of the production for the director. So, in fact, what she does is free the director from having to worry about all the minor details of the production; she thus operates very much as a first assistant. Anyone from another department in Thames who wishes to contact a director will speak to the PA working with that director first.

LC: 'If you feel there has to be an answer from the director then of course you get them to meet, or if you find out the answer from the director you let them know. It's a difficult liaison job keeping many people happy and keeping to a very strict schedule all the way through. And getting answers out of directors who don't want to give answers at the time because they'd rather give you all the answers the day before they do it, you know — when you have to know 2 weeks before, and all that kind of thing — you really have to pressure a lot in the nicest possible way'.

Before detailing the different aspects of the PA's job it is worth noting that it is a job always done by women, and the most usual way of becoming one is to start as a secretary for a television company. Once a secretary applies for such a job (as Liz Cadley did) and is accepted, she will be trained for approximately 9 months by the company. She will work with a principal production assistant for that period learning all the different aspects of the job and then will be assigned to a small production (like a children's programme). After that PAs will probably gain experience on a whole range of programmes until they reach Liz Cadley's position, which is a principal production assistant. As a PPA she had chosen what area of television she most wanted to work in, drama, but if necessary could, because of her experience, be called in at short notice to work on any type of programme.

In common with many television workers Liz Cadley commented on how work in television had changed since the days when programmes used to be transmitted live:

LC: 'I went to ATV and worked on all the very large dramas which went out live. The 90-minute dramas were terrifying things and we'd all come out either dying the death because it didn't really work as it should have done or tremendously elated because everything had worked and we were so pleased with outselves. A totally different atmosphere exists now that we record it all — a sense of excitement, achievement, urgency and all of the bite has gone, to a large degree, from the control room. I find now that my control room days are my most relaxed days; it's very odd really when it used to be the most tense moment that you could ever go through.'

Liz Cadley was a PA on 3 episodes of *Hazell* and worked on the first recording, *Hazell And The Weekend Man*. Thus Liz first heard that she was working on *Hazell* the November prior to January 1977, when she was working with Don Leaver on another programme. Brian Walcroft is responsible for assigning PAs to the different programmes that are scheduled — something which he does 3 months in advance although they will not be informed until 6 weeks later unless they are particularly interested to find out. A PA will be assigned to a particular programme or episode and she will work closely with the director. Thus a PA will work on a programme like *Hazell* for approximately 7 weeks — 3 weeks before first rehearsals, the 2 weeks of rehearsals, filming and recording, and the 2 weeks following when editing is done. The schedule may be tighter than that if the PA is having to finish some late editing on the previous programme (not uncommon given the busy commitments of most directors) and might have to begin work on the next before the present one is fully finished. Given the recording schedule of *Hazell* (2 weeks per episode) there is no way in which one PA could have been assigned to the entire series. Add to the scheduling problems their holidays etc., and it becomes clear that it is very difficult even to achieve a situation where, for consistency and continuity, only a few PAs are assigned to a series.

One of the first tasks that a PA has to carry out is to read the rough rehearsal script through with the director in order to time it. The script editor will already have done this but the PA will do it as well to check if it is likely to be over or under. This question of 'timing' is one of the PAs main concerns at all stages of the production right through to final editing. She will be constantly timing everything and will be frequently asked for timings, so she must have a constant and up-to-date knowledge of how long the show runs. As a result of reading the script the director might go back to the script editor and ask for something to be cut or added (although the latter is unlikely) and after that the script will go to rehearsal script stage. In the meantime the PA will be involved to some extent in casting, which can take up to 10 days, and she will also be present at some of the meetings that the director will have with the designers and wardrobe, make-up and lighting director. Liz Cadley mentioned one interesting problem that they had in maintaining continuity of make-up between film and studio recording:

LC: ' . . . we had the vicious fight scene in *Hazell Settles The Accounts*, his right eye slit and his nose bashed in; you have to find ways in which to ensure that continuity is absolutely perfect when somebody comes into the studio like that. So you go into quite a lengthy discussion with the make-up artist — in our case she was going to use blood that is synthetic and it wouldn't wash off easily. When we went into the studio he had to wash this off in front of the camera and he was going to be left with a big red face. So in the end we had to use the real thing, I don't know how they found it, but eventually that was the only way they could do it.'

It seemed a strange problem given that Thames must have been faking blood for years.

LC: ' . . . the reason was because we were going to make it a continuous scene. June didn't want to stop the take especially for that to be cleaned off, she wanted it to be continuous. Normally you could say, well he comes in like that, he's got to wash it off, we'll stop shooting when his head is down in the bowl, and then you could carry on.'

So in this period the PA will be organising meetings, ordering special pieces of equipment like hand-held cameras and answering people's queries so that the director need not be bothered with them.

Once the first read through has taken place she will spend approximately half her time with the director at rehearsals and the other half at her office dealing with correspondence and general organisation. At rehearsals she is responsible to the director and will again be timing each scene very carefully. Also the PA will deal with any problems the artists have about their money, travelling arrangements, etc.

This pattern of working is maintained until 2 days before the production enters the studio at which point the camera script has to be drawn up. Before this however the PA is involved in the 3 filming days.

The PA and filming

Originally PA's used to function as location managers — finding the locations, clearing them with the police, organising the facilities; but since those times, schedules have got tighter and tighter, resulting in the creation of more and more specialist jobs. Now, PAs liaise with the location manager over the film script, which it is their responsibility to copy and distribute. The film script contains only the location scenes, extracted from the original main script, and organised into 3 sections which correspond to the 3 days of shooting. Each day is duplicated on different coloured paper to avoid confusion and is organised according to the filming sequence, not to the narrative sequence. This will have already been decided between the director and the location manager and the order of shooting will be determined by the proximity of the different locations.

On the actual filming days the PAs change their roles slightly — they function as traditional film continuity girls. According to Liz Cadley this a bone of contention amongst PAs, who don't want to do the job because they haven't been trained for it. She pointed out that continuity is a very skilled job, particularly as scenes aren't filmed in sequence either on location or in the studio. This lack of a single person to watch continuity in television is one of the most striking differences between film and television and also one of the most surprising facts given the enormous problems of maintaining continuity. In fact, a number of people are all watching for different aspects: designers will watch for continuity of sets and locations; make-up will watch for continuity of hairstyles, etc; stage managers will watch for continuity of sets (and locations) and costume designers will watch for continuity of clothes; and the PAs will watch for continuity of dress and gesture on filming.

In the studio everybody will be watching for continuity in their own specialised area: e.g., lighting, sound levels, colour matching etc.

So on filming days the PAs write down everything which they think might be important for continuity while timing, taking down the film footage shot and logging which take is going to be processed (because takes which are obviously going to be poor are not printed up) and thus which sections of the sound tape are going to be used. The director will give this information to the PA who will record it, and inform the assistant cameraman and the sound team.

The camera script

The director writes the camera script which the PA will have typed up and duplicated. This is a version of the original script which contains only the sequences to be done in the studio and has every shot listed by number. It too is organised according to recording sequence not narrative sequence. This will be written two or three days before entering the studio, after a rehearsal session, and will be sent to all the technical staff but, interestingly, not to the actors. They can see it if they wish but Liz Cadley said that it might affect their performance to know whether or not the cameras were on them.

From the camera script the PA will also write out all the camera operators' cards. These are 4 individual sets of cards (if there are 4 cameras) which separately provide a complete list of what each camera will do. For camera 2 the card will list every shot that it will be taking, together with a description of the shot (whether it's a 2-shot, a close-up or a mid-shot). This will be attached to the camera for the operator to follow.

When production actually goes into the studio the PA remains for the whole 2 days in the control room. It is her responsibility to call out information to the relevant sections e.g., shot numbers. Whilst the director is on the floor on the first day his or her contact with the control room is directed via the PA and vice-versa. She will be previewing shots about to come up on the monitors, which the director can't do of course when on the floor.

Liz Cadley: ' . . . you're previewing each shot each time, so that they know what they're coming to; you tell them when a tape-stop is about to happen; you also pick up shots as you're previewing. You're calling out the shots that are going to happen and you might see that the cameraman has looked at his card incorrectly and there might be a single shot of somebody and you know that it should be a 2-shot. You would then say to the cameraman — I think this is a 2-shot here — very discreetly if you can! — and they might pick it up before it all grinds to a halt. This is in the rehearsal stage of course, when they are blocking (organising the actors' and actresses' movements) and this kind of thing can happen. Of course, when you record it should all go quite smoothly!'

At the same time the PA will be watching for continuity of dress and props related immediately to the actors (e.g., cigarettes, glasses) especially in studio scenes which match up with film inserts. Wardrobe also watch for continuity of dress and they do in fact have somebody who is called continuity dresser, thus the PA acts really as a reminder to that person if they happen to notice anything. Continuity of action (gestures, movements of the head) will be done by the PA.

One of the most important aspects of the PA's job in the studio is timing. She will constantly and very carefully time the rehearsals, keeping the director informed and therefore enabling him or her to decide whether any cuts are necessary or whether it will be enough to simply instruct the performers to put a little more pace into a scene. In fact directors demand more pace fairly regularly because there does seem a general tendency for things to slow down over a period of time and a number of takes.

On recording day the PA will catalogue every take together with timings and possibly odd comments about any problems that were experienced during recording. This is important because in a long take involving a number of shots a director may decide that s/he likes part of it and use it in conjunction with another take. Incidentally at the same time as the PA is listing all the takes for the benefit of the director, as an aid to editing, the video tape operator will also be doing the same thing and his list will go to the video tape editor with comments on the technical quality of each take.

With time-code editing the situation is slightly different. Apart from the BBC only one other Independent TV company other than Thames had time-code editing equipment and this form of editing, which caused the PAs dispute, was to affect the production of *Hazell* considerably. Until time-code editing was introduced all video editing was done by what is called the assembly method — adding each scene one after another by dubbing them on to a master tape in the correct order. This can involve a fairly laborious operation, isn't as precise, and many of the technical effects cannot be added at this stage. For time-code editing, whenever recording begins the PA presses a freeze button which imprints the exact time of day on the tape (down to tenths of a second). This is a 6-digit number, which the PA logs. This system creates more work for the PA but the advantages at the editing stage are enormous (see p 226 below).

Post recording

We asked Liz Cadley what she did the day after recording:

LC: 'The day after you try and avoid coming near the place because you're so shattered — but you do come in and then you have to start the complicated procedure of what we call "clearing the production". We produce a document which we call a "P as T" — Programme as Televised — which details all the information for payment as far as the show is concerned. You detail the amount of film you used — sometimes you use film which is library material and you have to find out which library it is from, how much you used and therefore how much you have to pay — you have to detail the amount of music that you've used and what you have to pay for it — that involves finding out who the composer is, who the publisher is, who the singer is — all those problems of clearing it world-wide have to be gone through before you can use it. You have to list all the hours that the artists have worked including all the rehearsal hours and what their overtime expenses are. You also have to note down all the extras because sometimes the extras you have used become walk-ons and that has to be logged.'

The director will decide how many people s/he wants in each scene and will then ask the PA to book so many extras. She will make out a booking sheet and that will go to Linda Butcher in the Casting Department who is solely responsible for booking extras. On the sheet will be specified the kind of people wanted — age group, length of hair, sex etc. — and also what type of extra is required. As we have seen, there are different grades of extras. Generally, of course, a director will know beforehand what sort of extras s/he requires but if something has had to be changed slightly in the script then it is quite possible for an extra to become a walk-on or a walk-on 1 to become a walk-on 2. It is the PA's responsibility to note all these small details and to deal with payment after recording has been finished.

LC: 'The next thing you do is get your script, which in the studio is out of sequence, re-shuffle all the pages and put the whole thing back into story order. And then you go through it and make a list of all the timings of the different sequences so that you obtain a total from this new order (which you double check of course) and then you have that duplicated and you send it out to all the relevant people (video editors, sound recordists, director) so that they don't have to work out of sequence. This doesn't always happen because they might do it themselves but if it is a difficult one we usually help them in that way.

'Then, also after the production, you have to issue a *TV Times* billing. This is a piece of paper which tells which artists must have block capitals, for instance — 'Nicholas Ball' is blocks — and then which are the A and B performers, etc. You also have to issue a synopsis of the episode and this is hysterical! At the end of each part you have to say what the atmosphere is, you have to decide whether it's anxious or loving, etc. It's for the adverts that they're going to put in, you have to give them an idea of what adverts would be suitable. Then you issue the timing report which goes to the master control people at Euston telling them exactly to the minute and the second how long each part runs and they then inform the network.'

Meantime of course the programme will be undergoing editing and dubbing and these sessions she will also attend. The timing information doesn't go to Euston until these stages are completed.

Editing

Firstly, film. After each day's shooting the PA and director will go back to the studios and draw up a shot list and a continuity list which indicate what's been done and in what order the shots must be placed. This is then sent to the film editor who will produce a rough cut from the answer print that the labs send back. An answer print is the first print produced by the labs. When the director sees it s/he will decide whether the colours are acceptable — if they're not it will be sent back, and the labs will be asked to process it differently so that, for example, a certain colour range will be accentuated. The rough cut is usually shown before rehearsals in the studio so that everyone can check their continuity. It was originally hoped with *Hazell* that, given the colour effects they were hoping to achieve would be different, it would be possible to have a final colour print in the studio in order to match up the studio colours with the film colours. In fact, the turn around of the programmes was too fast to allow the labs the time to do that and anyway the colours were in the end no different from normal.

178

Once an acceptable colour print is received the film will be fine cut and when the director enters the VTR (videotape recording) editing suite the first job to be done will be the transferring of the film on to video tape (complete with a numbered leader for each section). This process takes place in an area that is central to all the studios where most of the video recording and tele-cine equipment is located. This is also where the programmes are recorded and where some video editing can take place. However Thames also have a new video-editing suite, which is where *Hazell* was edited (see p 224 below).

Before going into the editing suite, the director will have a fairly precise idea of how he wants to cut the material together and also which takes he wants to use. This is possible because the VTR simultaneously recorded the studio sessions on the large 2″ colour video machine and on a small black and white ½″ machine. The editor and the PA can then watch this ½″ tape in their office in the period between recording and editing (which sometimes can be quite a considerable time). Thus he will have quite a lot of time to think over the problems and have a fairly clear sense of what he is going to do. This is important because there isn't really time to struggle with problems in the editing room as, like the studio, it will only be booked for 2 days. Any sound dubbing that is required will be done after the programme is finally edited together.

The PA will tell the video tape operator which scene or shot is required next and he will refer to the list that has been made by the operator who recorded the programme. If there has been any 'drop-out' in a scene resulting from poor quality tape, or any other such technical problem, he will inform the director as it might mean that one take cannot be used unless it's absolutely necessary. The PA will also be timing again (as well as the video-tape editor) and keeping the director informed as to how it compares with the studio running-time — usually it is a question of whether he is managing to save time by the tightness of his editing. Over the course of the programme it may be possible to lose quite a bit of time but if something does have to be cut this is the time when it must be done.

In a series that is designed to have 13 episodes like *Hazell*, it's very unlikely that a PA would be able to do more than 5 episodes at the most but it's probable that she would work on more than any one director will. This means that, as with so many other people who work regularly on a series, PAs sometimes know more than the director about certain aspects of the production.

179

The production assistants' dispute

From *Hazell*'s first entering the studio there was a clear possibility that the production assistants would get into a confrontation with Thames management over time-code editing. In the period while we watched *Hazell* being made there were in a fact a number of small disputes — one reason given to us for Thames having so many was that, as for the other big 4 companies, any new wage or contractual agreements achieved by the staff would have repercussions for similar workers in the smaller companies. Thus Thames, being the largest of all, becomes a kind of testing ground for new agreements. The introduction of time-code editing raised some major questions about the work and responsibilities of the production assistants and although only one company at the moment has an electronic editing suite (apart from the BBC) it is fairly clear that all of them will eventually obtain an electronic editing system of some sort. Thus any re-grading that the production assistants managed to achieve at Thames would represent a major achievement for all production assistants working in independent television.

The first 4 episodes of *Hazell* were recorded using time-code editing but only the first 3 had been edited before the PAs refused to operate the system in the editing suite because their demands were not being met. At the time it was too difficult to 'assembly-edit' tapes (the old system) that had been catalogued according to the time-code system and therefore the fourth episode was not edited for many months. The subsequent episodes were recorded using the old assembly method. The dispute reached a confrontation level just at the time the eighth script to be recorded reached the producer's run stage. This script was *Hazell Plays Solomon,* which is the episode that has to go first because it is the one in which all the characters are introduced. The production team found that they couldn't go into the studio the next day because the PAs had been given the sack or as the management preferred to put it, had terminated their contracts.

The production assistants' claim for re-grading

The production assistants' position rested on a number of points. In ITV generally the job of the PA had substantially changed, particularly over the previous 2 years, with developments in the methods and technology of programme production, which were not recognised by management in terms of job title, work scheduling, training provision, grading structure, promotional opportunities, staffing levels or salary.

Furthermore the job structure, title and salary are based on what the PAs claim to be a totally incorrect assessment of the job itself — the significance of the post lies in the fact that, apart from the producer, the PA is the only person in the production team involved throughout the production of a programme and is the only person other than the director who has to have a working knowledge of all the processes involved in production. The work of the PA provides the basis of the liaison and co-ordination work that is required throughout programme production between people inside the studio, between the different departments and in relation to all sources outside the company.

However, despite the specific skills of the PA the job is regarded as neither technical nor administrative and as not providing a qualification for any other job in TV production. The fact that the job is almost exclusively done by women is not unconnected to the fact that the work has been regarded as no more than an extension of the work of a secretary and personal assistant. Many employers still tend to insist on the central importance of the ability to type and the willingness to provide personal secretarial services — something re-inforced by the misleading title of the job. It was this position and the general adoption of discontinuous recording and of the techniques of film production in the television studio that forced into the open the fact that the nature and definition of the job had substantially changed and increased. The introduction of time-code editing early in 1976 provided the impetus and focus for the new demands to be made.

The changes that the PAs initially recommended, and subsequently demanded, included a change of title to programme co-ordinator, a removal of personal secretarial services, a request that the comprehensive nature of the job remain intact and that experience in the post should be regarded as relevant for moves into other areas of production, and finally that the salary and the attendant scales should be brought into line with other Thames employees having similar levels of responsibility.

The ITV companies have an association called the ITCA — the Independent Television Companies Association — one of whose functions is to deal with labour relations on national issues and negotiate for wage claims by a set of workers employed by all the companies. The ITCA will negotiate with the top officials in the different unions. Thames has its own group of staff responsible for staff relations. John O'Keefe is the controller of staff relations and under him there are a team of officers who have general responsibilities for the various unions. Thames was sympathetic to most of the demands being made by the PAs and appreciated their problems. However, under the Government's pay code it was necessary to prove that the PAs now had additional responsibilities if Thames were to give them the rise they requested. This the company felt it could do, and they also changed the job description. Apparently the union and company together decided that time-code editing provided the best area to concentrate on in order to demonstrate that the nature of the job had changed. They both drafted letters outlining the situation and sent them to the Department of Employment. The DOE turned the submissions down on the basis that the PAs had been working the system for a year and therefore the claim was invalid. The company accordingly told the PAs that the government had refused to allow them to pay more but that they would pay them as soon as the restrictions were lifted. The PAs' refusal to accept this position led to Thames invoking 'custom and practice' but to no avail. Thames gave the PAs 7 days' notice to return to normal working, i.e., operating the time-code editing system, and their refusal meant that on 23 May all the PAs at Teddington (though not at Euston) were dismissed and all production immediately ceased — the day that *Hazell Plays Solomon* was due to enter the studio. The possibility of the other ACTT members at Teddington coming out on strike was discussed but that would have meant loss of their salaries for little purpose — as it was, with all production halted, they were costing the company a lot of money in pay, while producing nothing.

The PAs were re-instated on 15 June and negotiations between the union and the company continued and at the time of writing, the problem was still not resolved. The PAs are working normally except that they are still not operating time-code editing. Whether Thames received any pressure to settle from the rest of the network, we don't know. Certainly, as the largest producer of ITV programmes a prolonged period of inactivity at Thames would present programming problems for all the companies so it was also in their interests to hasten the end of the dispute. And it would seem that for Thames to re-instate the PAs without them agreeing to use the time-code editing equipment meant that the company achieved little by dismissing them other than disrupting the schedules for 6 months, though in the management's view much had been clarified by the negotiations.

Once the PAs returned to work a decision about future scheduling had to be made by Jeremy Isaacs. Thames lost a number of programmes in that period of inactivity and certain of them had to be finished before *Hazell* could be completed, for example *The Norman Conquests*—a 2-hour, 3-part series. So either certain episodes of *Hazell* had to be cut or programmes scheduled for later in the year would have to be delayed. The decision was taken to cut 3 episodes because to have 'knocked on' the later programmes scheduled to begin production in the late autumn would apparently have created problems and would also have meant that *Hazell* would have reached completion very close to its projected transmission date. *Rumpole,* starring Leo McKern, was one important programme for Thames which it would have been difficult to re-schedule. It might also have been the case that Jeremy Isaacs was already fairly certain that *Hazell* would run to a second series and therefore the scripts that had been written for the first series could be used on the second.

The director

No-one has yet made out a detailed case for saying that television is a director's medium in the way that the so-called *auteur* theory* has argued for the primacy of the director in the cinema. Nevertheless, that the director is very important, as important as anyone except the producer, few would deny. So we have devoted more space to directors than to any other job (with the exception of the producer, to whom we have not devoted a separate section, preferring instead to describe her functions as they emerged at every stage of production). We spoke to all the 7 directors who worked on *Hazell,* but we have chosen to concentrate on 2, not because they were necessarily the most interesting but because one worked on the start of the series and one on the last episode. Originally it was intended to have only two or three directors working on *Hazell* in order to allow a consistent style, but due to the re-scheduling of the series and the fact that production was brought forward 3 months at a late stage in planning, this was not finally possible. Directors are usually freelance and tend to be very busy people; they can be committed to projects as much as a year in advance and so most of them had to fit *Hazell* in where they could. The PAs' dispute exacerbated this problem so that many episodes had to be edited and dubbed months after the recording date, either because the director concerned would be working on a programme for another

---

*This 'theory', first advanced in France, primarily through the journal *Cahiers du Cinema,* and then introduced into English through the writings of Andrew Sarris and others, proposes that films should be seen as the expression of an individual consciousness. This individual turns out almost invariably to be the director.

company, or because of the difficulties of scheduling the editing suite.

In the end there were 7 directors on the 10 programmes — 6 men: Don Leaver, Alistair Reid, Jim Goddard, Peter Duguid, Brian Farnham and Colin Bucksey; and 1 woman: Moira Armstrong. There must have been many factors that ultimately contributed to these 7 people being chosen but originally there were two basic principles from which June worked. Firstly she asked people with whom she had worked successfully before (e.g., Brian Farnham, Peter Duguid, Colin Bucksey and Jim Goddard, all of whom had directed episodes of *Couples*), and secondly she had a conception of who would do which script well. Jim Goddard and Alistair Reid have a reputation as good 'action' directors, for example, so it is not surprising that they did *Hazell Goes To The Dogs*, and *Hazell Pays A Debt* (though Jim Goddard said he didn't see himself as that kind of a specialist).

I

There is no set pattern that determines how somebody becomes a television director: there is little formal training available, nor is there any one particular job that a person needs to have done in order to become a director. Those who worked on *Hazell* had either been actors, or a floor manager, or a painter or a set designer. They were sometimes producers as well — Peter Duguid for example, or Don Leaver, who was going on to produce a series for Southern Television — but all had their own agents through whom they would either obtain work or, more usually, through whom they would negotiate their contracts on the jobs they were offered. One small generalisation one might make, however, is that they tended to be slightly more sensitive to the area of work from which they had originally come, so that a director who had been an actor would appear to be particularly good at working with actors and actresses and somebody like Jim Goddard, who is a painter, is particularly concerned about colours and visual patterning on the sets. This is not to say that they weren't good at all aspects of their jobs but simply that they seemed to be particularly concerned about an area in which they had special experience. One other general point to make about directors is that it is one of the few senior areas of television where women work.

To obtain an idea of how somebody becomes a television director we asked Alistair Reid to describe how he came to be working in this field. His account is not necessarily typical of other directors — it simply offers an interesting example.

AR: 'Well there is no easy answer to how one becomes a television director. I started acting at school. It was an all-boys school and a boy's mother objected to him playing the part of the maid in a play. At this point the English master pointed at me and said, Reid, you're playing that part. I did that and various other plays and I got up to my final year and I was by now the kind of leading light in the drama society and they more or less said now what would you like to do this year, Reid? And I thought, well, *Hamlet* it's got to be, hasn't it, you know, but instead I was foisted into *St Joan* and I was St Joan. Then I went to study fine art at Edinburgh College of Art — there I carried on directing plays and designing them and acting in them, doing the whole bit really. I also got interested in film. At the end of the war my father used to take me to a big film society in Edinburgh and we used to see all the really obscure European movies and then when I was at art school I started to make little documentaries and things like that mainly for the use of the school, for the Architecture Department and so on. In the middle of it, in about 1959 or '60 I went to Africa with another student who was at the University doing philosophy and we made a film which was financed by Scottish Television. It was supposed to be about education in emergent African states — Tanzania, Kenya and Uganda — and we travelled around and interviewed educationalists and politicians and so on, and in the process actually travelling through Rwanda- Burundi, which is part of the Congo. The Congo war started and we got trapped in Elizabethville in Katanga. In fact I was in Kitwi which is in the copper belt of Northern Rhodesia when Hammarschold was killed, and I was waiting there to fly the film out in a plane. So suddenly I was doing a lot more than just this education film.

At the end of my 4 years at art school, when I got my degree, they gave me a post-graduate scholarship which in fact I resigned, and I went to the Bristol Old Vic Theatre School, mainly because an actress called Annette Crosbie who comes from Edinbrugh told my mother that it was a good place to go. I went and actually didn't particularly like it — I was on a director's course — and so I gradually eased out of that into the University Drama Department which also had a film unit. So whilst I was there I co-made a 35mm film of an Ionesco play fir.. nced by the National Film Finance Corporation. Then I went to the Bristol Old Vic Company as an assitant director and out of the blue I got an invitation from ATV to go to an interview board for trainee directors and to this day I still don't know how it happened.

I'll never forget that, it turned out to be the shortlist interview — they'd interviewed hundreds of people already — and I arrived very late. There was a great board of directors sitting around a half moon table with one solitary chair in the middle and they said things like, If you were in my shoes what changes would you make to ATV? and I had to say. Well I'm sorry, I don't know what shoes you're in, I mean who are you? It was Lew Grade actually and I said, Oh well, I would get rid of *Emergency Ward 10* straightaway. He fell about, he thought I was the funniest man on earth. Then they said he's got to have the job and I finished up directing *Emergency Ward 10* for a year and a half and then producing it for a while after that. So in fact I was with ATV for about 4 years directing everything really. I mean all drama — *Emergency Ward 10,* single plays and love stories until I was fed up with it. I went to the Controller of Programmes and he gave me odd things like *Sunday Night at the London Palladium* and documentaries with people like Sir Kenneth Clark.

Then I left ATV for Rediffusion at the invitation of a woman called Stella Richman who moved there to be head of a department and we made a programme called *A Man of Our Time,* a series which that year won the British Academy Award. I was there for a couple of years and then about 1967 I left and wrote and directed a feature film, which is a terrible little skin flick, which I saw again the other night on the late, late show, called *Baby Love,* which cost all of $267,000. I remember exactly what it cost because it was sold to Joseph E. Levine of Avco Embassy in New York for a million dollars cash plus 33 $1/3$% of the world gross and was top box office film of 1969 in this country. What I got for writing the screenplay and directing it was something in the region of £700 and a new suit — and the only reason I got the new suit was that they didn't think I was well enough dressed to go on a promotion tour of America with it.

Subsequent to that I spent a strange 7 months in Hollywood working on an abortive film with a man called Abby Mann, the founder of Kojak, and then came back to this country and made a very strange, obscure film for Metro-Goldwyn-Mayer called *The Night Digger* with Patricia Neal, and written by her husband Roald Dahl, which got very, very good reviews in America and has only been seen in that country. It's not been shown in this country mainly because Patricia Neal, Roald Dahl and I all took deferred payments which would only come into

186

being if the film opened in this country. So it is actually very much in their interests not to release the film in this country, and I got involved with Robert Mitchum and various other luminaries into suing M G M on this basis, but we didn't get anywhere with it so the film's not been seen — there's one copy sitting at M G M and that's about it.

Then I made another rather bad film, the screenplay of which I wrote, called *Something to Hide,* also for Joseph E. Levine, with Peter Finch and Shelley Winters. I also wrote the screenplay of a film called *Shout at the Devil* which is a rather mundane film with Lee Marvin.

I worked doing odd plays at the B B C and first met Verity Lambert at London Weekend where I did a couple of plays for her. I generally spend my time flitting between this company, where I do maybe 2 plays a year, and the B B C, where I tend to do rather more — that's up-to-date so far.'

Alistair Reid considers himself to be a specialist drama director which means that he is not likely to switch to different types of programme such as *The Generation Game* unless he pushes to do something different. In 1977, for example, he started with *Hazell,* then he was off to do a documentary about a group of women Cambridge graduates in New York, *Gangsters* for the B B C, for 6 months (the fact that he did the first series partly encouraged Thames to ask him to do *Hazell*), and then in January 1978 he was booked to do a musical for the B B C on location, which was going to be entirely song and dance. Alistair talked about when he first heard of *Hazell:*

AR: 'I was doing *Romance* here about September or October last year and June Roberts, who knew of me although we didn't really know each other, just asked if I could have lunch with her and she put it to me. What they wanted me to do was direct about half of them. I think they basically wanted 2 directors. But they were just too late, I'd already been booked up to do *Gangsters* and so on — I mean you tend to get booked up more than a year in advance. I was also going to do some plays by Alan Plater for the B B C during this time and then the funny thing is that the Plater plays fell through. By this time they had cast other directors for *Hazell* and they juggled dates around so I could do one of them.'

In fact the *Hazell* project hadn't at first interested Alistair very much as he hadn't really liked the scripts, although he had seen their potential. However, once he became involved in *Hazell Pays A Debt* he did regret leaving it. Alistair said that it was quite normal to hear of a new project like *Hazell* in the way that he had and that it was quite rare for it to go through his agent. There was a strange coincidence about his agent in this case however:

AR: ' . . . the agent for the progamme, in others words the agent who sold the book to Verity Lambert and the agent who represents the writers and June's agent and my agent are all the same woman, so read into that what you will. She's a very clever woman, and she more or less tried to sell a massive package deal to Verity Lambert which would have included much more than in fact it turned out.'

The next stage for Alistair was to take away a script and the novels to read. He wrote back to say that he wouldn't be free to do most of them due to his prior commitment to *Gangsters.* He went on to make an interesting point in his letter:

AR: 'I said, "I think you ought to know that *Gangsters* is a prior commitment, that this is not dissimilar to *Gangsters,* and you don't want to get into a situation of divided loyalties." Actually I don't think that they could care two hoots about that. I mean they were quite obviously, it seems to me, towards the end, especially from Verity Lambert's point of view, asking me because I was responsible for *Gangsters* and hopefully we would put a similar sort of look into this.'

When setting up *Hazell* June (along with Verity Lambert and Joan Rodker) wanted to create a different and innovatory series in order to break away from *Private Eye, Callan, The Sweeney.* That was one important reason for asking Alistair to do the show: that he had directed a crime series which had broken to an extent with realistic conventions. For the same reason, Brian Farnham, who had also directed a highly stylised series, *Rock Follies,* was originally asked to do several episodes of *Hazell.*

Alastair wasn't really involved in thinking about or working on *Hazell* again until mid-January when he came back to London to see June. Within a day of starting work at Thames he saw the first episode that had been recorded — *Hazell And The Weekend Man.* He described his reaction at the time.

AR: 'I saw the first one which I thought was disastrous, I hated it and I told June that I hated it and I said that Nicholas Ball was disastrously miscast. But she also showed it to Jeremy Isaacs and Jeremy Isaacs told her she had a winner! That actually didn't change my attitude because I just think that he didn't really know frankly. It could be that June did have some sort of a winner, but it doesn't change the fact that Nicholas Ball is disastrously miscast and I've told everybody including him that. However he's a good guy and now that he's cast they will have to bend in the direction that Nicholas Ball is taking it. He's not Hazell as written in the book. He's too young basically. However he's got a certain charming *naïvete* together with a sort of toughness which is good and he's beginning to make the part his own.'

We asked Alistair how he thought that Nick coped with his telling him that, and whether it was something all actors and actresses had to cope with:

AR: 'Yes, because you've got to be basically honest with him and he respects honesty and actually he's continually coming to me even now when I'm finished with the production. He realises I suppose that he's not what they were after, which was a sort of Michael Caine, somebody of that age, that cool and so on. Nick isn't that but he'll bring something else to it, you know, which should be quite valuable. It's impossible for me to estimate what the public reaction to him will be. I think they'll find him quite an amenable character'.

We asked Alistair what his next move was:

AR: 'I went to a pre-production planning meeting where they expected me to tell them everything about how I was going to do it and I couldn't — I wasn't prepared to and I suddenly got the idea that they were trying to push this programme through as a pot-boiler, you know, and I wasn't prepared to accept that. I regard myself as above working on pot-boiler programmes now anyway and I wasn't going to buy that. I was prepared to work at the company's pace but I was going to make this programme as good as I could and one of the things was that I thought there was a vast amount of film in it — it was about half film. At the production planning meeting they held up the script and they looked at me and said You are joking aren't you? I said that I didn't write the script and that we were going to need 'x' number of days. They said, you only have 3 days. I thought sod it, you know. I will bloody well show them, I will shoot it in 3 days and I did. Having shot it in 3 days and getting 30 minutes of film in that time I was then accused by the company of shooting too much film, because the Editing Department couldn't cope with it. They said, what did you go out and shoot 30 minutes of film for? How can we possibly edit 30 minutes of film in the time allotted? So either way you see you can't win. Then they said, well since you have shot 30 minutes of film in 3 days it means that you have only got 25 minutes to shoot in the studio so things will be much calmer and so on. So I thought no, sod that, I am going to shoot everything on a single camera, on hand-held cameras in the studio and, as you know, it was very, very hairy.'

The problem with this is that every section of the company has to be very carefully geared to each of the others and precise work loads calculated. The fact that one section — the film crew — is only available for 3 days means that the editing suite booking is very precisely related to that. If a bit too much film is shot then that poses work load problems. Hence June's and Richard Harris' fussiness about timings and locations. Thus when Richard said to us one day that he wouldn't have written so many pub scenes if he had been responsible for the series (although this will seem an odd restriction for a series such as *Hazell*), this is clearly a response to personal experiences of what is and is not possible within a particular time schedule.

Alistair worked in the studio in a very different way from the other directors on *Hazell*. As he states he shot nearly everything in the studio in single takes on one camera. He had only one hand-held camera but he used it a lot, placing it in all sorts of strange places. Thus when using it and the heavy rostrum cameras he shot as if he were in a film studio. We asked Alistair if it was normal for him to use a hand-held camera in this way.

AR: 'Yes, I quite often do, for this sort of material. I did for *Gangsters* as well, but I also did for the *Romance* that I did here, and in each case it has caused tremendous ructions because they think that Alistair Reid is trying to break the system down. It's the same at the BBC, in fact the one that I used there (the BBC in Birmingham) was hired here to do *Romance*. I said to them that I'd like to get a hand-held camera. Oh we don't have such a thing, they said, so I phoned up Bosch and they sent the same camera. Then, and this shows you the sign of the times, I again said that I want the hand-held camera — this, by the way, is just using it as a small camera where you fit it into difficult places and so on, not necessarily using it hand-held — and I phoned Bosch again and they said that they had sold it to the BBC! However they did have another one on an OB unit here, so I said, OK, and that's how we got it.'

In fact the camera didn't work on the first day they were in the studio though eventually they managed to get one that did. Alistair was annoyed by this, since he had booked it 3 months before he went into the studio, and angry memos were sent to the head of department.

Since he was an ex-designer himself we talked with Alistair about the sets he was using on *Hazell*. He was very keen to use all 4 walls in rooms because, he said, 'it was like a real room'. Some sets were fairly minimal but Alistair explained that it was more usual to have such sets on what he called fantastical programmes like the Graham Greene series, *Shades of Greene*, where just a table and a backdrop would be sufficient. Despite this drive towards realism, it was interesting to note that in the pub scene where a fight takes place the flimsy set walls were not specially reinforced but instead the walls had scene shifters behind them ready to take the impact when people fell against them. Alistair had also requested that most of the sets had ceilings.

AR: 'I'll tell you the real reason why I approve of ceilings — apart from seeing them — and that is it stops the lighting director lighting from the top. There are very good lighting directors around now but there are still some living in the days when television was all heavy, top lighting, and I hate that so much that I make it impossible for them to do it by just having ceilings. You see my principle is to have lots of windows in the place, especially in a pub, and a lot of light should apparently come in the windows. If people are half-lit, fine, that's the way it should be.'

Alistair's attitude to direction in general was very much that of Alfred Hitchcock, who claims that the film is finished when it first goes into the studio; i.e., he's made all the decisions and choices and all that is left is the, to him, somewhat tedious task of having to film it.

AR: 'Yes, my attitude is that the most boring part of direction is going down and shunting the camera and getting the right angle. It more or less directs itself if you cast all the parts right. And so if all these elements are working together, then I ought to be able to sit back and let it all happen.'

Unfortunately, it didn't quite work out that way on *Hazell Pays A Debt* (see p.238 below).

II

Brian Farnham is an interesting director to compare with Alistair Reid because he is committed to television as a medium in the way that Alistair obviously isn't — Alistair is still very much, like Colin Bucksey, a film-maker. As a result of the production assistants' action Brian

191

Farnham ended up doing only the last episode, instead of the 3 that he was scheduled to do. Thus their experiences were likely to be very different in that Alistair Reid was to determine a lot of what was to happen in the future in terms of constructing some of the stock sets and advising Nick and the rest of the regulars about their acting. By the time Brian came on the scene all the stock sets were designed and built and all the regular characters knew their parts better than he did. If he wanted to change something in their performance he would have to work hard at it *and* not contradict anything that had already been done earlier in the series.

Although it was being recorded last, his episode, *Hazell And The Walking Blur,* would be transmitted in the middle of the series, so any slight deviation from the norm would be very noticeable.

We asked Brian to go through the processes of his work when he first comes to a programme.

BF: 'Well in an ideal world you get the script before it comes to its final draft. But in a series like *Hazell* you're lucky if that happens. You usually get the script in its final draft, but that's still not too late for you to say look, I don't think this works, wouldn't it be better if we did so and so? It depends a great deal on whether you know the writer beforehand, I find. On this it was just marvellous because I knew Richard Harris; not that we had to do many alterations, in fact. The script was fairly good to start with. There were slight shifts of emphasis, that was all — about characters. It was a bit overwritten in places — which is good — and bit too long, so basically it was a cutting-down, which is nice. I'd much rather get a script which is too long rather than too short. You can tighten it and I think when you see the finished product you'll think it is quite tight, even though it is still slightly overlength — 1 minute 29 seconds over, to be precise.

And then there's discussion with the designer. You've got a certain number of stock sets which you're lumbered with, which are murder in most cases by the time you get to the end of the series. The stock sets have been designed for the first two or three episodes and probably fit them very well, but you get to the last episodes and you find scenes have been written that just don't fit in a stock set and there's nothing you can do with them. A case in point is the scene in this one in Gregory's office. They come for the first time with the money and they're going to put the money in Gregory's safe. If I'd designed that set I would have made it much bigger because there was nowhere that I could tuck the Scotsman out of the way where he couldn't overhear what Gregory and Hazell are saying to one another. I think it worked in the end but it could have worked much better if I had designed the set. In this series it hasn't worked too badly in fact, but in some series that I've worked on, if you do some of the latter numbers you really are lumbered and things don't in any way fit in with the stock sets. Apart from that problem you do have to discuss the new sets with the designer, of course.

When there is filming you've got to sort the locations out and often the locations have to match the interiors or sets, like the scene in the cabby's hut which have to match exterior/interior. Also the outside of the banqueting hall had to at least match in style — although it wasn't a direct match — with the interior.'

As described elsewhere, it is the location manager who actually does the initial searching for locations. He will then make suggestions to the director who, if he knows the place, will say yes or no. If there is any uncertainty the two of them will go together (and possibly the designer as well). Brian described the unusual situation that he inherited on *Hazell*.

BF: 'With the Soho montage we just walked round Soho together and obviously at that time most of it is in my head. On this one we had to work very fast because as you probably know I went away on holiday thinking we were doing one script and then came back and found we were doing another, which I received on holiday two days before we came home. And I said I'm not reading it now, I'll read it coming home on the plane — there was nothing I could have done about it anyway. So in that case Eamonn had luckily done a lot of the work on the locations.'

Brian had referred to the problem with stock sets (which he mentioned several times) but he also inherited a set of characters, a set of actors and actresses and production people. This provided a contrast to Don Leaver, who had not wanted to make too many hard and fast decisions, had wanted to play it 'by ear' precisely because he didn't want to lumber the subsequent directors with things that would hamper them.

BF: 'Oh, I inherited a whole team, I inherited a set of actors and actresses, a set of costumes, which didn't worry me. In a sense you see, that makes it easy if you come in late — I've done it both ways, I've started off a series and I've finished one. In a sense if you come in halfway through it makes it easier provided the script-writer's got it right. If the author's got it wrong then you're in trouble. But if the author knows his characters, and here we were lucky because we'd got Richard as the script editor on the series anyway, then you're all right. I wasn't worried in this instance. I inherited a set of actors who knew their characters. There are certain things that you find they help you on — I blocked a thing and I put Hazell's desk on the opposite side from where it normally was, it seemed to look better in the scene. When we came to rehearsal they said, Oh no, Hazell's desk was never there, it's over there. So I said all right, O K, reblock the scene, lovelies. It was quite simple, but then it's not difficult with a set as small as that and with actors who know the part. But I think that it does help that Nick, I think, felt much more secure by the time he came to mine, so he was able to do things, and I was able to make him do things, in this script which he probably wouldn't have dared risk doing earlier on. He's much more relaxed, he's much more flip, and I think, having seen some of the other episodes, that he's much funnier because he's much more relaxed and he's able to flick the lines off. They all said to me how much trouble they'd had with the voice-overs and there had been voice-over sessions which went on for ever and ever and when they got the final thing it was rotten and they had to re-record him. We literally recorded the voice-overs for this episode in three quarters of an hour straight through and it was almost the first take every time, and they're the ones we've used. We aren't re-recording any, which is a big bonus. Also a lot of credit must go to Richard, who knew the character and was writing for an actor he knew as well, of course, which makes a difference.'

Richard Harris ended up writing 3 of the *Hazell* scripts when originally it had been June's intention that the script editor shouldn't write any scripts (one of the things that Kenneth Ware was unhappy about at the time that he was working on it) but then Richard had been commissioned for 3 and had already written 2 before he was asked to script edit. In fact Richard was very unhappy about his first script — *Hazell And The Weekend Man* which, after a long discussion, he wanted to scrap. One of the problems was that it read very well but on the screen it did seem a rather slight story. Brian Farnham commented on the fact that he had read Richard's other script, *Hazell And The Rubber-Heel Brigade,* which he hadn't liked at first, but when he saw the finished product directed by Peter Duguid he thought it worked really well and 'looked smashing'. He did, in fact, see a number of the episodes before starting work on his episode and we asked him if he was influenced by other people's camera style or cutting.

BF: 'Not really, I don't think. If you're doing a series and the producer says I want it done such and such a way, well then obviously the other programmes will be like that. I never ever said consciously to myself that I must do this scene in this sort of style. I think we were aware of the style and the style came out of the script, and I think I was lucky because the script was right and I think we got quite close to the original idea. I've been slightly involved with the series right from the beginning, you know. June told me about it ages ago and wanted me to do it. Then it evolved; it's got a long way since that time. The original ideas, I don't know where they went, a lot of them, they just vanished, but I still think in ours we paid homage to those 40s movies in the right way — I think there were echoes which were quite nice. It came over marvellously to me in the Griffiths scenes which were dead right and it all crystallised — also in the Minty scenes I think we got the lighting right and the mood was right.

I talked to the lighting director in this case at great length and in great depth because I had worked with him before and what had happened before hadn't, as far as I was concerned, been a very happy result. I thought he overlit everything so I actually did go into great detail and we discussed every scene, what sort of lighting I wanted and in certain scenes I just said I want to see faces, show me faces, that's all I'm asking. Backgrounds, in this, are not important. This was true in a lot of the script except, for example, in the Tudor Room set, where the background was significant early on and we took big wide shots to show it off. But still it was darkness and I wanted underlighting and lighting men, I realise, have problems because they have to reach a certain level otherwise it won't go out, it won't reach a signal and then they get told off and they get graded by the IBA or a technical committee or something, but you can suddenly find yourself in tune and the lighting director will take risks.'

Brian Farnham was particularly concerned about this question of the technicians having some technical code to work to because he had worked on *Rock Follies* on which a fair amount of unusual lighting set-ups were used. The lighting director had commented to him that episode 2 of the first series of *Rock Follies* which was the first that Brian had done and was one that he was quite happy about) had been graded 2 technically. This meant that they had achieved a sub-standard grading for something that, as far as Brian was concerned, had worked very well artistically. In common with all the other directors we spoke to, Brian was vitally interesting in getting the lighting for the show right.

BF: 'It annoys me intensely that light sources are ignored and I always like to say, right, we've got a window there and that's the light source, therefore most of the light should come from there. If we've got a night scene we've got a standard lamp there and a lamp over here — now I'll be aware of those lamps and I will position my actors in such a way that they will be lit. If I position them in such a way that they are not it's because I don't want them lit, I want them in silhouette. This is why in the first hotel scene in *Hazell And The Walking Blur* I sat Hazell with his back to the window when he first comes into the room. He walks into the room to meet this man and he immediately goes and sits himself with his back to the window so that the light is shining on the man's face, but Hazell is almost in silhouette. Obviously you've got to cheat a bit so you can see him but clearly he puts himself in a position of power immediately. It's the old interview technique, it's as simple as that.'

Although Brian is here demanding a high degree of control over what he is doing and indicating the extent to which his decisions are conscious and intentional, even so he will not 'go the whole way' — he still feels that you have to 'cheat a bit' in order to show Hazell, which is not a concession that the directors who worked in the *film noir genre* were prepared to make. For example, in *Gilda* Charles Vidor shot a scene between Rita Hayworth, Glenn Ford and George Macready in the latter's house where George Macready's silhouette is so extreme that the audience is encouraged to wonder 'how is it that a shadow can have a cigarette that glows'.

Generally Brian talked a good deal about, and made extensive references to, *Rock Follies,* which marked possibly a personal departure and experimentation period for him as it obviously did for Thames. Thus to the vision mixer on a programme like *Hazell* he hadn't talked too much about cutting, whereas on *Rock Follies* he talked to the vision mixer at great length in order to get the complex *musical* cutting correct.

In talking to Brian about the rehearsals we commented on the fact that there seem to be two main areas of attention. One is the concern for motivation of the characters — why they are doing what they are

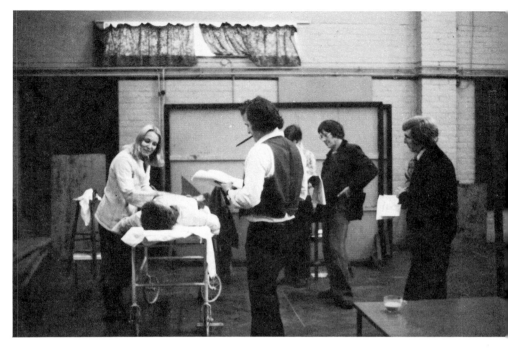

in rehearsal for Hazell And The Walking Blur: (l. to r. Katharine Schofield, Nicholas Ball, Brian Farnham, Mary Lewis, Gordon Toms, Ken Tester-Brown

doing — and the other is the question of pace — everybody is concerned to make their episode snappy.

BF: 'Well that was really a directive from June. The series right from the beginning had to be snappy and especially this script — it really had to move, it had to be paced. Yes, and the other thing of course *is* motivation. You've got to tell the people what they were doing before the script started, what they were doing before the first word of the script. In a series like *Hazell* of course, a lot of the characters know anyway. Your stock characters will know but a lot of your new characters need to have built some sort of background, what sort of person they are, what sort of wife they've got, whether they are married, what sort of job they do, what sort of place they live in, the background they come from, and I think that's all very important. It shows.'

This naturalist attitude to acting is the dominant mode in both theatrical and television acting in Britain and it's difficult to extract more from that line of questioning in our experience when talking with actors and directors. It simply seems to be generally assumed that the characters should behave as much as possible like real people — despite the fact that many of the characters in *Hazell* are 'larger than life'. About acting and casting generally:

BF: 'I find that a lot of what I do is instinctive, a lot of what I do happens on the floor and obviously you read a script and you have your idea about the actor and you cast your actor for that idea. But I'm a great believer in letting the actor express himself, so maybe when I'm watching a rehearsal, I don't say too much to start off with. For a start you learn a lot at the read-through — you learn whether you've mis-cast for a start, that's the first thing. I did say once, many years ago, look chum, I've made a terrible mistake, I've totally miscast you, no hard feelings, but do you mind? I've actually done it and there were no hard feelings, the fellow was as aware of it as I was. It's an expensive mistake and not one to be encouraged, but in that case the producer agreed with me totally and we'd cast him as a semi-running character anyway so it obviously had to be altered because things aren't going to get any better, they're only going to get worse since he's going to be unhappy because it didn't work for him.

You cast for a particular character and sometimes you will, or at least I will anyway, cast someone against type. I think to myself that will make them work, that will make the person they're playing with spark off. It's a great thing if you're doing a series to cast a really good actor against type when he's playing a scene with a character who's getting bored with the part, doing the same thing every week. I think, well I'll make him sit up and I'll cast someone against type and everyone starts to think, Christ, he's going to take the bloody scene away from me so I'll bloody well bring out my performance. That was the case with the Griffiths character — that's not the normal role for Michael Elphick to play.'

The Griffiths character was something that Brian changed.

BF: 'The character of Griffiths was built up to be a much bigger, much more powerful man than he was originally. He was just another Soho gangster in the script, but I thought it would work much better if, given that the beginning was so funny anyway, we had a man who obviously really was a threat to Hazell without ever stating it — that way we got a much better turn around in the last part. For example, there was originally a line in the scene in the cell where Minty said "You've heard of Tommy Griffiths" and Hazell's reply to that was "Oh yes, one of your veritable Mr. Bigs", which in my mind didn't do anything. It just said that he was an organiser, whereas in the final thing what actually happens is Hazell doesn't say a word in response to Minty — you just take a reaction of him and the reaction says it all. By saying "One of your veritable Mr. Bigs" you inevitably diminish the man. By just taking a reaction shot and saying to Nick, "think of Ronny Kray", you don't have to say any more. The Griffiths character is built up much more and then when he appears there's more of a threat there.'

We asked to what extent the producer would comment, especially over the course of the fortnight before the producer's run.

BF: 'I usually ask them, but a lot of times, actually eight times out of ten, you find if you're not sure of something then the answer is cut it, because I find if I'm not sure then it ain't working. But you don't normally see the producer very much — I saw June more often probably because it was the end, the last one, and she'd got more time to come to rehearsal. Normally one wouldn't see a producer unless you'd asked them to come down. There are occasions when you say look, I'm in big trouble. Things aren't working, for the life of me I can't see why they're not working. I've tried. You'll do it with the author, you'll get the author down and say I've got a scene that isn't working, I don't know why. Sometimes the author will realise why — sometimes you get so close to it that you can't see the wood for the trees. But normally you wouldn't see the producer except under those circumstances. Otherwise you see them at casting and in the studio.

In fact June was unusual in that she spent a good deal of time at the rehearsals on all the episodes (Brian wasn't to know that of course).

On working methods in the studio:

BF: 'I always work on the floor, as you probably noticed, but I always try and keep in touch with the control room by talking to them through the neck mike that I usually wear. I think the old style television directors always used to stay up in the gallery the whole time and never come down on the floor, but I think the tendency now is to work on the floor when you're blocking cameras. I think it's just totally unfair to the actors. They've had you there in rehearsals for 2 or 3 weeks, and you've been there and they've been referring everything through you, and suddenly you're gone and all they're faced with is a great battery of cameras. I think you've got to be there to translate, to be the intermediary between the cameras and the actors; for them to suddenly lose you totally I think is wrong.'

Thames uses 4-camera studios and the cameras are fitted with standard zoom lenses. There are a whole range of lenses that are available and on something like *Rock Follies* many of them are very likely to be used. However, on something like *Hazell* the only additional type of lens that a director like Brian is possibly going to ask for are 'K' lenses, which will remain in focus on extreme close-up. The director is more likely to request other types of equipment specifically e.g., hand-held cameras and different types of camera pedestal. It depends on the scene and way in which each director works as to how many cameras are used in a scene. We observed scenes being shot with 1 (rare), 2, 3 or 4 cameras. Given that there are 4 cameramen in the studio, if less than 4 are used in a number of scenes they will be rotated to give them a rest — it can be heavy work lugging the cameras around a crowded studio. We asked Brian why 4 were often used, given that it frequently meant they were simply placed in a row — it often looked quite easy to simply ask one or two of them to pan when they were not on shot.

BF: 'Well I would use all 4 because it avoids movement and distraction for the actors, it's as simple as that. You can quite obviously sometimes do a scene in 2, but as I've got 4 cameras I'd rather use all 4 if I can get them in. On the cabby's hut scene, which is a very tiny set, I used 4 cameras because there was a lot of concentration as far as the actors were concerned in that scene and there would be less distraction than with cameras whizzing from side to side to get into position. If you use 4 cameras you hardly have to move and they just click their shots.

There were a number of points concerning direction we discussed with Brian Farnham, and in the rest of this chapter we have simply reproduced our interview with him.

INT: *In terms of the way you shot the scenes in that hotel room, every time it's from a different direction. That presumably is to give some variety?*
BF: To give some variety — again this comes back to the original discussion with the designer. We looked at it and said, well it's got to be a small pokey hotel room, it's one man, single bed, pokey hotel in Earl's Court. That visually is going to be boring by the end of the episode because there's so much action in it and we can't have him walking the

same lines for ever, so we finally designed a 4-sided set from which you could take different bits out and take from different angles — just for visual variety, and also a variety of movement. Of course there are certain central areas that will never move, like the chair and the bed and the sink, but one can still shoot those in different ways. There would be no danger of the audience being confused by shooting from different angles because it was obviously the same hotel room anyway, with hideous green wallpaper.

INT: *Was it also for variety that you shot the scene of Nick and the fiancée in the mirror, because that took a certain amount of setting up?*

BF: Well yes, quite. The mirror was there, and there's always a terrible temptation to use mirror shots anyway, but I deliberately avoided it until the fiancée scene where I thought it would tell you most. I didn't want to have to cut in the fiancée scene anyway, so I just saved the mirror for that one shot. We did slightly use the mirror in a later shot where Nick leans in and you've got a nice double reflection. But again it comes to variety, by then too the audience will know that room backwards, so there will be no danger of disorientation.

INT: *Weren't you deliberately bringing a style to this . . .?*

BF: I don't know whether I was exactly, because obviously there's a style anyway which is innate to the series. I think I was very lucky with this episode because I think the way it was written dictated the way it was done, and I think that was the right way for the series.

INT: *We would like to come to this business of style by another direction perhaps. If you're watching something on television presumably you would, quite often, have a fairly good idea about who would have directed it. Obviously you don't know all the directors in television but you might quite often be watching a thing and think so-and-so directed this because . . .*

BF: Oh yes, people have said this to *me*. People have said I knew that was you before the credit came up. I wouldn't know how they knew it was me but they knew it was.

INT: *OK, you wouldn't know how they knew it was* you, *but supposing you were watching something done by someone else, how would you know it was* them? *What king of things would tell you . . . ?*

BF: I haven't the faintest idea. I mean someone like Alan Cooke, for instance, is very plush and you would know because it was very plush. Herbert Wise you would know — there are long, big developing shots and it's all very sinuous; and then there are the big action directors like

Jim Goddard, who directs action like it's coming out of his ears, you know, it's beautiful, it's marvellous, he makes it work in a way that I never can. I try and analyse it but I think he just does it, again it's an innate thing. Waris Hussein is the greatest studio director there is, for my money. He shoots studio cameras like it's going out of fashion, and I can always tell, there's a sort of luxuriousness about it.

INT: *But you can't tell what your own style is? Although other people can.*

BF: I couldn't tell, no . . . because it's not conscious. You see I take the script and the script dictates the style, the way I shoot it.

INT: *What you're saying is, you have a functional style, you do things because that's what the script dictates. I suspect actually that that is what all directors would say, and yet they all have different styles, so there is a paradox there.*
BF: Oh, there's a terrible paradox there, yes, absolutely. In the final analysis you come back to the script again, because the script does dictate the style, well I find it always does.
INT: *Except that in* Hazell *obviously not all the scripts are the same, yet the episodes are more like each other than they are like other television shows, presumably . . .*
BF: We hope so; we hope for instance that it's not going to look anything like *Target,* to name but one . . .

Well, when the series was originally planned the idea was to get 2, 3, writers at the most; 2, at the most 3, directors. Now that is an ideal situation, because then, I think, you stand a better chance of evolving a consistent style. Here there are 10 episodes and there are 7 directors. It's impossible to get a unified style unless, as I say, you start at the beginning. You get a producer and she says, or he says, I will have 2, at the most 3 writers on this, and I will have 2, at the most 3, directors, and we'll all get together at the beginning and we'll all talk and decide the ways the sets are going to be designed, the way the scripts are going to be written, the way everything is going to be shot.

I hope that in a certain way we did it on *Rock Follies.* There we were lucky, we only had the 1 writer and we only had 2 directors, and we only had 6 episodes, in a sense it was different, but I think there was a certain unity of style. It's very difficult, this style thing is innate, it's something which you do, I don't sit down and say, this is the script, this is what the scene is about, this is what the actors are giving me, this is how it should look, and that's the way I shoot it. In any case you have to remember that T V is much more of a close-up medium than film, and that dictates the style.

INT: *If you had more time and money what would you do differently; supposing you had, say, more rehearsal time or twice as much time in the studio?*

BF: 'I don't think in something like *Hazell* one needs more rehearsal time — I don't think I needed any more. It would have been no different, no better, it may even have been worse. One always complains about rehearsal time and in many cases you are short of time, but actors and directors do inevitably pace themselves to the amount of rehearsal time they've got. The thing I'm doing now, you need more rehearsal time. We definitely do, because it's the kind of play where I need in fact to improvise — improvisation I don't think really plays any part in a series like *Hazell,* whereas with certain one-off plays it does. There are scenes in it for which I would dearly like twice the amount of rehearsal time we've got — I would have liked to improvise scenes which aren't in the piece but which are bridges between people. I would like to be able to say to people, right, that scene is in the play, now just show me how you got from A to B, let's improvise a bit. But, in a series it's very different, you don't have time, you know you haven't got time. I don't know, if one had more money, I suppose one would have spent more money on sets, one would have liked in a sense to make certain sets more lavish, I would have made Ingrid's set a bit more lavish. I don't know really, I can't think of many ways in this episode where I would have liked more money and time. The usual complaint is about extras, which isn't important in *Hazell,* but in a television series in general, you do a crowded pub scene with seven extras and you drive yourself out of your mind shooting them backwards, forwards, sideways, from down here, from up there, they're coming in from here, they're coming in from there; you know, that is one of the main worries.'

13 Making an Episode

At this point it may be useful to summarise the recording schedule. Originally *Hazell* was to have been a 13-part series (13 of course fitting neatly into a 52 week year of viewing). It was intended to go into production in early April 1977. At a late stage this date was brought forward to the beginning of January. Half way through production, in the summer of 1977, an industrial dispute involving the production assistants at Thames led to a decision to restrict the series to 10 episodes.

As is usual the recording order differed from the transmission order. The first to be recorded, *Hazell And The Weekend Man,* was intended to be transmitted near the end of the run, the reason being that inevitably the first episode will have teething problems and if it turns out to be less strong than the others it can be supported in the sequence of transmission by more successful episodes on either side. For the same reason the first episode to be transmitted, which had to be *Hazell Plays Solomon* because this one introduced the characters, was the next to last to be recorded. By this time it was hoped (correctly as it turned out) that everyone would have got well into their stride and produce an episode that would give the series the strong send off it needed if it was to be successful in the ratings.

Hazell And The Weekend Man was chosen to go first because at that time it was felt to be one of the most successful scripts, was written by a professional TV writer, and presented no major problems in production. It is also a rather quiet script in terms of mood and it was felt that this would help the actors ease themselves into their parts.

After the first recording there was a break of a month during which time the episode would be edited and available for discussion, to see what lessons could be learnt before proceeding to the next. Each episode was produced on a 2-week schedule, which normally ran as follows: Thursday, read through and first rehearsal; Friday, rehearsals, with the possibility of more on Saturday and Sunday; 3 days of locations filming on Monday, Tuesday, Wednesday; back to rehearsals on Thursday, which might be attended by the lighting director, lighting charge hand, camera crew and boom operators (this is the 'technical run'); on Monday the 'producer's run', while the scenery is being erected in the studio. Tuesday and Wednesday recording in the studios. On the Wednesday afternoon another group of people would be having the technical meeting preceding the rehearsals for the next episode starting the following day. For those people such as actors involved in all the episodes it's a gruelling schedule.

Into Production

After several months — indeed nearly a year — of planning and preparation, of seemingly countless discussions about concepts and scripts, casting and design and all the rest, *Hazell* was at last ready to go into production. On Tuesday 4 January 1977 the first episode, *Hazell And The Weekend Man*, began rehearsal. In this chapter we detail the cycle of events involved in the completion of a single episode, using the first one as a typical example though feeding in incidents which occurred in later episodes where this seems relevant.

Usually before the first rehearsal there will be one more meeting, the 'technical meeting', at which the director will outline any particular technical requirements so as to give those who may be involved, such as the lighting people or the technical supervisor, advance warning. The next day rehearsals begin with a read-through of the script, normally attended by the director and producer, the script editor and author, floor and stage managers, wardrobe and make-up, plus, of course, the entire cast. Thames have very limited rehearsal facilities at Teddington (only 2 rehearsal rooms) so outside halls usually have to be booked. Rehearsals therefore take place in the rather bleak and spartan surroundings of British Legion halls and boys' clubs, though the first episode was lucky enough to be booked into the slightly more appropriate setting of the Ballet Rambert rehearsal rooms.

There's little actual rehearsal at the initial read-through, the director simply sitting back and listening to the cast go through their lines. It's more an occasion for mutual introductions. However, there may well be some late changes in the script to communicate to the cast. Rehearsal schedules for everyone will be determined and the dates of the location filming confirmed. Frequently performers will be appearing in stage plays and their rehearsals will be scheduled for convenient times.

Perhaps the most important work to be done on this occasion concerns wardrobe and make-up. At this first read-through the director (Don Leaver), the producer (June Roberts), the costume designer

(Frank Van Raay) and the make-up artist (Audrey Proderick) went round to each of the actors and actresses in turn to discuss the appearance of the character they were playing. Care was taken, especially since this was the first episode, over the smallest details and this time too each of the running characters had to be looked at. Later, once the appearance of these characters had been set, less time would be needed for them.

The director will play a large part in these discussions. Don Leaver constantly referred to his own experience of how certain types of people in the real world actually looked. He commented on how the clerks in his bank dressed and was particularly concerned with the colour of the uniform to be worn by a milkman in the episode. The intention had been to dress him in blue; but blue is a colour that many directors will try to avoid on the screen because of the intensity with which it shows up. Accordingly the designers, Dave Ferris and Bill Palmer, were asked to go out and photograph some milkmen and their floats to see what such a character might typically wear. As it turned out the uniform adopted was based on a local dairy and was a kind of aubergine colour — not, perhaps, all that typical.

Once such details have been sorted out there will be a break for lunch and rehearsals will start in earnest in the afternoon. During the afternoon rehearsals will normally be quite short; Don Leaver preferred to finish by 3 if possible. This gives the director and others the chance to get back to the studio for meetings with designers, production assistants and so on.

Filming

At some point during rehearsals, usually as early as possible, 3 days were set aside for location filming. Several people on the production seemed to feel that this was a less than generous allowance for a series that aimed to make a feature of its London setting, since 3 days would not normally produce more than about 15 minutes of screen time on film. Alistair Reid, as we have seen managed to obtain 26 minutes of edited film for his episode, but this was considered quite exceptional.

The filming involved a completely different set of people from those who worked in the studio, apart from a very few personnel. Agreements with the unions require, besides a director and assistant (a function performed by the location manager), 2 people on camera, 2 on sound, an electrician and stage manager*. All filming is with standard 16mm. equipment. Since the film crew was almost invariably different from episode to episode, the onus was placed on the director to explain as quickly as possible what was going on — film crews appeared never to be involved in any meetings prior to shooting, except that the director might take whoever was in charge of the camera along when he went looking for locations. The fact that film crews were so little involved in preparations, and the rapid turn-over of personnel, undoubtedly does lead to difficulties, not least in continuity, as explained later. But these conditions of working also meant that on a series such as *Hazell,* where special trouble was taken to achieve a unified style, the film sequences could never be entirely integrated into the studio work. As regards lighting, for example, it was impossible to achieve in the film seequences the same effects as were being obtained in the studio because the studio lighting directors took no part in the filming.

There were particular problems about the kind of filming required on *Hazell.* Location work in Central London is never easy to organise. Certain places can't be filmed at all; police stations, for example. London Transport will not allow filming on the Underground, which meant that a sequence in the last episode which should have been set in the Underground had to be shot in a pedestrian underpass. There is also the perennial difficulty of parking, especially when you have a large generator lorry (to provide lights for night shooting, of which there was quite a bit), in addition to the equipment van, a mobile dressing room and the various cars to be used in the scenes. The location manager, Denver Thornton on the first, Eamonn Duffy on the rest, will therefore try to organise as many locations as possible within a small area, so as to cut down the number of special parking permits required and also because it saves previous time spent on having to pack up and drive through heavy traffic to new locations. Thus on *Hazell And The Weekend Man* it was important in terms of the plot that Victoria Station was used for the scene in the 'superloo' (which was booked by Thames for the day, and closed to the public). But the first scene has Hazell dropping off a lady at her hotel, and the location manager, Denver Thornton, couldn't find a large smart hotel of the type required in the immediate vicinity of the station. So to avoid

---

*While not being purist about the use of the term, we have been concerned in this book with the making of a *television* series. We have therefore not directly discussed the parts played by those who were only involved in the film inserts, since information about the work of a film crew is more readily available elsewhere.

having to move to another location for this one scene it was decided to use the brand new and very plush-looking BP building just round the corner instead. The designers stood by in case it wasn't possible to shoot the scene without getting in the tell-tale BP sign, in which case they would have made a new sign to put on top. (Normally a fee will be paid for the use of a building, though it doesn't seem a large one; £30 was one figure we heard mentioned.)

Five minutes of screen time in a day may not sound a lot, but it in fact leaves little time to spare. For the scenes shot in the 'superloo' the lighting cameraman, Norman Langley, had to walk round quickly making snap decisions where the lights were to be placed, decisions based mainly on what fittings were available to fix them on. He also had to walk round with the director and camera operator looking for possible flare spots — areas where the light would be reflected off glossy surfaces such as the vitreous enamel. There had been no opportunity to plan this in advance.

On *Hazell* there were a lot of scenes which took place at night, and all of these were actually shot at night (instead of being shot 'day for night', i.e., shooting during the day with a filter over the lens to simulate darkness). This made scheduling more complex (for example, there are union regulations about the number of continuous hours of filming that can be worked) and also more expensive, since people have to be paid extra at night. And on one episode, the third recorded, June wanted to get the same kind of effect that had been achieved in the feature film *Taxi Driver*, which had used no artificial light at night, only what was available in the streets. Shooting with available light is possible if a very fast film is used, but most laboratories won't promise to obtain an acceptable result in the processing. So at considerable expense the film shot in this way was sent to the lab in New York which had processed *Taxi Driver*. Clearly shooting this way was taking a risk, since there could be no guarantee that what was produced would come up to an acceptable standard, but it was felt worth taking the gamble for the extra 'realism' achieved.

Once the film has been shot the director will find time during rehearsals to view the rushes. The next stage is for the film editor to produce a rough cut and the director will then be involved in the final cut of what has been shot. Ideally a satisfactory print should be ready by the time the show enters the studio, both so that it can as far as possible be matched with the material shot on tape and also for continuity purposes. In practice on *Hazell* the tightness of the schedule meant that this was not always possible; surprisingly, perhaps, in view of the fact that the matching of film inserts and videotape is felt by many people in television to be quite a problem on shows employing both technologies. To them the differences appear obvious, even glaring. To what extent the audience is aware of the discrepancies must be an open question.

Rehearsals

Rehearsals are usually scheduled in such a way as to minimise the amount of time the artists are kept waiting about in generally uncomfortable rehearsal rooms, though since Nick Ball was in every scene he didn't get much of a rest. Most of the work of the director at this stage seems to involve three main concerns. Firstly, a lot of time is spent on the characters' motivations; what would a person like this do, how would they react, why are they behaving in this way? The next thing is pace. Scenes in *Hazell,* the directors were constantly impressing on the cast, had to be snappy. As rehearsals progress and the actors became familiar with their parts the length of the whole show, meticulously recorded by the production assistant, became shorter and shorter. The third important point was 'blocking'. The movements of the actors have to be organised not only in relation to the actions the plot requires of them and the physical location of the sets and props, but also in terms of the way the director intends to shoot the scene.

Obviously there's a lot more to it than this; we certainly don't mean to imply that anyone could do it, far from it. Directors wouldn't be paid their (comparatively) large salaries if they could. But the mechanics if not the art of direction appeared to us to come down to these factors, which can be summarised as firstly making the action believable and entertaining and secondly making it work technically. As examples of what the director can contribute towards the first one can cite two admittedly simple suggestions which Brian Farnham made during rehearsals of his episode, *Hazell And The Walking Blur.* Hazell's client in this case, the Walking Blur, is a bewildered and occasionally drunken Scotsman, played by Bill Henderson, who has come to London and unwittingly got caught up with some Soho gangsters. At one point Hazell finds himself wrestling with his client in a hotel corridor. Brian asked for, and got, a couple of extras to play the parts of an Arab and his wife who happen to be walking past at the time and observe this piece of strange behaviour. At another point Hazell comes back to the hotel to report to his client on the things he has unknowingly been involved in during a drunken binge. Richard Harris' script had suggested that the Scotsman might be washing his socks.

Brian enthusiastically endorsed this, and ordered that the set be constructed accordingly.

BF: 'I just liked the idea. There's this poor little man, he hasn't got many socks and he's got to wash them. His Mammy normally does it for him which is why he's not really making a very good job of it. It also gives a nice contrast to Hazell's report, because Hazell's come back to say that while he's been drunk he's been involved with gangsters, massage parlours, prostitutes, all those dreadful things.'

It's another example of how much effort goes into details, since the idea necessitated a plumber building into the hotel room set a wash basin that had running water and drainage.

Lighting and Technical Runs

Some 3 days before the production enters the studio the lighting director will attend a rehearsal and will follow it through with a floor plan of the studio with all the sets marked out. He'll ask the director about camera positions, and make notes on exactly where to place the lights. This information will be transferred onto a studio grid plan, which marks all the overhead grids along which the lights can be moved, and this will be given to the charge-hand electrician. The electrician will then come to the technical run the next day to see for himself how it works out.

Present at the technical run also will be the cameramen, boom operators and sound engineer, who will go round with the director as the actors run through the scenes, checking against their plans the positioning of their various equipment. By the end of this run-through everybody should be happy about what and who is going where. Of course it doesn't always work out perfectly once they get into the studio; it can happen for instance that there turns out to be no convenient place to get a sound boom in without causing awkward shadows. But at least the major problems should have been anticipated.

The technical run also serves a useful function for the cast. It's the first time they will have met the technicians they will be working with, and also it will be the first time that anyone from outside has seen the show. On *Hazell* people seemed to take great encouragement from the technicians laughing at the jokes.

The last day of rehearsal will be the producer's run. Usually the writer and the script editor were present also. By this time the work is all but complete and any adjustments can only be concerned with making improvements here and there. (Obviously if something major had been going wrong it wouldn't be left to the producer's run to talk about it.) After the producer's run there was always a discussion, sometimes quite lengthy, and this was usually concerned largely with the performances of the cast. Anything that is felt to be not quite right about the acting will have to be raised now because once the production enters the studio the director will have other things to think about.

While this is going on the sets will have arrived from Manchester, where they are built, and will be erected in the studio by the scene shifters. More than once the sets were late in arriving and work had to go on until midnight and even into the first day of production in the studio to get the sets up. At the same time the electricians will be rigging the lights.

Discussion of producer's run

As a small example of the kind of discussion which took place we can cite the following brief interchange. It occurred after the run of *Hazell And The Walking Blur*. In one scene Hazell is trying to retrace the steps of Alec, the Drunken Scotsman, played by Bill Henderson, and is interrogating a cockney taxi driver who had picked up Alec. Richard Harris, the author, was worried about the taxi driver's accent:

RH: 'I'd envisaged when the taxi driver is quoting Alec's words, "the broads, take me to the broads", that it would be said in Brooklyn.'
Brian Farnham: 'Don't you think it's funnier doing it in broad Scots? He actually did do it in Brooklyn but I made him change it.'
RH: 'Did you? Well, this was purely the way I saw it.'
BF: 'What I said was, I think you should do it in Alec's version.'
RH: 'Well, I think Alec would try to do it in Americanese.'
BF: 'But I think it should also have that touch of Scots there.'
June Roberts: 'Why doesn't he do half the lines in Brooklyn and the odd line in broad Scottish?'
BF: 'We actually have got more and more Scots, in fact we got Bill to say the lines for the taxi driver. I got Bill to do the lines in American and then he tried to copy him. I think it's funnier, we get more of a picture of this drunken Scotsman if we get a hint of the Scots.'
RH: 'My argument is that we know who we're talking about and it's funnier if we get him suddenly going into Brooklyn.'

BF: 'I think it *would* be funny if he went into Brooklyn. I don't think it's as funny if someone is reported as going into Brooklyn. But I know what you mean. I'll try to get him doing a combination of the two. What it should be is a Scotsman attempting to do Brooklyn. Which is pretty difficult for an Englishman to do.'

June's concern in these discussions, apart from her comments on individual performances, tended to be with maintaining a certain continuity between any one episode and the series as a whole. She was after all the only person in a position to do this. Thus she was immediately anxious if she felt that any of the regular roles started to go 'out of character'. She was also concerned with preserving a balance between the characters in any one episode, and ensuring that no-one is being acted out of a scene through another performer coming on too strong. In one episode, *Hazell Pays A Debt,* one character, O'Rourke, the most one in the story besides Hazell, ended up being of only marginal importance due to the way the scene was shot and edited. This had nothing to do with the performances, however, but was a result of the difficulties experienced both in the scripting and in putting it together in the studio. But no-one except the director is in a good position to know what the show will actually look like until it's on the screen — by which time it's very difficult to change it.

Studio days

The working area of Studio 1 at Teddington measures something like 100 ft. by 70 ft., with about 30 ft. between the floor and the lighting grid. (Studio 2 is somewhat smaller.) At one end, overlooking the working area, are the 3 control rooms, usually known as the gallery. In the centre room there are half a dozen seats facing away from the studio and towards a battery of monitor screens. One monitor is hooked up to each of the 4 cameras, one displays whatever shot is being recorded, and there are others showing material coming in from outside, such as film inserts, test cards and so on. In this room sit the technical supervisor, the vision mixer, the PA, the producer and the designer, script editor and writer if they are present. To the right, again facing away from the studio towards monitors, is the sound control room, accommodating the sound supervisor and the grams operator. To the left, in the other room and in front of another row of TV screens, sit the vision control operator, the lighting director and the person operating the lighting console together with, on occasion, the costume designer and make-up artist.

Grouped nearby, in a central complex serving all 3 studios, are the various technical facilities. In one area are the tele-cine machines, on which film material is converted into electronic signals to be transmitted onto monitor screens or recorded onto videotape. At Teddington there are 2 35mm machines and 2 16mm ones. These machines have their own separate colour controls, allowing the operator to adjust the colour of film to what is being recorded on tape in the studio. The machines can also compensate for variations in the colour of different film stocks. There are also 3 machines which will perform the same operation for still pictures made up into slides. These are used for such things as opening and closing titles and credits.

Another area contains the videotape recorders (V T Rs). For recording there are 5 machines, for the 3 studios, with a further 3 in the editing suite, all recording on 2" tape. Normally on a drama production there will simply be 1 V T R recording the show and the operator of the V T R is responsible for making sure that each scene has in fact been properly recorded before going on to the next. The operator needs to check not only that there is a picture but that it is technically acceptable. So with a drama production each scene is played back after recording. On light entertainment, apparently, there is not always time to do this, since it would involve keeping the studio audience waiting too long, and only the end of each sequence may be checked. With the old system of editing, known as the assembly method, the V T R operator has to log the number of every take against the footage counter on his V T R; on the new system, time-code editing, this logging is done automatically. (For an explanation of the two techniques, see 226 below. Before starting work the V T R operator has to 'line up' the machine; this involves, firstly, putting on a standard tape, always with the same pictures, to check that the machine is working correctly. Then the recording tape is put on and the operator has to ensure that its quality is acceptable — tapes are subject to wear and tear, and frequently have to be rejected. An hour is allowed for this process before recording begins.

To the outsider the electronic equipment appears almost unbelievably complex, and since this book is not a technical manual we don't propose to explain how it works, only give some explanation of what it does. But some idea of the sophistication of the technology involved is indicated by the fact that last year Thames spent £1.1 million on replacing and improving equipment, of which £¼ million went on the VTR suite at Teddington. The general function of all this equipment is, of course, to produce as faithful as possible a recording of what the cameras on the studio floor 'perceive', and then to make its retrieval and subsequent assembly as quick, easy and inexpensive as possible. An indication of the lengths to which engineers (and those who purchase their equipment) will go in the search for technical perfection is given by the fact that the VTRs have built into them an electronic system which automatically compensates for small defects in the tape. The oxide material with which the tape is coated occasionally gets rubbed off in parts, and this will show up on the recording as small specks of black, where no picture has been recorded at that point. But at the flick of a switch the VTR will scan such gaps and fill them in with the correct lines and colours.

As well as the VTR the cameras too have to be lined up before recording starts. This is the responsibility of the vision controller (or 'racks' as the job is often called, apparently from the time when the vision controller used to sit in front of racks and racks of equipment. Now he sits in front of a few monitor screens, the electronics being housed in a separate room.) Lining up cameras is done both visually and electronically. The main thing is to make sure that each camera is producing a picture with the same visual qualities as the others, with the same (and correct) definition and colours. To do it visually all the cameras on the floor are turned on to a dummy woman's head, and the picture from each matched up. (A human figure is used because flesh tones are the most crucial colours of all.) In the control room during recording the vision controller has 2 colour monitors in front of him, on one of which he can punch up the picture coming from any of the 4 cameras and on the other of which he sees the picture selected by the vision mixer to go out to the VTR. Thus he can at any time compare the various shots being taken to ensure consistency.

Studio 'norms'

Some weeks before the show goes into its first recording Brian Walcroft, the Drama Department manager, will agree with the producer and the heads of the technical sections what is called the studio 'norm'. This is the breakdown of the various staff and facilities which are needed for this particular show in the studio. The norms for are set out on pp. 216-7.

214

There are two ways of organising the recording of a show. You can either spend the first of your days in the studio rehearsing both the artists and the technicians, and the second day going right through recording each scene in turn. This was the pattern adopted on almost all the episodes of *Hazell*. Alternatively you can do what is called rehearse-record, which means that the rehearsal for each scene is followed immediately by its recording. The second method is much closer to that adopted in film-making, and it's perhaps not surprising that it was employed by Colin Bucksey in the episode he directed, *Hazell And The Maltese Vulture,* since Colin's previous experience had mostly been in films. (There was, however, another reason for using the method on this episode, which was that some heavy and complicated equipment was required and it was easier to get the shots involving this out of the way on the first day.) On another episode too, *Hazell Pays A Debt,* one scene was recorded on the first day. This involved smashing some fish tanks with a shotgun, and scheduling it for the first day meant that if anything went wrong the tanks could be set up again for the next day.

There is some debate as to which system is preferable. John Lopes, floor manager on several episodes, favoured rehearse-record.

JL: 'It's physically more tiring, I think, but I prefer it because then a scene is finished, it's in the can and out of the way. I also think that rehearse one day, record the next is leaving something to chance in that, though I don't have any statistics to prove it, we may not have quite as much time for re-takes as when we do rehearse-record.'

For other people it may not be such a good system. At least two of the directors expressed a preference for leaving all the recording till the second day. Apart from the fact that with rehearse-record they are likely to spend 2 whole days rushing from studio floor up to the gallery and back down again, in order both to keep in touch with the actors and see what it looks like upstairs, there is the more important consideration that with the recording all on one day the actors can to an extent save themselves and give it everything on the second day. The tension that results from having to tape the show in a single day is also felt by some directors to raise the adrenalin level, and produce better performances all round. Actors, on the other hand, seem to prefer rehearse-record. That way they feel they see more of the director during actual recording (if the second day is entirely recording the director will

215

Production: HAZELL			
STUDIO SCHEDULE		(HRS)	
DAY 1	CREW TECH. RUN/TECH. RIG SET AND LIGHT		SOUND (No Rig) CAMERAS ELECTRICIANS
DAY 2	Camera Reh 09.30 — 13.00 Lunch Break 13.00 — 14.00 Camera Reh 14.00 — 18.30	8 HRS	OPERATIONAL SL STUDIO ATTEND. CAMERAS VIS. CONTROL SOUND VIS. MIXER SCENES PROPS.
DAY 3	Line Up & Make Up 08.30 — 09.30 Camera Reh/VTR 09.30 — 13.00 Lunch Break 13.00 — 14.00 Line Up Check 14.00 — 14.30 Camera Reh/VTR 14.30 — 18.45 Tech Clear 18.45 — 19.00 Tech Ops Supper Break 19.00 — 20.00	7¾ HRS	FLOOR ASSISTAN FLOOR MANAGER STAGE MANAGER MAKE-UP WARDROBE LIGHTING DIR
POST-PRODUCTION FACILITIES			
	VTR EDITING		Editor Engineer
	SOUND PREPARATION		Grams Op
	SOUND DUBBING		Sound Sup Grams Op

216

	SHEET No: 12F

. OF REW.	NOTES
5	*STUDIO 1* — 4 CAMERA NORM OR *STUDIO 2* — 4 CAMERA NORM Special video effects and chroma-key facilities available on both studio mixers
	FACILITIES — DAY 2 Telecine and colour slide facilities available 09.30 — 09.45 for checking opening and closing titles. Other technical requirements to be booked through Central Planning. 1 x 35mm B/W slide machine available all day. REQUIREMENTS OUTSIDE THIS NORM TO BE DISCUSSED WITH STUDIO SUPERVISOR.
ɔject to ipt	FACILITIES — DAY 3 Telecine and colour slide requirements to be booked through Central Planning. 1 x 35mm B/W slide machine available all day. 1 x VTR 09.30 — 18.45 to record in simplex. REQUIREMENTS OUTSIDE THIS NORM TO BE DISCUSSED WITH STUDIO SUPERVISOR.
	2 days per programme
1	1 day per programme
1 1	1 day per programme

217

tend to spend most of it in the gallery). Actors also feel they're more likely to forget points made to them the previous day.

Whichever system is adopted the technicians will arrive at 8.30 a.m. to line up the equipment, and the director, the stage and floor managers will check that the sets are properly dressed. The artists are called onto the set by the assistant floor manager at 9.30, having previously put on their costumes and been made up. Painters, scene shifters, electricians, carpenters will all be doing last minute jobs. Once rehearsal begins the director will remain on the floor, though paying more attention by this stage to things like cameras and lights than to the cast. The director will watch the rehearsal on one of the monitors hung from the studio ceiling, often with his/her back to the set, since the important thing is not what is happening on the set as such but what view of it the cameras are getting.

A few days before the production enters the studio the director will have written out his camera script. This is the script which details all the camera movements for each scene, and is organised according to the sequence in which each scene will be shot. This may well differ radically from the order of scenes dictated by the logic of the plot, and will be determined by, for example, whether an actress needs half an hour for a costume change, in which case another scene can be slotted in while she is in the changing rooms.

It's quite common while work goes on in the studio for the director to decide that extra shots are required or for a cameraman to find that he experiences difficulties with a particular movement or angle, and accordingly adjustments will be made to the camera script. But by the end of the first day everyone should have a precise knowledge of what is expected of them during the following day's recording. Sets will be touched up and any last minute problems dealt with (for example, glare reflected from a window-pane).

Sets and props

Directors will have discussed in detail with the designers the kind of sets and props they want, but until they actually get onto the set it is unlikely they will see what has been produced. (The same will generally be true of costumes.) So the first day on the set the director is apt to walk round the studio floor taking a good look. Don Leaver on the first episode entered every set asking questions like, 'Is this real? Do we believe this curtain/that chair in the hall? Would such a person live/work in this room?' He went through Maureen's office saying this or that object wouldn't be found in an office, and asking for its removal.

Directors may also find they need to change the position or the height of the furniture in order to get the exact framing they want. Furniture can be raised on '4 blocks', pieces of wood with 4" steps cut into them.

One problem that arose on *The Weekend Man* props concerned some porcelain figurines which Hazell has to examine. As he does so he comments on them: 'Those two are imitations, I reckon. That looks like a Sampson. They specialised in copies, very deceptive. Now that one . . . that's a Ralph Wood, I reckon. That's what I call art, that's something special.' In fact the props people found that Ralph Wood figurines were too difficult to get, so Meissen ones were substituted. But when Don Leaver wanted to zoom in close to them someone pointed out that those in the studio were also only copies. Don was annoyed by this and wanted to know why they weren't real. He demanded that some real ones be got, and quick! Someone muttered that the real ones were only to be found in museums, though all the same there was a general scurry of movement towards telephones. But in the end copies had to be used after all.

Realistic detail seems to count for a lot. On one episode Hazell has to hand over a large sum of money to Gordon Gregory. For the scene a large amount of actual cash was borrowed from the studio accounts office, and a security guard stood by till it was returned. On *The Weekend Man* people went to a lot of trouble over some photographs. One of them had to represent an adult character in childhood. The picture is only on screen for a few seconds, but a still photographer was hired for a day to go out on location with a minibus, a child actor, the costume designer and make up artist to take the photograph.

On *Hazell And The Maltese Vulture* Frank Van Raay, the costume designer, produced some very elaborate costumes for two girls who had to appear in a short blue-movie sequence. Dressed up as chickens they are pursued by another character dressed as a fox. Besides the time spent making up the costumes, the scene took quite a time to set up and shoot. In the event, however, it appears on the screen only at some distance on a television set that Hazell is watching, and in black and white (it being argued that the character who had made the film wouldn't have had access to colour facilities). To an outsider it seemed to involve a lot of trouble and expense, but obviously such attention to detail is felt to be worth the effort.

Recording

On the second day, when recording was taking place, the director would spend most of the time upstairs in the gallery. There is direct contact via a radio mike with the studio floor and in particular the floor manager, who acts as the director's representative while the director is in the gallery. If the previous day has been spent 'blocking', with no recording, the usual pattern will be for there to be one swift rehearsal of a scene and then a take. A clock, with the number of the scene on it, will be shown on the monitor screens to count down the seconds till recording starts. Three seconds before action is due to begin the vision mixer fades the clock to black and then punches up the picture from the camera taking the first shot.

The usual practice in television is to record a sequence of several shots in a single take (whereas in film, of course it is normal, given that there is only one camera, to break down a scene into a number of shots and take each one separately, pausing after each to reposition the camera). During the sequence, then, the vision mixer will, following the camera script and any additional instructions from the director, cut between the various cameras until the end of the sequence is reached.

the same scene as on p. 197, now in the studio

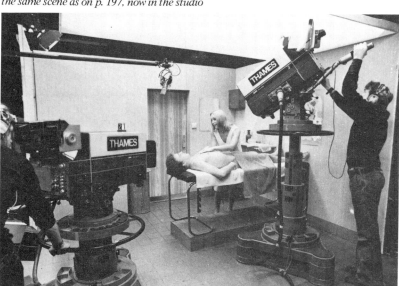

Hazell And The Walking Blur in the studio

At the end if the director is satisfied s/he will indicate to the technical supervisor, who will order the V T R operator to stop the tape. This will then be replayed and the director will decide whether it's a good enough tape to go on to the next scene or whether another take is needed. However if something goes wrong during a take such as an actor fluffing a line, the director may ask to keep the tape running and go back to the start. Directors don't much like asking for the tape to be stopped if there has been a mistake, since there is then a delay while the tape has to be rewound, the clock punched up and the whole count-down gone through again. Technical supervisors, on the other hand, prefer to stop the tape. This is partly because unless the clock is put on again there can be confusion as to which number take has which shots on it, and partly because each videotape runs for only 90 minutes. This should be enough to record the 35 minutes or so of studio screen time and the transfers of the film inserts, but if the tape is kept running too much eventually it will run out and a fresh one will have to be lined up. This can take at least half an hour of valuable studio time, during which everyone else has nothing to do but hang about. It happened once, on *Hazell Pays A Debt*, at a time when the show was already running behind schedule, and produced some rather tense moments in the gallery.

It will be clear that the multiple camera set-ups of the television studio are an inherently faster system of working than that adopted in film-making, though in order to produce this speed certain sacrifices have to be made. For example, the fact that the set has to be lit in such a way that it can be shot from up to 4 camera positions at once must involve the lighting director in certain compromises. However, not only is the system faster in itself; less time is allowed than would normally be the case on a film set for retakes. Whereas on a film it is not unusual for there to be 5 or 6 takes of a single shot, in a television studio it is very rare, unless something is seriously going wrong, for there to be more than 3 takes of a scene. On some of the episodes, towards the end of the day when time was running out, some quite lengthy scenes were shot in a single take; though the kind of pressure this puts the actors under couldn't be supported throughout a whole day.

Once the director is satisfied with a scene the whole company moves on to the next set. If the one that's been finished with is a stock set (i.e., one that will be used again on other episodes) all the props will be stored in large lockable trolleys ready for next time. Sets that will not be wanted again will be struck, the flats sent back to the set constructors to be used again and the hired props returned. Anything else, such as specially made props, will probably be scrapped. Thus as the day goes on the studio floor, which began by being extremely crowded, with sets all round the side leaving only the centre of the floor clear in which to manoeuvre equipment, will become progressively emptier. (It's remarkable, considering how little space there seems to be on the studio floor, just how small many of the sets are. The pub set in *Hazell Works For Nothing*, which on the screen looks sizeable and busy, was nothing but a pillar, a small length of counter, a couple of door frames and a few tables and chairs.)

Recording usually finished at 6.45. By 7 o'clock the whole company was in the studio bar. To outsiders it's noticeable that though there is a certain amount of fraternisation during the immediate after-show euphoria, after a while the company would usually split up into technical staff and 'production' staff. In part this was no doubt merely a reflection of a difference of interests and the fact that technical crews usually work together on a variety of shows and thus know each other well, while production staff may have a certain continuity on the one show but may not work together again once it is over. But it is also clear that television, like other occupations, has its own caste system.

14 Editing and Dubbing

A television studio is organised around the principle of live transmission. The personnel employed, the location of the control rooms and the division of labour within them, the use of multiple cameras and the headphone system of communication are all designed to enable last minute changes and decisions to be made whilst a programme is on the 'air'. With the development of modern production techniques and the introduction of V T R, programmes rarely go out live and thus the situation has changed somewhat. Generally speaking, studio practices have remained much the same — television teams have not reverted to the modes of working of a film crew — but the possibilities of television have increased as the technology has become more sophisticated. It is now possible to 'capture' in 2 days in a television studio what would take a film crew weeks.

The initial form of video-editing — what is termed assembly editing and at Thames is referred to as 'Editech' (the name of the company that made their equipment) — which is still in use, is fairly clumsy to operate and therefore encourages the retention of sequential recording, even if the programme is recorded dis-continuously, for the sake of speed and ease. The recent development of electronic systems of editing has meant that there is now no need to record in sequence and that video has become as flexible as film if not more so. But first we will describe assembly editing.

On a series like *Hazell* an average of 35 minutes will be recorded in the studio and together with the 15 minutes of film that have to be transferred on to tape (again on average they will usually use 2 tapes — allowing for re-takes etc. Professional V T R tape is 2" wide and is divided into 4 sections. One is an audio track for the soundtrack, one is the cue track onto which are placed the edit pulses for synchronising·purposes, one is the control track that governs the speed of the tape and the fourth, which constitutes approximately 1.75" of the tape, is the video (image) track. Bot the P A and the V T R operator will catalogue the recording so that when it comes to editing every take can be located quickly and efficiently. If at all possible the editing suite will be booked for the 2 days in the week following recording. Long hours will be worked on those days

— on the first it is normal to work for 12 hours and on the second for 9. The people present will be the director, the PA, the video tape editor and one or two video tape operators.

The procedure is as follows. Three video tape recorders are used. The intention is to transfer what has been recorded, which normally exists on 2 tapes, onto a third master tape on which the programme will be 'assembled' in the correct order. (On modern equipment the loss in quality that always occurs when video dubbing is negligible on a 'first generation' transfer.) Thus the 2 recorded tapes are placed onto adjacent machines, the director will request the first scene, the PA will provide the reference for the operator and he will locate it. If there is only one operator, which is often the case, only one machine will be used due to necessary union regulations but this does make for a very time consuming operation if a director wishes to cut from a scene at the end of one tape to a scene at the end of the other tape. The rewinding of each tape will take 12 minutes and each tape will have to be lined up every time it is used.

Meanwhile the editor will have lined up his own VTR and the master tape — exactly the same procedures are involved as lining up the equipment on recording days. All this work will be done by hand in that the tapes will be marked with a special pencil (as in audio tape editing) and will be finely positioned by manual movement of the spool.

The first task to be undertaken when editing is the transferring of the edited film stock to video tape via a tele-cine machine. Then, the opening credits will be placed on the master tape and editing can begin. The director will already know fairly precisely what he wants to do and which takes and bits of take that he will want to use due to the fact that he will have watched what was recorded a number of times on a ½" machine in his office. This is done to save time that would be expensively spent if he was making decisions in the editing suite.

Under the assembly editing system any special effects that are required such as fades or wipes have to be put on the tape by the vision mixer at the recording stage. Assembly editing simply allows the transferring of material from one tape to another in a different order. In the pub scene that Moira Armstrong shot in *Hazell Works For Nothing,* she wanted to use a number of wipes to indicate the passing of time. The scene had to be re-run a number of times in order to get the wipes exactly as she wanted them. This is not the case with electronic editing as will be explained in the next section.

Once a scene has been transferred to the master tape, to the director's satisfaction, then they will move on to the next shots required and in this way the programme will be gradually 'assembled'. If a director wishes to 'drop' one or more shots into the middle of a complete take, it is possible but extremely tricky and can mean losing the original dub if a mistake is made i.e. the previous take will have to be transferred again.

During this whole process the PA (and the editor) will be timing the programme. The director will already know (from previous timings) if time has to be saved or extended and will be constantly watching for moments which can be cut or allowed to run, and will therefore want an accurate and up-to-date timing.

Time-code editing

Time-code editing is a good deal more sophisticated than the manual assembly method. In essence it allows you to use video tape as though it were film. The first 4 episodes of *Hazell* were recorded on this new system and the first 3 were edited before it became fairly definite that there was going to be a dispute between the PAs and Thames over its use. Thus the subsequent episodes were recorded using the old system.

What happens with time-code is as follows. Through the VTR room already described is another room which looks something like a tiny television studio control room. There is a large console at which sits the VTR editor and his assistant and behind them sit the director and the PA. In front of them are the TV monitors and speakers. (The tapes are on the machines outside, with just one operator watching them.) The director will ask to see the first scene and the PA will read off the code number. This the operator will punch up on his controls and the machine will automatically locate the scene because that information was printed into the tape when it was recorded. The director will then ask to see either the next scene or shots that s/he might wish to drop into the middle of the first scene (e.g., close-ups). Time-code editing allows a director to 'drop in' much more easily than the older method will; the machine will also allow the director to edit down to a single frame and with an accuracy that is not possible by hand, however skilled the operators. In addition all the technical effects like mixing, fading, wiping, superimpositions, negative reversals, etc., can be added at this stage, which is not possible in assembly editing. This means that a director can try out all sorts of different effects if wished and still decide against them. In the studio these effects take up time and the

226

director has to be certain that s/he wants to use them. Once done they can't be changed without recording the scene again. Thus time-code editing can save money because the most important stage of production in television is in the studio when time is at a premium and you have anything up to 100 people to be paid. In the editing suite there are 5.

The V T R editor sits behind a control panel and punches up the codes for the different sequences and shots and also the code for whatever type of cut or effect the director requires. In addition, because the equipment is so precise it is possible to easily cut scenes together out of a pile of single shots, as Alistair Reid did on *Hazell Pays A Debt*. This meant that in the studio he recorded the programme virtually as if he had been shooting a film.*

As we have said, the editing suite will be booked for 2 days in which time *Hazell* has to be finished. It is extremely difficult to find more time both because of the tight scheduling for the facilities and also because directors are usually freelance and much too busy to be able to easily find the time to keep coming back.

Dubbing

As a result of programmes being recorded dis-continuously and out of sequence it became necessary to adopt a method of processing the sound track after the final video tape edit. If, for example, continuous background music is required to run throughout a scene which has been recorded in short sections then it won't be possible to record the music at the same time as the dialogue. Thus post-production sound dubbing is necessary in the modern television studio. The system that Thames has used for the last 7 years is the 'Medway' system (*M*usic, *E*ffects and *D*ialogue *Way*); this, with the introduction of time-code editing, is being replaced by the Studer system.*

The procedure for sound recording at Thames is that each

* Film works on the principle that 24 frames pass through the gate of the projector every second, whilst television works on the principle that an electronic dot scans the lines of the television screen alternatively, covering them all 25 times every second; i.e. the dot will cover odd numbers 1-625 followed by even numbers 2-624 25 times a second. Both systems thus produce the illusion of movement by running together a series of discrete static pictures.

* The Studer TLS 2000 System was adopted largely because of the introduction of the time-code edit system for video editing, as it uses exactly the same code system. The Medway system doesn't use that code, but less efficient system, which meant that on time code edited tapes the cues have to be erased and replaced by the Medway code for dubbing. If it was subsequently decided to re-edit a programme this made for great difficulties. The other big advantage of the Studer System is that it offers 16 tracks which makes it an altogether more versatile system.

programme has allocated to it a sound supervisor and grams operator who will stay with the programme through all stages of production including pre-recording sessions (necessary, in the case of *Hazell*, for the voice-overs) and all post-production work. They will change however, from episode to episode. Once a programme has been edited (as described in the previous section) it will undergo a sound dub, usually the following week, and, as with the video editing suite, the dubbing theatre will be booked for 2 days.

A copy of the edited programme will be made on a 1" helical scan tape (thus leaving the expensive 2" VTRs free for recording and editing) which will be used as the guide, and the sound track (i.e., the dialogue) transferred from the 2" video tape onto an audio tape. On the first 'preparation' day of the dubbing session the director, PA and gram operator will select, record and edit the music and special effects onto ¼" sound tape. It is not normally necessary for the sound supervisor to attend this session and he therefore will only do so if something complex is involved. The incidental music for *Hazell* was almost entirely taken from the library, which contains records of music recorded in different styles expressly for this purpose. As mentioned in the chapter on music and titles, if any commercially distributed music is used there can be problems clearing the British and foreign rights.

Once these tracks have been recorded and timed to coincide with the video-tape (and on the 1" machine the 'time' is placed on the image so that the operator always knows exactly where he is) the different sound sources will be placed onto adjacent tracks of the Medway 6-track tape. One track will take the dialogue, one the music, one the special effects, one will be the cue track (as on the video tape). The different sounds will be placed on to these tracks so that they synchronise with the image — although sometimes a director might precisely not want the two to be synchronised. For example, in order to heighten the effect of O'Rourke's death Jim Goddard (in the dubbing of the re-edited version of the programme) placed the gun shot sound slightly out of synch with the image. The gun shot itself had been re-recorded using a sound from the effects library because the microphones in the studio are designed to record the dialogue and will automatically compensate for, and thus soften, any loud noise.

Once these 3 tracks are mixed and laid down to the director's satisfaction then they will all be mixed together and transferred to the sixth, composite track. The laying down, synchronising, mixing and transferring of the different sound sources on the 6-track machine will be done on the second day with the sound supervisor present. Whilst the gram operator will be operating the tape machines with the tapes prepared the day before, the sound supervisor, as in the studio, will be operating the mixing equipment and the 6-track machine. Once this has all been completed and one composite track produced this will be transferred back onto the audio track of the edited master video tape.

The fifth, miscellaneous, track can be used for one of two purposes. It can be used either if there are some very complicated special effects, or to record foreign language dialogue after the programme has been sold to a foreign language country. If it is necessary to have both then there are problems which the Studer system solved.

As mentioned earlier all programmes have the studio sound recorded simultaneously on a ¼" tape recorder. This second sound track might not be used at all but is there as a safeguard in case short sections of dialogue need to be replaced (and a scene which is intricately edited might end up with a range of different voice levels), or if there is slight damage to the edge of the V T R tape.

As a way of illustrating some of the relations between editing and dubbing technique and the aesthetic choices involved, we are printing part of our interview with Brian Farnham. As the reader will see, at certain points we tried to press him to analyse why he edited *Hazell And The Walking Blur* in the way that he did; we cannot claim to have been more than partly successful, since it is clear that we were asking questions about what is largely an instinctual process.

BF: One of the great difficulties of tape editing as opposed to film editing is the pace of the thing as a whole, and in the final analysis with today's recording techniques, where everything is recorded in a fragmentary fashion, scene by scene, bit by bit, the only person who really knows what the end piece is going to look like is the director. Therefore the pace of the thing is always put together in the editing, but you've got to be aware of that a long way before, while you're actually shooting it; you've got to be aware of the fact that here's a scene which of necessity must go slower, it must be a longer, slightly more drawn-out scene, therefore shape-wise we can't have too many of those together because otherwise the audience are going to go to sleep. It's just the whole shape of movement, of pace, of holding something up and then suddenly rushing forward to get the audience excited, to sort of move them on — now that is much more difficult in my experience in tape editing than it is in film editing. With film you can take it apart and put it together again, you can cut a scene together and say, right, that's it, no it needs to go quicker there, it needs to do this, we need more close ups, we need to cut it faster or we need to do it slower. Tape editing, you really get basically one go at it, and that's the final assembly. In a way, in the studio you can tell whether the pace of a scene is right, but whether the pace of the thing as a whole is right, is much more difficult to tell.

INT: *Presumably there simply isn't time to take a scene to pieces if you think it isn't right, and re-edit it — it's mostly a question of editing scenes together, isn't it?*
BF: In some cases there's time, but it's also a question of money. You see the only way you can really find out is when you've got the whole thing together and then you look at it a day later and say Oh, Christ, it's slow there, it really needs to move much quicker there. Film is very easy to adjust, tape is much more difficult, because you've got to go back and you're going down what they call a generation again, because it's got to be re-recorded one more time onto another tape, so you're losing definition, although that's not important nowadays because the quality is much higher.
INT: *You can cut bits out but you can't add in . . . Do you ever try to cover yourself that way in the studio rather like you would with film — do a bit again in case you need it.*
BF: Yes, I did slightly on this. I overlapped certain scenes or ran the whole scene twice — a couple of scenes in the hotel bedroom where I shot it once and then took different walls out and shot it another way, just in case. Also in case something different happens I might do it, especially when you get someone like Bill Henderson playing a drunk. He is very much an instinctive actor — you know he might suddenly do something on one take that he's never done before, and you think it's marvellous, hang on to it, one needs it, one's got to use it even if the rest of the scene wasn't right — if you've got time. Obviously time is very limited, if you haven't got time, well, then you don't.
INT: *It's quite interesting that you mention that because it could happen that Bill would do something you might think is marvellous, but he might not actually be in the shot . . .*
BF: Oh quite, I might be on Nick . . . It's the luck of the draw, it's as simple as that. One has on occasions said — this is where you've got to know when to say it and when   to say it — you did so and so there and it's absolutely marvellous. And Bill will say, what'd I do? And you can't explain what he did, I mean he just did it, he instinctively

did it because he's an actor and that's what he's there for — you just hope he does it again the next time.

INT: *Suppose that happens and you're on Nick (just taking Bill as an example) would you ever take that scene again only this time on Bill?*

BF: Yes, if I had time . . .

INT: *Even though it's not scripted . . .*

BF: If I had time I would. I mean I always map out anyway for myself a plan when I know I should be at such and such a shot by such and such a time, and if I think according to my own schedule that I've got time, then I would, but nine times out of ten it wouldn't happen again because Bill wouldn't know what he'd done anyway. Somehow once he's aware of something that he's done instinctively and it's good, and he hasn't really been aware of the fact that he's done it, then it becomes false because he's trying to give you what has happened just like that. There are many cases in this one where something just happened, and it happened just at that moment, the shot was right, Bill was right. That marvellous moment when he said, 'Oh you're not a bad fellow.' I'd intended taking that on a totally different shot, on a close-up of him, in fact, but what we got was him full length . . . sprawled out on the bed in a raincoat, which is much funnier, much better. So in fact my first instinct was wrong, I'd intended to be in there, close . . . 'Oh. You're not a bad fellow Jimmy' — but it's much funnier to see the man sprawled out full length on the bed.

INT: *It's interesting watching Bill to see how it was different almost every time.*

BF: Oh, yes absolutely. You see this is the great difficulty, the most difficult thing is to play a drunk, and to play a man who is drunk most of the time as Bill had to be, and keep it fresh in his own mind. This is again where the director has got to decide just how much you rehearse the scene because with a scene like that you could over-rehearse it, so that the actor gets so fed-up with it and nothing begins to happen, he's just over-rehearsed — one just has to know. Because television is so much a one-off thing (it's unlike a film in that you can do 2 or 3 takes in television, but you can't really go up to the 17, 18, 19 takes which you can on film), I always like the actors to go into the studio feeling that they are just slightly under it, because it gives them an edge, otherwise they feel too confident.

INT: *Another question about editing; there's a scene where Hazell is talking to the fiancee, and you cut into the next scene which is the Stag coming down the Edgware Road, and the first time that you cut that in the editing room, you cut straight into Hazell's voice-over, and you and the VTR editor seemed to think that wasn't quite right, and so you re-edited it with a pause. Can you say why?*

BF: I can analyse why, though it's an instinctive thing . . . I mean you can either put stuff together or you can't. But analysing it, the reason is to give the audience a chance to say — there's the Stag going down the . . . they don't know it's the Edgware Road, they just know it's moving fast in traffic and overtaking another car . . . and then, oh, there's the voice-over. What was happening was that we were getting voice-over and car together, and they would have missed the first bit of the voice-over — I swear the audience would not have taken in the first half dozen words of the voice-over. And they need time to react to the gag of 'you can take a cheque?', 'no, no . . .' which the actors did so beautifully anyway, so that one wanted to hold on to the end bit anyway, and then give the audience a chance to say, 'change of scene . . .'

INT: *I think that's one of the things that interests us a good deal about the whole process — an awful lot of people are doing things that they instinctively think are right — the question is . . . why is it right?*

When we were watching you, you were overlapping, you were having somebody in the next scene speaking for half-a-dozen frames of the previous scene — why? It's a nice effect . . .

BF: And it does give pace . . . I mean it just moves the thing on.

INT: *And yet what's strange about that is that it's a highly artificial thing (which is fair enough, there's no reason why it shouldn't be), and yet a large part of most people's time seems to be concerned with making it 'real' and as close to life as possible, and yet here you are actually using very artificial techniques.*

BF: Absolutely. An interesting case in point occurs after they walk down the subway and they talk to the busker the first time we meet her. He comes back to Hazell and says, where are we going now? And Hazell says, first of all we're going to lock the car up and then get the loot. It's the first time the Scotsman's ever thought of the money he's found as loot, and he says, Loot?! And then we overlap with the beginning of the next scene — £1,420, Gregory is saying, and we overlapped it. I guarantee that 99% of the audience would never be aware that we overlapped that, but the fact that we did would tie up totally with the fact that his reaction to the money being loot was determined by the amount of money involved.

INT: *So it's not instinctive . . .*

BF: There, no. That wasn't instinctive, it was an absolute deliberate thing, but the case that you were talking about earlier *was* an instinctive thing. The only person who knows, or thinks he knows, what the show is going to look like in the end is the director, because he's the only person who can put it together. It may well be, and it happens quite frequently, that when it's put together, and the producer and author and Head of Drama see it, then they are going to say, that doesn't work, that's got to come out. They may have very good reasons for it, and if they justify those reasons to me, then I've got no objections. If they can't justify their reasons then I put my foot down, then I say, No. Over my dead body. Although theoretically I suppose the person who does have the last word is the Head of Drama, which is Verity in this case. If she had really felt very, very strongly she could have taken a scene out. In *Rock Follies* she said, I think a scene should go. I said I don't think it should go, the producer said it should go, I said I don't think it should go; the writer said it really should stay. So there we were. There you've got four people, and it was two and two, and in the final analysis I looked at it and I said No, I think it should stay; I think it needs at that point in the script to slow down and just be gentle for a minute — and they let it stay. Whether I was right or wrong I don't know. Neither Verity nor Andrew Brown felt strongly enough to want it taken out, but I felt strongly enough to want it left in.

INT: *You were talking about rhythm and so on in editing, and the fact that you are aware when you're actually working of some kind of rhythm . . .*

BF: Oh yes, which you often have to adjust when it comes down to the final analysis. You can have thought that is going to be a big close-up, but then the actor is giving you so much that in a big close-up it looks ridiculous so you pull it back and do it in ordinary close-up, you know. That is a constantly evolving thing, and that's why you've got to be awake the whole time in the studio. And you find that certain actors will walk through their parts virtually in rehearsal and dress run, and it'll come to the take and suddenly they will burst forth . . . and you will think, what's going on here? Which is very unfair to the people they're acting with, for a start, to be suddenly bombarded with. But it does happen and then you go back and say, I think we'll do that again. Quite often you'll cut from 2-shot to single, 2-shot to single, 2-shot to single, and then single to single, because you'll want to make a point with that. The audience would never be aware of that, but it would make the point. Without them being aware that it had happened, that you're trying to control them — Television is much more a directors' medium than an actors'.

INT: *Is it your concern that the audience isn't aware?*

BF: Oh yes, I would hate to think that the audience was aware. I mean if the audience is ever aware of camera technique and the fact that I'm doing such and such, then I've failed, I think. Except in certain circumstances where you want deliberately to alienate them, or deliberately distance them and make them say, look . . . here are these people doing this, aren't they silly, here they are and here's my camera watching them. But not on something like *Hazell* — if they're aware of camera techniques on *Hazell* then I think it's gone wrong.

15 Post-mortem on the First Episodes

Hazell And The Weekend Man, the first episode to be recorded, was unusual in that it was the only one to be both recorded and edited before another episode was begun. This was done deliberately in order to afford an opportunity for the production team to discuss this first effort in some detail and to learn from their experience. (At one time it had been intended to have a break of some 2 or 3 months between the recordings of the first and second episodes but rescheduling produced a gap of only 5 weeks. There was also to have been a similar gap half way through the series, but again rescheduling proved necessary and production had to continue straight through.)

Present at the discussion after this first effort had been viewed were Gordon Williams, Terry Venables, Nick Ball, Richard Harris and Tony Hoare, with June Roberts coming in towards the end. Much of the discussion centred, not surprisingly, round the character of Hazell himself. Gordon took the view that part of the attraction of characters such as Hazell and his ancestor Philip Marlowe was the air of mystery that surrounded them. To give away too much about the character would be to remove this mystery. But others pressed for more clarification. Richard Harris wanted to dig deeper into Hazell's motivation. What, for example, was the purpose of Hazell's non-stop wisecracks? Were they a defence and if so against what? Richard pressed for more revelation of the darker side of Hazell's character — the marriage breakdown, the drinking problem. (This first episode, which of course Richard had scripted, is certainly fairly light in tone, both in the sense of putting Hazell into some comic, even farcical, situations, and of having as its central 'villain' a mild-mannered bank clerk who doesn't in the event commit any crime at all.) Gordon's response to this was to suggest that the last scene could have ended more sharply. At the beginning of the episode Hazell gets an unwelcome visit from a very young tax inspector. At the end, having completed his investigation of the bank clerk (who had intended to run off with some of the bank's money) Hazell returns to his office where he again encounters Mr Arnold, the tax man. The scene ends like this:

ARNOLD:Just happened to be passing, Mr Hazell.

HAZELL: Yeah, well, unfortunately, Mr Arnold, I'm just on my way out.

ARNOLD: Oh. Will you be long?

HAZELL: Actually, I'm gonna rob this bank and piss off to Jamaica wher de rum come from.

ARNOLD: You're what?

HAZELL: People do, you know. And if they don't actually do it they dream about it.

ARNOLD: I don't quite understand what you're saying, Mr Hazell.

HAZELL: Not now, maybe . . . but in a few years time you'll understand, believe me . . . come on . . . you can buy me a cuppa tea and I'll tell you all about it.

Gordon remarked that if the scene had ended with Hazell telling the tax man to piss off while wearing a broad but unfriendly smile one would have got some sense of the hardness that lies beneath his apparently affable exterior. As it turned out Richard's response to this discussion was to write into the next episode he scripted (*Hazell And The Rubber-Heel Brigade*) a less light-hearted story line, in which Hazell is investigated for possible corruption during his service in the police and also comes into contact with his former wife.

Gordon was also concerned at the discussion that London itself didn't feature strongly enough. The location shooting had been done in the suburbs with the exception of some sequences in the gents' at Victoria Station, and Gordon felt this wasn't quite what he had had in mind when he had wanted London to feature as the second 'star' of the series. He suggested that a lot of stock material of London street scenes without Hazell in them should be shot, to be inserted into later episodes. This was done for one episode, but the idea wasn't followed up much. The problems of what could be done within the constraints of a television series — budgetary and otherwise — to give London the presence on screen that Gordon was seeking was never perhaps to be fully resolved. The director of the last episode, Brian Farnham, was to remark that by the end of the series London seemed to have shrunk to Soho and that it was getting difficult to find (literally) new angles on it.

There was also discussion of how to handle the running characters. In part this took the form of an argument as to whether Dot and Maureen were actually meant to be lesbians. Several people seemed to want this resolved one way or another, so that, for example, decisions could be made about the decor of their office and the kind of clothes they were to wear. But a more important problem for the writers was to know what to do with these characters in terms of creating meaningful roles for them in the plot. Gordon felt that already Maureen (the part, not the actress who was playing her) was in danger of becoming a piece of talking furniture. Again, despite efforts on June's part to encourage the writers to integrate the running characters into the plot there remained some difficulties to the end.

There was undoubtedly some feeling of disappointment with this first episode, possibly increased by the fact that the script had been generally well received, Gordon for instance remarking when he read it that it had got closer than any so far to the essence of what he and Terry had been trying to do. In part the problem was one of the direction, in that Don Leaver had deliberately not given it a highly distinctive visual style for fear that this would bind later directors to a 'look' that they might not be happy with. He had made the style as neutral as possible so as to leave open for as long as possible a decision on this question. But June possibly put her finger on one of the main difficulties with this first episode. She pointed out that it was untypical of the series as a whole in that it showed Hazell in the alien territory of suburbia, of quiet, tree-lined streets and lace curtains, and people to match. Hazell's true milieu, it will be remembered, was to consist of characters who are 'larger than life' and such livelier settings as Soho at night, East End pubs and dog tracks. This first episode would only really work by contrast with the others. She also felt that perhaps they had not been successful in bringing out strongly enough Hazell's feelings of unease in suburbia and that if the money had been there it would have been worth doing some of it over again. In the event this wasn't possible, but as we shall see the learning process continued into the second episode, parts of which were eventually to be re-done.

It may be true that the problem of doing justice to the concept of London as a star of the show could only have been fully solved had the whole series been done entirely on film, as some had wanted from the start, though it may well be the case that this would have led to the sacrifice of some of *Hazell*'s other qualities; it would have been hard to resist, for example, the pull towards the 'car-chase' syndrome which June and others had been at such pains to get away from. But in any case discussions after the first episode could only be concerned with details, however important. The basic format was by now set.

Remaking Hazell Pays A Debt

This book has given quite a lengthy account of the problems involved in getting a set of satisfactory scripts. To redress the balance, perhaps, it's worth including a short description of some difficulties encountered in the production, as opposed to the writing, of one of the episodes, *Hazell Pays A Debt*. This was the second to be recorded and presented problems of a rather different order from those encountered on the first. Jim Goddard defined the problem in this way:

JG: 'Basically, it was that the story was supposed to be about O'Rourke and his revenge on Hazell and was also designed to introduce Vinnie Rae (who was important) but somewhere along the line what actually happened was that the O'Rourke story became a bit obliterated by the idea of Hazell becoming a debt collector. There were also a lot of extraneous characters and I should think that as the thing developed both Gordon and Alistair in a way lost confidence in the central theme of the story. I think that everybody including Verity, Gordon and Alistair realised that the story was wrong. I've never yet seen a script for television, or a screen play or a play in a theatre, in which you can have two stories of identical weight — one has got to be dominant because if you don't make one dominant the audience will split and the play will only have half the impact. Although the audience may tolerate this they will choose the story that they're really interested in. If the stories are equally split then they have the maximum amount of frustration because the story they actually want to watch is only going to be fifty per cent of the play — for their input of attention over an hour they are only getting half-an-hour out. The writer and director do have complete control over this situation because they can simply make one story more dominant and then even if some of the audience prefer story A, if the director and writer decide that story B is more important, story A will become less important.'

We quote Jim Goddard because he was the director who was asked to re-make *Hazell Pays A Debt* — as the director who had been responsible for a number of episodes *(Hazell Goes To The Dogs, Hazell Settles The Accounts* and *Hazell Plays Solomon)* it was felt that he was in a good position to do this. What Jim did was to get together with Verity, June and Richard and spend a whole evening discussing what they all thought was wrong with the episode. As Jim said ' . . . we not only discussed the play and its content, scene by scene and word by word but we actually discussed the way in which each scene was done in detail, shot by shot'.

238

Basically it was felt that O'Rourke didn't figure strongly enough both in terms of the amount of time that he appeared on the screen and in terms of the fact that his potential for violence wasn't strongly enough presented. For example, the first time that he is seen in the episode is in the first pub scene. In the original version he doesn't appear until near the end of this scene and then only in long shot through a crowded bar. Jim re-edited that scene slightly but in addition shot a new scene, on film, in which O'Rourke is seen approaching the pub. He needlessly pushes aside two men who are standing outside having a conversation but when one of them goes to physically protest the other stops him and points to his head, indicating that he knows O'Rourke to be a nutcase. This established the menace of the character but also, interestingly, marks the only deviation from a rule that had been established, and rigidly adhered to, for the series — that is, that it is unacceptable to show something that Hazell doesn't witness or personally experience. In order to re-inforce this point Jim Goddard also re-shot the scene where Hazell discovers that his dad's walking sticks have been broken by O'Rourke — Jim replaced them with a pair of aluminium crutches that have been tied in a knot!

The other important change that Jim made was to re-shoot the death of O'Rourke. The point about the death is that Hazell has to argue and prove that he shot O'Rourke in self-defence. In the original version Alistair recorded the scene with Hazell pumping three bullets into O'Rourke's back. Gordon Williams had been very unhappy with the way this had been done. Apart from the possible difficulty of pleading self-defence having done this, the fact that that was the way in which he shot a man would significantly change Hazell's character as Gordon and Terry had defined it. He would no longer be a man who was worried by his own capacities for violence and who was frightened of the possibility of enjoying violence. This would thereby place his actions in the rest of the series in a very different light as well as contradicting what was in the novel and in the script.

Given the expense of re-shooting studio sequences it is not surprising that the two main scenes that were re-recorded (the scene in Hazell's parents' house and in his flat) were those which used stock sets. Other studio-shot scenes were merely re-edited and some small sections cut out. A certain amount of re-filming was also done, but that is less expensive in that it doesn't involve the building (or re-building) of costly sets.

Despite the number of changes and cuts that it was felt necessary to make (and Jim cut a number of minor characters and incidents that he felt were extraneous to the story) Jim had a very positive attitude to the whole situation:

JG: 'You know it just astounds me in television how often people get things right first time. When you are making a new series like this one where you introduce a character that nobody has ever seen before — only Gordon and Terry have seen him in their heads — you are actually creating something. It will be derivative, it must be in a way because you can only lead an audience from the known to the unknown, but you are still trying to create something completely new for television.'

After this episode, the next 8 to be recorded proceeded without major upsets, though in a series of this nature no-one would expect unanimity on every major decision.

16 Publicity and Sales

Programmes not only have to be made, they have to be sold. The activity of selling within an IT V company takes two forms: the potential audience has to be persuaded to watch the programme, and advertisers have to be convinced that the programme would be a suitable location for their commercials.

This work is split between two departments at Thames: the Advertising and Publications Department and the Press and Public Relations Department. The latter, as the title suggests, is concerned with gaining coverage in the press for Thames programmes. Stories and photographs are provided for journalists, and the main purpose of this work is to ensure that Thames programmes are written about and therefore that the public knows about them. The Advertising and Publications Department, on the other hand, takes care of any paid advertising, whether in the press, on commercial radio or other means such as posters in the London Underground. It also deals with spin-offs from programmes such as records or books; anything, in short, which either costs money or makes money. The controller of the department is Mike Phillips.

In terms of press publicity, as opposed to advertising, the three people immediately concerned with *Hazell* were Donald Cullimore, controller of press and public relations, Sue Cassell, the press officer for drama productions, and Jack Breckon, who is responsible for picture coverage of all Thames' shows (his actual title is Head of Pictures). The objective of Donald Cullimore's department is, he says, 'to persuade as many viewers as possible to watch the programmes. I don't care what anybody says about them as long as on the morning of transmission every paper in the country is saying, "for God's sake whatever else you do tonight, watch *Hazell*." That's the ultimate target.'

The general pattern is for publicity activity to increase once a show gets on the studio floor. Jack Breckon will arrange for a stills photographer to be present throughout recording and the pictures taken will be made primarily with an eye to their appeal to the press. Sue Cassell 'will want to have reports of what happens in the studio because that makes the kind of gossip story that will be useful for the television correspondents to write about when they come to urge their readers to watch a show.' Thus material is collected at the time of production, but usually not put into circulation until shortly before the programme is due for transmission. Some 6 weeks before there will be discussion in the department as to the particular way a programme is to be handled, and then some 2 weeks before transmission the stories and pictures will be fed to the press in time for the papers to catch their various deadlines (some of the Sundays may have deadlines a fortnight in advance of publication). Some publicity material, however, will appear before that time.

Sue Cassell: 'Once it became known that we were going to do *Hazell* there was tremendous interest in who was going to play the lead. We get notification from the casting department of who is going to play all the parts. As soon as Hazell himself was cast there was a lot of interest in the press, and there were interviews, which we arranged. It's so far ahead of transmission that it's not going to cut us out of any publicity later, but we don't go out of our way to set this up. If there is an interest we'll respond to it, but the main effort comes later. It can have a value, though, in that it gets the journalists interested, so that when *Hazell* comes up and we send out invitations to the preview they are going to say, oh yes, that's *Hazell*, we've got to go to that.'

There will invariably be a big press preview, usually of the first episode, a few days before the first transmission, and this will be attended by the stars of the show, the writers, producer, etc.; anyone, indeed, who might provide the critics with useful material.

Press coverage of television programmes, then, is carefully managed. The popular press in particular, whose television pages are primarily geared towards previews rather than reviews, will be fed with a variety of pictures and stories to follow up and interviews, in particular with the stars of the show, will be arranged. Unfortunately this book has had to go to press too early to give any details of the coverage which resulted from the publicity efforts for *Hazell* but we assume readers will be familiar with the kind of thing that is likely to happen. Some material, of the kind Sue Cassell doesn't go out of her way to promote but is not averse to, has already appeared. For example, there was a piece in *The Sun* in September 1976 entitled 'Strewth! A Sleuth With A Heart Of Gold!', which began: 'He's tough, funny, and as cockney as a plate of jellied eels. His patch is the sleaziest streets of London, where knuckledusters and knives are standard issue.' It mostly concerned

Terry Venables and Gordon Williams, as did a rather more restrained feature in *The Guardian* some time later. And Nick Ball has already been interviewed in *The Sun*. In late November Thames held a press show of *Hazell Plays Solomon* specially for women's magazines, since it was hoped that part of the appeal of the series, and in particular of the leading character, would be to the female audience.

The Advertising and Publications Department will want to get involved before the show goes on to the studio floor because at the stage when contracts are being drawn up thought will need to be given to the possibility of spin-offs. In the case of *Hazell* Thames didn't have the opportunity to produce a novelisation of the series since three books were already in existence. Nor is there likely to be, as there was in the case of *Rock Follies*, for example, a profitable line in records of the show. There is, however, the possibility of some merchandising spin-offs (toys, games, clothes) if the series is successful. The main concern of the department as far as *Hazell* goes will be in placing press advertisements, in posters and in material both for Thames Television International, who will sell the programme overseas, and for potential advertisers on Thames.

Press advertising can have two functions. It can be simply to bring the programme to the attention of the public and to urge them to watch it. Or it can be intended more as an exercise in building up the company's image. Thus at the time we talked to Mike Phillips Thames had been advertising its production of *The Norman Conquests* in the *Evening Standard*.

MP: 'That wasn't really done to increase ratings, that is if you like public relations advertising. We want to be seen to be proud of this particular programme.'

Posters on the other hand are more likely to be aimed at increasing the audience. At the time of writing Thames had 2 posters on the London Underground, one for their revamped local news show *Thames At Six,* and another for their production of *London Belongs To Me*. It seems certain that there will be a poster for *Hazell* too. Interestingly, it is likely to feature a photograph of Nick Ball taken by the Advertising and Publications Department in a style reflecting the *film noir* influences on *Hazell*; it's in black and white with heavy shadows across his face and a Humphrey Bogart style trench coat slung over his shoulder.

This picture has also been used as the cover of a magazine put out by the department. This magazine, *Studio News,* is produced primarily for the advertising agencies, though copies also go to Thames staff. Its purpose is to alert advertisers to forthcoming Thames productions. Once a programme has been definitely scheduled the department will probably make up a selection of clips from the show which would also be made available to advertisers. On occasion though, as Mike Phillips explains, they may wish to see a whole episode.

MP: 'Whereas the advertising business used to be very much concerned with cost per thousand viewers, these days a number of agencies are less concerned with actual numbers and more with whether a programme is appropriate for their kind of product. Some agencies will pay top money to be in a programme that maybe isn't getting very good ratings but which they feel is just right for them. And some agencies these days want to see whole shows; they've chucked out the calculator altogether and make all their decisions on gut reactions, so we'll send them a complete cassette.'

Officially the position on IT V is that advertisers cannot specify which programme they wish to advertise on. The IB A feels that to permit this would open the way to direct sponsorship of shows, on the American system. Nor can advertising be directly linked to programme content. Thus because Hazell drives a British Leyland car, that company would not be allowed to advertise on the programme or within half an hour on either side of its transmission hour. All an advertiser can do therefore is to book a slot in, say, the first commercial break after 9 o'clock on a Monday evening. But since the advertisers know what shows are scheduled, they are likely to know that at that time in the schedule Thames will be showing *Hazell.* In order to deal with advertisers who wish to book in a certain slot, Thames have a pre-empt rate card system. Under this arrangement there is no set rate for any particular slot; instead there are five or six rates on the card for any slot. If the advertiser books early enough the booking can be made at the lowest rate. But if someone comes along in the meantime and offers more money for that slot they will get it, except that the original booker has the chance to up the offer. There is, however, a top rate of £4,500 for 30 seconds, beyond which no-one is allowed to go, so that if someone decides that 20 9 o'clock Monday spots are essential for a campaign, they are entitled to book at the top rate right from the start so that no-one can outbid them. Advertising rates vary quite widely from time to

Hazell on the cover of Studio News

STUDIO
News

FROM THAMES TELEVISION · APRIL 1977

Hazell -'the biggest bastard who ever pushed your bell-button'

time according to the demand, which of course is dependent on the general state of the economy and the time of year. The lowest rate is £100 per 30 seconds. The rates are fixed by Thames' Sales Department, which is separate from publicity.

Almost all commercials are placed with the companies by recognised advertising agencies, who receive a commission of 15%. Thames' booking system is now fully computerised, allowing the sales staff to instantly punch up onto a screen the state of booking for any commercial slot. The display will show not only how much time there is available and how much of it has been booked, but will also give a forecast of the rating for the show in question. This will be broken down into a figure for the numbers of men, women, housewives (not synonymous!) and children. This allows the advertiser to decide whether it's a good time slot in which to advertise a certain product. Thus those articles mostly bought by housewives will be advertised more in the afternoons, when a higher proportion of those watching will be in that category. The proportion of men watching rises later in the evening. *Hazell* is likely to be seen as appealing equally to men and women and so will attract a wide variety of products. There will also be considerable competition for its available slots if the advertisers believe it will be as popular as its makers hope, and Thames certainly hope to sell all the time available on *Hazell* at the top rate. Because commercials have to be booked some time in advance, however, the advertisers can't simply wait and see how it's doing. It's for this reason that the company shows forthcoming programmes to advertisers in advance of transmission dates. Advertisers too can only cancel a booking if they do it 4 weeks or more in advance, so with a new series there must be an element of forecasting of the ratings on their part.

All commercials have to be passed by a vetting committee of the Independent Television Companies Association (ITCA), and the IBA has a Code of Advertising Standards and Practice, some details of which are given in its publication *Television and Radio 1977*. The IBA also lays down regulations about such matters as the amount of advertising permitted (7 minutes an hour in peak time programmes). Advertising itself as the basis for a whole system of broadcasting raises many crucial questions, but reluctantly we have to conclude that they fall outside the scope of this book.

One other job carried out by the Advertising and Publications Department is to provide Thames Television International with material to help them sell programmes overseas. This may take the form of a small illustrated booklet. At the time of going to press the major effort to sell *Hazell* abroad had not yet begun, but Muir Sutherland, head of Thames Television International, told us that he hoped to be able to sell it in several European countries besides traditional markets for British television such as Australia. America, it seems, is more of a problem. Most of the sales of British television programmes to America have been to the educational or public broadcasting networks, who have proved a ready market for 'cultural' productions such as *Upstairs Downstairs. Hazell,* however, hardly qualifies for this category.

Two other major forms of publicity not so far mentioned are *TV Times* and what is called 'on-air promotion', in other words announcements in between programmes of future attractions. Although *TV Times* is owned jointly by the ITV companies, it appears that its editorial policy, though obviously dedicated to presenting all ITV programmes in a good light, operates independently of any single company. Thus whether or not Hazell himself appears on the front cover will be a decision of the editor of the journal, and though of course it is open to the various companies to make requests and suggestions, from what we were told at Thames *TV Times* jealously guards its rights to make such decisions. It also has it own photographers, who took pictures on the set of *Hazell* independently of those who were employed by Jack Breckon.

On-air promotion is also handled separately at Thames from paid advertising. Clips from shows will be made up to be networked throughout the ITV companies.

Liaison between the various publicity personnel and the rest of the company takes place partly through a regular series of meetings. There is, for example, a Programme Liaison meeting each month attended by the Managing Director, the Director of Programmes, the Sales Controller, the head of on-air promotions and people from both departments concerned with publicity. Such meetings are concerned with 'polishing the image of the company', as it was described to us. There are also regular meetings between Mike Phillips and the controllers of production departments, and between individual press officers and the controllers of the departments for which they are responsible, to discuss what can be done for forthcoming programmes. But all the publicity people we spoke to felt that most of their information came from informal contacts with heads of departments and producers. Though Thames is the largest of the ITV companies it employs only one tenth of the number of people employed by the BBC and the feeling seems to be that it is small enough for a producer who wants to discuss publicity to ring up someone in the press office or to meet casually for a drink.

Producers therefore have no problem in reaching the publicity people and putting in any requests they may have. However, it seems that the publicity departments have a considerable measure of indepenance in making decisions.

Donald Cullimore: 'The programme judgements of someone like Mike Phillips or myself are regarded as valid because we are there to please an audience, not merely to accept the programme judgments of producers. We're, if you like, nearer the audience perhaps than some producers are and we're better placed to decide — not always but sometimes — whether a programme deserves publicising in a certain way. This isn't final; obviously the programme-makers, particularly the Director of Programmes and the heads of the programme-making departments, have valid judgements to offer as well, and the company collectively through the Board and Executive Directors. But the programme judgements of the publicists are not to be ignored.'

We asked what happened if there was a difference of opinion with a producer over publicity.

Mike Phillips: 'Well, we don't ignore the pressure from them because we have to bear in mind that we have an internal public relations role to fulfil as well. But if there is a strong difference of opinion, we would see our main concern as trying to influence the public and if we were being urged to produce an advertising campaign for something that we didn't think was worth it then, whatever the producer said, we probably wouldn't do it.'

It's instructive to note, then, that despite all the producers' struggles to control the nature of their shows during production, once the programme has been made it is to a great extent out of their hands. This is not to suggest that the publicists consistently publicise shows in a manner against the wishes of their producers. It merely demonstrates that production is a separate activity within the company from the marketing of those products both to the audience and to the advertisers. Of course in terms of overall company policy there must be a relation. A situation could not exist for very long in which departments were producing programmes for which the Sales Department couldn't sell advertising time. But the relationship is an indirect one and will be

248

handled at the level of general company policy as formulated by the Board and as communicated to the programme-makers from the Board through the Director of Programmes to the heads of production departments down to the producers. Producers don't market their own products, neither do sales and publicity people decide what programmes are made. And any feedback from the ratings to production policies can only operate in the long term because of the length of time needed to plan and produce a major series.

One detail is suggestive of the way the relationship works. All the way through production those involved in the conception of *Hazell* were at pains to mark its differences from other programmes in the crime series *genre*. *Hazell* would be different from *The Sweeney, Callan, Public Eye* or whatever. The publicity people saw *Hazell* as 'not dissimilar to *The Sweeney* in the potential audience appeal', but were enthusiastic to be associated with new products, and to promote Thames as a company with an adventurous production policy. The advertisers, on the other hand, so one person told us, would probably like Thames to go on producing *The Sweeney* for ever, since it virtually guaranteed top ratings. It is possible that Thames' sales staff, whose job it is to sell air-time to those advertisers, might sympathise with this view. There will thus always be a certain tension between the search for new ideas and a pressure to stick to the tried and tested. The net result is, of course, programmes which are very often different but the same. Wholly new *kinds* of programme are comparatively rare on television.

17 Conclusion

As Dr Johnson said, 'We that live to please, must please to live.' From the start *Hazell* was conceived of as entertainment, whatever the particular motivations of the people who worked on it. So at the end of it all there were two questions on everyone's mind: has it turned out the way we wanted it to, and will it be a hit? Those of our readers who have got this far should by now have an answer to the first question. *Hazell* as the audience will see it is not quite what any single individual envisaged at the beginning, but the nature of the production system makes this inevitable. Many people described this system to us as always involving a compromise between what they ideally wanted and what was possible. Jim Goddard prefered to put it this way: 'A compromise is when you go to the producer and say I can only do this scene properly if I have more money, and the producer says you'll have to do it with what you've got. What you ought to get on a good programme is a *fusion* of various concepts. It's really being egoistic to say if a show doesn't exactly reflect your individual concept that it's a compromise.' So although *Hazell* turned out differently from what some people may have wanted, many of the key people involved appeared to be reasonably satisfied, in the sense that it 'worked'.

Strangely, though, considering that those who made *Hazell* are in the entertainment business and must please a large public to make a living, there seemed to be some reluctance to predict the precise degree of success which the show would achieve. Measuring the ratings is now a sophisticated and accurate process, but predicting them is still an inexact science. The general consensus was that *Hazell* would probably do well, though we didn't find anyone betting that it would achieve the rating of 40 which Jeremy Isaacs had originally been hoping for. Possibly what this uncertainty about the audience reception argues, however, is not so much that people don't know what the audience wants as that, though they are working within the general imperative of pleasing the viewer, in the actual process of production people were working more to please themselves. In other words, they were trying to produce a show which *they* thought was entertaining, and then hoping that the audience would like it too. Doubtless there are people producing television programmes which they believe to be rubbish but who do it because they can make a lot of money. As a general rule we did not think that this was the case on *Hazell*. We're not trying to suggest that there was a spirit of lofty dedication, only that people did set out to produce something that would meet their own standards. If the viewing figures were high, so much the better. A model of popular television which sees it either as cynical manipulation or a straight-forward identity of tastes between producers and audience (though there must be cases of both) would be, based on our experience of *Hazell*, an over-simplification.

We do not mean to suggest that during the course of production no-one ever gave a thought to the question of making the programme popular. Decisions about casting, scripting, standards of design and so on were all made within a context of giving *Hazell* an appeal to a wide audience. But the kind of judgements people were making when they said that something was 'right' or that it 'wasn't working' were judgements that appeared to reflect their own immediate feelings, rather than an objective assessment of what the viewing public would think. What this seems to suggest is that television professionals have their own system of values, their own ideology of entertainment; but of course it will overlap to a varying degree with that of the audience at large, and in a commercial system can never stray too far from that held by the majority.

Clearly enough people at Thames, and specifically Jeremy Isaacs and Verity Lambert, believed *Hazell* would be a success, because a decision to make a second series of 13 episodes was taken in November of 1977. This was scheduled to go into production in May 1978, and was to be produced by Tim Aspinall, June Roberts having taken up another post with Granada Television. At the time we spoke to him the new producer had scarcely had an opportunity to talk to anyone involved, or had the chance to sort out his own ideas on the series, though it seemed likely that some of the writers from the first series would be involved and of course Hazell would continue to be played by Nick Ball.

One thing he was prepared to commit himself to, however, was a view on the importance in a series of this kind of seizing on what it is in the central concept of the series that you believe in. For him, as for those who had made the first series, it wasn't a question of assembling a whole number of things which would appeal to an audience and then trying to paste them together. Rather, he felt, you had to find what it was that really drew you to the programme (and for him this was essentially the character of Hazell himself) and build on that. What he would be searching for, he implied, was the thing that attracted him to Hazell and made him believe in him. After only a few days he didn't feel he had got there yet, but he was sure that there was such a centre, otherwise he would not have been drawn to the character in the first place, or taken the job.

If this sounded like a more 'realist' conception of *Hazell* than June Roberts' had originally been (Tim Aspinall talked about getting at what made Hazell a relevant character in terms of contemporary life, and he seemed likely to drop the attempt to fit Hazell into the Humphrey Bogart-Raymond Chandler tradition), it nevertheless showed an attitude towards the production of entertainment similar to most of those involved with the first series. If anything he took it further, implying that you couldn't do anything which was really good unless you had some commitment to it. What exactly that commitment would be to, the second series of *Hazell* will reveal.

Postscript

We showed a draft of this book to half a dozen of the people most closely involved in the production of *Hazell*. This was partly out of courtesy and partly because we were anxious that they correct any errors of fact or interpretation (though they are not responsible for any errors in the book). But we also asked them if they would like to make a final comment on their experience of the production. Gordon Williams had this to say:

Working in television for the first time, by a fluke, my overall impression is a conflict between the need for team-work and the different career and status pressures on individuals. A lot of problems seem in retrospect to have arisen from poor communications. There has been a slight drift towards jokiness from the 'book' *Hazell* but by and large the episodes I've seen so far are very, very good.

Of the directors who did scripts I was involved in, only one, Jim Goddard, made a specific point of consulting writers. If I were a full-time television writer I'd take a GLC night-class in direction, so as to meet directors on their ground. One sure thing — if you want artistic and creative control of a television series you become the producer.

Having had two novels mauled by film directors, I am very appreciative of Thames' determination to spend time and money on getting *Hazell* right, both from their own point of view and from Terry's and mine.

18 Credits

All the episodes will be transmitted on Mondays at 21.00

Hazell Plays
Solomon   16th January 1978
Hazell Pays A Debt   23rd January 1978
Hazell And The
Walking Blur   30th January 1978
Hazell Settles The
Accounts   6th February 1978
Hazell Meets The
First Eleven   13th February 1978
Hazell And The
Rubber-Heel Brigade 20th February 1978
Hazell Goes To
the Dogs   27th February 1978
Hazell And The
Weekend Man   6th March 1978
Hazell Works For
Nothing   13th March 1978
Hazell And The
Maltese Vulture   20th March 1978

Hazell And The Weekend Man Recorded in Studio 2, 18/19th January 1977
Writer: Richard Harris
Designers: David Ferris, Bill Palmer
Story Editor: Kenneth Ware
Producer: June Roberts
Director: Don Leaver
Production Assistant: Liz Cadley
Floor Manager: John Lopes
Stage Manager: Dennis Redwood
Costume Designer: Frank Van Raay
Make-Up Supervisor: Audrey Proderick
Floor Assistant: Fiona Waters
Assistant Stage Manager: Giles de Gatacre
Costume Assistant: Mandy Harper
Graphics: Bernard Allum
Technical Supervisor: Dave Sparks
Lighting Director: Ken Tester-Brown

Cameras: Albert Almond
Sound Supervisor: Brian Hibbert
Grams Operator: Roger Laycock
Vision Mixer: Nick Bigsby
Vision Control: Alan Harradine

Cast
Hazell: Nicholas Ball
Dot: Barbara Young
Maureen: Maggie Riley
Mrs Bradley: Pat Heywood
Mr Norman: George Waring
George Bradley: Roger Sloman
Mrs Ford: Gwen Taylor
Hammond: Eamon Boland
Finch: Michael Sheard
Mr Arnold: Sam Dale
Mr Doddimead: Martin Neil
Ruth: Gracie Luck (Film only)

Walk ons/Extras
4 bank employees, 4 bank customers (1 young girl, 1 black man, 2 men); cafe customers — 4 men plus 1 man from bank customers; cafe owners — 1 man, 1 woman, 1 son.

Hazell Pays A Debt Recorded in Studio 2, 1/2nd March 1977
Writer: Gordon Williams
Designers: David Ferris, Bill Palmer
Story Editor: Richard Harris
Producer: June Roberts
Director: Alistair Reid

Production Assistant: Jill Watts
Floor Manager: Kerry Mann
Stage Manager: Mary Lewis
Costume Designer: Frank Van Raay
Make-Up Supervisor: Audrey Proderick
Floor Assistant: Richard Shackleton
Graphics: Bernard Allum

Technical Supervisor: George Coates
Lighting Director: Dave Motture
Cameras: Peter Coombs
Sound Supervisor: Peter Willcocks
Grams Operator: Jim Wilde
Vision Mixer: Nick Bigsby
Vision Control: Alan Harradine

Cast
Hazell: Nicholas Ball
Mr Hazell: George Hilsdon
Mrs Hazell: Betty Hardy
Rodders: Leo Dolan
Slippery: Karl Howman
Cousin Tel: Desmond McNamara
Minty: Roddy McMillan
Billy Begg: Maurice O'Connell
O'Rourke: Derrick O'Connor
Dornford: Richard Murdoch
Vinnie Rae: Celia Gregory
Pub Manager: Roland MacLeod
Barmaid: Arbel Jones

Film only
Dot: Barbara Young
Maureen: Maggie Riley
Mrs O'Rourke: Tina Martin
Swimming Pool Attendant: Oscar James
Roger: Leon Lissek

Musicians
Lennie Hastings (Singer), Stan Gregg
(Pianist), Martin Guy (Drummer), Len
Skeats (Bass)

Extras
16 pub customers, 1 policeman,
O'Rourke's mate.

Hazell Settles The Accounts Recorded in
Studio 2, 15/16th March 1977

Writers: Gordon Williams, Tony Hoare
(Note: Gordon and Tony decided to split
the screen credits for their scripts between
them, but this list indicates who actually
wrote which scripts.)
Designers: David Ferris, Bill Palmer
Story Editor: Richard Harris

Producer: June Roberts
Director: Jim Goddard

Production Assistant: Liz Cadley
Floor Manager: John Lopes
Stage Manager: Diana Paskin
Floor Assistant: Ivor Ramsey
Costume Designer: Frank Van Raay
Make-Up Supervisor: Audrey Proderick
Costume Assistant: Mandy Harper
Graphics: Bernard Allum

Technical Supervisor: Campbell Keenan
Lighting Director: Bill Lee
Cameras: Peter Howell
Sound Supervisor: Julian Ford
Grams Operator: Roger Laycock
Vision Mixer: Martin Perret
Vision Control: Bill Marley

Cast
Hazell: Nicholas Ball
Minty: Roddy McMillan
Dot: Barbara Young
Maureen: Maggie Riley
Dobson: Freddie Jones
Mrs Dobson: Patsy Byrne
Creasey: Alan Lake
Graves: John Rhys Davies
Gloria: Pamela Stephenson
Jennings: Patrick Durkin
Jay: Harry Landis
Japanese: Sabu Kimura

Extras
4 young hostesses, 12 male punters, 2 other
barmen, 4 wives, 4 Japanese businessmen,
1 West Indian char, 1 policeman, 1
Minty's boss.

Hazell Meets The First Eleven Recorded in
Studio 2, 31st March/1st April 1977

Writers: Gordon Williams, Tony Hoare
Designers: David Ferris, Bill Palmer
Story Editor: Richard Harris
Producer: June Roberts
Director: Moira Armstrong

254

Production Assistant: Paddy Dewey
Floor Manager: John Lopes
Stage Manager: Mary Lewis
Costume Designer: Frank Van Raay
Make-Up Supervisor: Sally Thorpe
Floor Assistant: Ivor Ramsey
Costume Assistant: Mandy Harper
Design Assistant: Jane Krall
Assistant Stage Manager: Giles de Gatacre
Graphics: Bernard Allum
Production Buyer: Leslie Fulford

Technical Supervisor: Peter Sampson
Lighting Director: Ken Tester-Brown
Cameras: Peter Coombs
Sound Supervisor: Brian Hibbert
Grams Operator: Eddie Elmhirst
Vision Mixer: Peter Phillips
Vision Control: Ian Jones
Film Editor: Peter Elliott

Cast
Hazell: Nicholas Ball
Vinnie Rae: Celia Gregory
Gordon Gregory: James Faulkner
Diane: Fiona Mollison
Pamela Courtney: Elizabeth Power
Charles Courtney: Bryan Coleman
Jonathan Clayton: David Robb
Sarah Courtney: Lalla Ward
Mark Woolridge: Reggie Oliver
Shop Assistant: David Gooderson
Henry Courtney: Howard Taylor
Mai-Lin: Fiesta Mei Ling

Extras/Walk ons
16 men and 15 women to be party guests, barman and library assistant.

Hazell Goes To The Dogs Recorded in Studio 2, 13/14th April 1977

Writers: Gordon Williams, Tony Hoare
Designers: Bill Palmer, David Ferris
Story Editor: Richard Harris
Producer: June Roberts
Director: Jim Goddard

Production Assistant: Liz Cadley
Floor Manager: John Lopes
Stage Manager: Diana Paskin
Costume Designer: Frank Van Raay
Make-Up Supervisor: Sally Thorpe
Floor Assistant: Andrew Rothschild
Costume Assistant: Mandy Harper
Graphics: Bernard Allum

Technical Supervisor: Del Randall
Lighting Director: Ritchie Richardson
Cameras: Mike Solomons
Sound Supervisor: Peter Wilcox
Grams Operator: Roger Laycock
Vision Mixer: Nick Bigsby
Vision Control: Alan Harradine

Cast
Hazell: Nicholas Ball
Minty: Roddy McMillan
Dot: Barbara Young
Cousin Tel: Desmond McNamara
Wally Wiggins: Dave King
Ida Wiggins: Marjie Lawrence
Melina Stassinoppolus: Marina Sirtis
Gladys: Irlin Hall
Porter: Kenneth Colley
Patrick Coyne: Frank Coda (film only)

Musicians
Andreas Markides plus 2 others

Extras
15 working class people for the pub scenes
20 mixed middle class to include the following walk ons: 1 barman, 1 maitre d'hotel, 2 waiters for the Taverna

Hazell And The Rubber-Heel Brigade Recorded in Studio 2, 26/27th April 1977

Writer: Richard Harris
Designers: David Ferris, Bill Palmer
Producer: June Roberts
Director: Peter Duguid

Production Assistant: Dottie Rice
Floor Manager: Kerry Mann

255

Stage Manager: Mary Lewis
Costume Designer: Frank Van Raay
Make-Up Supervisor: Sally Thorpe
Floor Assistant: Ivor Ramsey
Costume Assistant: Mandy Harper
Graphics: Bernard Allum

Technical Supervisor: John White Jones
Lighting Director: Ken Tester-Brown
Cameras: Peter Coombs
Sound Supervisor: Brian Hibbert
Grams Operator: Paul Vincent
Vision Mixer: Peter Phillips
Vision Control: Alan Harradine

Cast
Hazell: Nicholas Ball
Minty: Roddy McMillan
Gordon Gregory: James Faulkner
Dot: Barbara Young
Maureen: Maggie Riley
Det Supt Bull: John Phillips
Mrs Hazell: Betty Hardy
Dave Ryman: David Daker
Bett Ryman: Patricia Francis
Jackie: Suzan Farmer
Judith: Belinda Sinclair
Det Sgt Fenner: Colin Burns

Walk ons
1 stripper and 1 barman (oriental casting)

Extras
5 drinkers and 1 client for stripper

Hazell Works For Nothing Recorded in Studio 2, 11/12th May 1977

Writer: Peter Ransley
Designers: David Ferris, Bill Palmer
Story Editor: Richard Harris
Producer: June Roberts
Director: Moira Armstrong

Production Assistant: Sue Mahoney
Floor Manager: Kerry Mann
Stage Manager: Diana Paskin
Costume Designer: Frank Van Raay

Make-Up Supervisor: David Morgan
Costume Assistant: Mandy Harper
Graphics: Bernard Allum
Production Buyer: Frank Evans

Technical Supervisor: Peter Sampson
Lighting Director: Ritchie Richardson
Cameras: Albert Almond
Sound Supervisor: Brian Moray
Grams Operator: Bob Davis
Vision Mixer: Nick Bigsby
Vision Control: Jim Fergus-Smith

Cast
Hazell: Nicholas Ball
Minty: Roddy McMillan
Cousin Tel: Desmond McNamara
Maureen: Maggie Riley
Dot: Barbara Young
Glad: Betty Hardy
Fred: George Hilsdon
Sadie: Alibe Parsons
Bernie Franks: Michael Graham Cox
Mrs Franks: Anne Kristen
Linda Franks: Lorraine Brown
Pearl: Gretchen Franklin
Moira: Alexandra Dane
Radio Announcer (V/O only): Neil Landor
Hospital Clerks: Sheelah Wilcocks
                  Doremy Vernon

Extras
2 policemen, 1 staff nurse, 1 sister, 5 hospital patients, 1 WPC, 2 hospital porters, 2 doctors, 2 patients in the VD clinic, 1 man on a hospital trolley, 9 visitors in hospital to double in pub, 1 man in bar, 1 barman, 1 WVS woman with tea trolley, 1 man and 1 woman in pub (continuity for filming), 4 prostitutes in the pub.

Hazell And The Maltese Vulture Recorded in Studio 1, 21/22nd July 1977

Writer: Trevor Preston
Designers: Bill Palmer, David Ferris
Story Editor: Richard Harris

Producer: June Roberts
Director: Colin Bucksey

Production Assistant: Sue Mahoney
Floor Manager: Peter Piddick
Stage Manager: Diana Paskin
Costume Designer: Frank Van Raay
Make-Up Supervisor: Audrey Proderick
Floor Assistant: Mandy Harper
Production Buyer: Leslie Fulford
Graphics: Bernard Allum

Technical Supervisor: Del Randall
Lighting Director: Ken Tester-Brown
Cameras: Peter Coombs
Sound Supervisor: Brian Hibbert
Grams Operator: Stan Lee
Vision Mixer: Peter Phillips
Vision Control: Alan James

Cast
Hazell: Nicholas Ball
Minty: Roddy McMillan
Cousin Tel: Desmond McNamara
Maureen: Maggie Riley
Dot: Barbara Young
Gordon Gregory: James Faulkner
Vinnie Rae: Celia Gregory
Sheena: Dana Gillespie
Lepper: Nick Edmett
Attard: Sam Dastor
Big Arti: Pat Roach
T P Eades: Ben Aris
Tina: Vicki Hodge
Sally Durham (film only): Tina Marian
Vic Preece (film only): Luke Hanson

Walk ons
2 plain clothes policemen

Extras
4 teddy boys, 1 teddy girl, 1 man behind bar

Hazell Plays Solomon Recorded in Studio 1, 5/6th August 1977

Writers: Gordon Williams and Terry Venables

Designers: David Ferris, Bill Palmer
Story Editor: Richard Harris
Producer: June Roberts
Director: Jim Goddard

Production Assistant: Paddy Dewey
Floor Manager: Peter Piddick
Stage Manager: Sarah Prebble
Costume Designer: Frank Van Raay
Make-Up Supervisor: Sally Thorpe
Floor Assistant: David Morgan
Assistant Stage Manager: Julian Meers
Costume Assistant: Mandy Harper
Graphics: Bernard Allum
Production Buyer: Frank Evans

Technical Supervisor: Dave Sparks
Lighting Director: Ken Tester-Brown
Cameras: Peter Howell
Sound Supervisor: Brian Moray
Grams Operator: Dick Bradford
Vision Mixer: Nick Bigsby
Vision Control: Alan James
Film Editor: Roy Hayden

Cast
Hazell: Nicholas Ball
Gordon Gregory: James Faulkner
Minty: Roddy McMillan
Dot: Barbara Young
Maureen: Maggie Riley
Diane: Fiona Mollison
Cousin Tel: Desmond McNamara
Georgina Gunning: Jane Asher
Toni Abrey: Susan Littler
Cliff Abrey: George Innes
Kathleen Donaldson: Daphne Heard
Tricia Abrey: Lisa Moss
Housewife (film only): Yasmin Pettigrew

Extras
4 children at party

Hazell Pays A Debt (re-recorded inserts) Recorded in Studio 2, 10th August 1977 and in Studio 3, 11th August 1977

Writer: Gordon Williams
Designer: Bill Palmer

Story Editor: Richard Harris
Producer: June Roberts
Director: Jim Goddard

Production Assistant: Liz Monkton
Floor Manager: Peter Piddick
Stage Manager: Sarah Prebble
Costume Designer: Frank Van Raay
Make-Up Supervisor: Sally Thorpe
Floor Assistants: Fiona Waters
                David Morgan
Graphics: Bernard Allum

Technical Supervisor: Campbell Keenan
Lighting Director: Ken Tester-Brown
Cameras: Gerry Whitney
Sound Supervisor: Peter Willcocks
Grams Operator: Norman Barnes
Vision Mixer: Martin Perret
Vision Control: Ian Jones

Cast
Hazell: Nicholas Ball
Mr Hazell: George Hilsdon
Mrs Hazell: Betty Hardy
Cousin Tel: Desmond McNamara
Keith O'Rourke: Derrick O'Connor
Vinnie Rae: Celia Gregory
Maureen: Maggie Riley

Walk on 2
O'Rourke's mate

Hazell And The Walking Blur
Recorded in Studio 1, 25/26th August
1977

Writer: Richard Harris
Designers: Gordon Toms, David Ferris,
           Bill Palmer
Producer: June Roberts
Director: Brian Farnham

Production Assistant: Dottie Rice
Floor Manager: Peter Piddick
Stage Manager: Mary Lewis
Costume Designer: Frank Van Raay
Make-Up Supervisor: Sally Thorpe
Floor Assistant: Ivor Ramsey
Costume Assistant: Mandy Harper
Graphics: Bernard Allum

Technical Supervisor: Peter Sampson
Lighting Director: Ken Tester-Brown
Cameras: Geoff Whitney
Sound Supervisor: Ron Ferris
Grams Operator: Dick Bradford
Vision Mixer: Martin Perret/
Vision Control: Bill Marley

Cast
Hazell: Nicholas Ball
Minty: Roddy McMillan
Dot: Barbara Young
Maureen: Maggie Riley
Gordon Gregory: James Faulkner
Diane: Fiona Mollison
Alec Galbraith: Bill Henderson
Griffiths: Michael Elphick
Sybil: Diane Fletcher
Pattie: Susie Baker
Harry: David Cardy
Bouncer: Dicken Ashworth
Ingrid: Katherine Schofield
Micky Bowers: Kevin Lloyd
Policewoman: Diana Rowan
Fiancee: Steve Hodson
Cabbie: Lloyd Anderson

Walk ons
Heavy No 2, Arab man and woman, taxi
hut cook

Extra
Driver in Minty's car

Bibliography

Burns, Tom, *The BBC: Public Institution and Private World*, Macmillan, 1977
A study, conducted through interviews with its personnel, of the largest broadcasting organisation in the country. There is as yet no equivalent work on the ITV companies.

Cantor, Muriel G., *The Hollywood TV Producer*, Basic Books, New York, 1971
A study of drama producers, working in the rather different world of American television.

Elliott, John, *Mogul: The Making of a Myth*, Barrie & Rockcliff, 1970
An account by a participant of the production of a successful drama series.

Elliott, Philip, 'Media Organisations and Occupations', in Curran, Gurevitch and Woollacott (eds.), *Mass Communication and Society*, Edward Arnold, for the Open University, 1977
A useful survey of what sociolgists know about the way in which mass media artefacts are produced, with a bibliography.

Elliott, Philip, *The Making of a Television Series*, Constable, 1972
A sociological study of the production of an ITV documentary series.

Garnham, Nicholas, *Structures of Television*, BFI TV Monograph 1, British Film Institute, 1973 (new edition forthcoming)
A concise description and analysis of the structure of British broadcasting.

Golding, Peter, *The Mass Media*, Longmans, 1975
A good survey of the general field of mass media.

Miller, M. & Rhodes, E., *Only You Dick Daring*, Wm. Sloane Assocs., New York, 1964
Descriptions of the experiences of a writer on a drama series on American TV.

Murdock, Graham and Golding, Peter, *Cultural Capitalism: the Political Economy of Mass Communications*, Routledge & Kegan Paul (forthcoming)
An analysis of the pattern of ownership and control of mass media in Britain.

Shubik, Irene, *Play for Today: the evolution of television drama*, Davis-Poynter, 1975.
By a BBC television producer.

Taylor, Cecil P., *Making A Television Play*, Oriel Press, 1970
An account by the author of the production of his play *Cromwell*. Sketchy in parts.

Television and Radio 1977, IBA, 1977
Contains much information (though not enough) on the ITV companies and the IBA's role in the system.

Thomas, Howard, *With An Independent Air*, Weidenfeld & Nicolson, 1977
Memoirs of the Chairman of the Board of Directors of Thames Television.

Whitfield, Stephen E. & Roddenberry, Gene, *The Making of Star Trek*, Ballantine Books, New York, 1968
An eccentric though often highly revealing account of the production of the popular American television series.

Williams, Raymond, *Television: Technology and Cultural Form*, Fontana, 1974
Especially good on the social determinants of mass media technologies.

The Educational Advisory Service of the British Film Institute will be producing some further materials, both visual and printed, designed for teachers who intend making use of Hazell *in their classes on television. Any teachers wishing for more information are invited to get in touch with the EAS, at 81 Dean Street, London W1V 6AA.*